This volume explains, from various experts' perspectives, how China and the United States should defend their respective interests, manage differences, mitigate crisis, and avoid conflict in various strategic domains including maritime, nuclear, cyber, and space. As the book correctly points out, "The central challenge to improve strategic stability between the United States and China is finding ways to enhance collaboration and mitigate sources of tension." This book has made highly valuable efforts toward achieving this goal. The U.S.-China relationship will significantly impact the 21st century, therefore, this book merits careful study by all those who are concerned with the future of global stability.

—Chen Xiaogong (Lt. General, Ret.), former Deputy Director
of the Foreign Affairs Office of the Central Committee of
the Communist Party of China and former Deputy
Commander of the PLA Air Force

Having assembled experts from leading Chinese and American research institutions and think tanks, this volume presents a series of the most cutting-edge joint research findings across the following six strategic domains: maritime, nuclear, cyber, space, military-to-military relations, and people-to-people exchange. This book, through in-depth theoretical analysis, provides an authoritative answer to the centennial question of whether or not China and the United States are destined to fall into the 'Thucydides Trap.' I firmly believe that this volume will become one of the classic studies on China-U.S. strategic relations. It should be read by anyone who is concerned about the future of China-U.S. ties, and thus, I hope it reaches a wide audience.

—Zhou Wenzhong, former Vice Minister of Foreign Affairs,
former Chinese Ambassador to the United States

The 2018 National Security Strategy of the United States defines the reemergence of long-term, strategic competition with China as the central challenge to U.S. prosperity and security. This volume is an indispensable resource in understanding the nature of this challenge and of the U.S. strategy, a key component of which is to set the military relationship between China and the United States on a path of transparency and non-aggression.

—Former U.S. Assistant Secretary of State,
Ambassador to China, J. Stapleton Roy

A landmark study. An admirable work by a group of leading experts from both the U.S. and China that aims to tackle some of the most sensitive, most difficult, and most thorny strategic issues facing the U.S.-China relationship. A must-read for anyone who is concerned about the prospects of U.S.-China relations.

—Former Commander of U.S. Pacific Command,
Admiral Thomas Fargo (U.S. Navy, Ret.)

Avoiding the 'Thucydides Trap'

As the relationship between China and the United States becomes increasingly complex and interdependent, leaders in Beijing and Washington are struggling to establish a solid common foundation on which to expand and deepen bilateral relations.

In order to examine the challenges facing U.S.-China relations, the National Bureau of Asian Research (NBR) and the Institute for Global Cooperation and Understanding (iGCU) at Peking University brought together a group of leading experts from China and the United States in Beijing and Honolulu to develop a conceptual foundation for U.S.-China relations into the future, tackling the issues in innovative ways under the banner of U.S.-China Relations in Strategic Domains.

The resulting chapters assess U.S.-China relations in the maritime and nuclear sectors as well as in cyberspace and space through the lens of P2P and mil-to-mil exchanges. Scholars and students in political science and international relations are thus presented with a diagnosis and prognosis of the relations between the two superpowers.

Dong Wang is Associate Professor at the School of International Studies and Executive Director of the Institute for Global Cooperation and Understanding (iGCU), Peking University. He has written extensively on U.S.-China relations and China's foreign policy.

Travis Tanner is President of the U.S.-China Strong Foundation. Based in Beijing, Mr. Tanner has more than 15 years of experience working on U.S.-China relations. Mr. Tanner is the author, contributing author, or co-editor of numerous publications on the strategic, economic, and political dimensions of the U.S.-China relationship, including five volumes of the Strategic Asia series.

China Perspectives

The *China Perspectives* series focuses on translating and publishing works by leading Chinese scholars, writing about both global topics and China-related themes. It covers Humanities & Social Sciences, Education, Media and Psychology, as well as many interdisciplinary themes.

This is the first time any of these books have been published in English for international readers. The series aims to put forward a Chinese perspective, give insights into cutting-edge academic thinking in China, and inspire researchers globally.

To submit proposals, please contact the Taylor & Francis Publisher for China Publishing Programme, Lian Sun (Lian.Sun@informa.com)

Recent titles in politics partly include:

Fiscal Policy and Institutional Renovation in Support of Innovative Country Building
Jia Kang

Avoiding the 'Thucydides Trap'
U.S.-China Relations in Strategic Domains
Dong Wang and Travis Tanner

Syrian Civil War and Europe
Zhao Chen, Zhao Jizhou and Huang Mengmeng

Re-globalisation
When China Meets the World Again
Dong Wang and Dejun Cao

China in the Eyes of the Japanese
Wang Xiuli, Wang Wei and Liang Yunxiang

For more information, please visit www.routledge.com/China-Perspectives/book-series/CPH

Avoiding the 'Thucydides Trap'

U.S.-China Relations in Strategic Domains

Edited by Dong Wang and Travis Tanner

Routledge
Taylor & Francis Group

LONDON AND NEW YORK

First edition published 2021
by Routledge
2 Park Square, Milton Park, Abingdon, Oxon, OX14 4RN

and by Routledge
52 Vanderbilt Avenue, New York, NY 10017

Routledge is an imprint of the Taylor & Francis Group, an informa business

British Library Cataloguing-in-Publication Data
A catalogue record for this book is available from the British Library

Library of Congress Cataloging-in-Publication Data
A catalog record for this book has been requested

ISBN: 978-0-8153-8309-3 (hbk)
ISBN: 978-0-367-63838-2 (pbk)
ISBN: 978-1-351-20667-9 (ebk)

Typeset in Times New Roman
by Apex CoVantage, LLC

Contents

Figures

Contributors

Elbridge A. Colby is the Robert M. Gates Senior Fellow at the Center for a New American Security (CNAS).

Dong Wang is Associate Professor in the School of International Studies and Executive Director of Institute for Global Cooperation and Understanding (iGCU), Peking University.

Jessica Drun is a Bridge Award Fellow at the National Bureau of Asian Research.

Xiao He is an assistant research fellow at the Institute of World Economics and Politics in the Chinese Academy of Social Sciences.

Xu Hui is Commandant of College of Defense Studies / Director of Center for Strategic and Defense Studies, National Defense University, People's Liberation Army, China.

Roy D. Kamphausen is President of the National Bureau of Asian Research.

Tang Lan is Deputy Director at the Institute of Information and Social Development, China Institutes of Contemporary International Relations.

Tiffany Ma is Director of Political and Security Affairs, the National Bureau of Asian Research.

Zhao Minghao is a Senior Research Fellow at the Institute of International Studies, Fudan University.

Wu Riqiang is Associate Professor in the School of International Studies at Renmin University in China.

Adam Segal is the Maurice R. Greenberg Senior Fellow for China Studies and Director of the Program on Digital and Cyberspace Policy at the Council on Foreign Relations.

Travis Tanner is President of the U.S.-China Strong Foundation.

Brian Weeden is Technical Advisor at the Secure World Foundation in Washington, D.C.

Yu Ying is Assistant Research Fellow, Center for Defense and Strategic Studies, NDU.

Christopher Yung is the Donald Bren Chair of Non-Western Strategic Thought at the U.S. Marine Corps University.

Acknowledgments

We wish to thank the Carnegie Corporation of New York and the China–United States Exchange Foundation for making this project possible. Additionally, we wish to thank the Institute of International and Strategic Studies at Peking University and the East-West Center for their support during this project.

This project has benefited from interactions with several key interlocutors, including June Teufel Dreyer (University of Miami), Thomas Fargo (former holder of the John M. Shalikashvili Chair in National Security Studies at NBR), Gao Zugui (Central Party School), Geng Kun (China Aerospace Science and Technology Corporation), Hu Bo (Peking University), Dan "Fig" Leaf (Asia-Pacific Center for Security Studies), Li Chen (Renmin University), Jamie Metzl (Atlantic Council), Denny Roy (East-West Center), Ruan Zongze (China Institute of International Studies), Wang Jisi (Peking University), Yuan Peng (China Institutes of Contemporary International Relations), Zhu Feng (Nanjing University), Zhu Yinghuang (China Daily), and experts at U.S. Pacific Command. We also would like to recognize Abraham Denmark's project leadership during his tenure as the senior vice president for political and security affairs at NBR.

Finally, we would like to acknowledge the hard work of NBR and Peking University staff, including Tiffany Ma, Alison Szalwinski, Joshua Ziemkowski, Jessica Keough, Craig Scanlan, Xiaodon Liang, Brian Franchell, Kyle Churchman, Alex Jeffers, Wu Xiangning, Tang Jing, and Mou Yi.

Dong Wang
Associate Professor and Executive Director
School of International Studies
Institute for Global Cooperation and Understanding (iGCU)
Peking University

Travis Tanner
President of the U.S.-China Strong Foundation

Introduction

Dong Wang and Travis Tanner

The U.S.-China relationship is becoming increasingly complex and interdependent, and leaders in Beijing and Washington are struggling to establish a common foundation on which to expand and deepen bilateral relations. While both sides seem to agree on the general need to cooperate and manage competition, the details of how to move the relationship forward remain unclear, particularly in areas where progress has already been difficult to achieve. The international stakes of how the two nations work together and collaborate are monumental. Given that the global challenges facing the world today cannot be resolved without both the United States and China, calculations in the cyber, maritime, nuclear, and space domains are increasingly consequential and carry implications for other nations. Military-to-military (mil-mil) and people-to-people (P2P) interactions also have the potential to influence outcomes across a range of these and other key policy areas.

Peking University's Institute for Global Cooperation and Understanding (iGCU) and the National Bureau of Asian Research (NBR) partnered on a project to produce an examination of the challenges to establishing greater trust and cooperation in U.S.-China relations in strategic domains and bilateral exchanges. The project—"U.S.-China Relations in Strategic Domains"—assembled a study team of leading experts from China and the United States to develop a conceptual foundation for U.S.-China relations. Employing an innovative approach to represent both U.S. and Chinese perspectives, the members of the study team jointly examined opportunities for collaboration by identifying areas of divergence and convergence across four strategic domains and two modes of bilateral exchange. The project also enlisted two groups of senior advisers—composed of top scholars and current and former senior officials—who provided guidance and direction to the project and feedback to members of the study team.

The study team interacted and held discussions through seminars in Beijing and Honolulu, as well as through tele- and video conferences. The resulting chapters published in this edited volume assess the U.S.-China relationship in the maritime, nuclear, cyberspace, and space domains as well as through the lens of P2P and mil-mil exchanges. The project team sought to go beyond the rhetoric of cooperation to examine side by side U.S. and Chinese interests in each strategic domain and bilateral mode of exchange. Each chapter identifies areas of convergence and recommends cooperative initiatives and mechanisms to manage tensions. The central challenge in improving strategic stability between the United States and China is finding ways to enhance collaboration and mitigate sources of tension. The project aims to help policymakers and strategists identify the terms and conditions through which the two sides can better understand one another, avoid conflict, and facilitate cooperation.

Today, the U.S.-China relationship is stronger than it has ever been but also faces an increasing number of sources of tension and disagreement. Taiwan, North Korea, and territorial disputes between China and several U.S. allies in the East and South China Seas all present significant potential flashpoints. In addition, general strategic mistrust plagues the relationship and carries the potential, along with several other factors, to quickly exacerbate tensions and bring about a harmful deterioration of the relationship or even conflict.

Even the economic domain, which has traditionally served as a linchpin for the relationship, is no longer as rock-solid as it has been in the past. The U.S. and Chinese economies are inextricably linked, and economic success or failure for one generally equates to benefits or harm for the other. The prospect of a maturing and slowing Chinese economy, volatility in the Chinese stock market, and depreciation of the yuan all carry negative implications for the United States and the global economy. Similarly, U.S. measures to restrain Chinese efforts to assume a leadership role in Asia and globally do not bode well for the bilateral relationship. Notably, 2014 was the first year in recent decades when the majority of both societies viewed the other side negatively.

So what is to be done to ensure a stable and productive U.S.-China relationship in the future? How can both nations enhance cooperation in areas of shared interest and reduce tensions in areas of disagreement to foster a more productive relationship? What efforts can be undertaken to strengthen dialogue, encourage mutual understanding, and identify common ground? Finally, in which security-related areas can the two countries actually collaborate in ways that will strengthen the bilateral relationship? These are the important and timely questions that this project addresses. Better understanding the dynamics of bilateral relations and taking appropriate actions are the recipe for ensuring a stable long-term relationship between the world's two great powers.

Strategic domains

Maritime. Dong Wang and Christopher Yung paint a clear and comprehensive picture of the strategic area that involves some of the most consequential issues for U.S.-China interactions in the upcoming century—the maritime domain. The stakes for potential cooperation or conflict are incredibly high. The maritime domain is a critically important dimension of the bilateral relationship and has the potential to shape much of how the broader U.S.-China relationship develops in the coming years. Therefore, Washington and Beijing must clarify their strategic intentions and avoid misunderstandings and misperceptions. The two sides share common interests and responsibilities to ensure freedom of navigation as well as maintain regional peace and stability.

Open and safe passage in the seas is a key priority for both nations. The United States and China derive a significant amount of their economic prosperity from the economic and commercial activities that occur in the East and South China Seas. Therefore, ensuring open sea lines of communications is a vital common interest. In addition, both countries define the maritime domain as a critical component of their respective strategic interests. Since the end of World War II, the United States has viewed its role in the Pacific as one of a balancer. It has sought to occupy the center of a hub-and-spoke system through which it cooperates and supports its Asian allies. Thus, the sea serves as a vital zone of operation. China views the maritime domain as critical for ensuring the protection of its territorial integrity as well as legitimate maritime rights and benefits. Thus, identifying a path forward in which both countries operate side by side and pursue their respective interests in the maritime domain is important for the future stability of the U.S.-China relationship.

The authors assert that the United States and China must implement robust crisis-prevention management systems and carefully maintain and coordinate the increasingly numerous and sophisticated confidence-building mechanisms. Signing the air-to-air annex to the U.S.-China Memorandum of Understanding on the Rules of Behavior for the Safety of Air and Maritime Encounters would be a major step in this direction. Significant potential also exists for enhancing cooperation through coast guard cooperation on law-enforcement missions and naval cooperation on humanitarian assistance and disaster relief exercises.

Nuclear. Elbridge Colby and Wu Riqiang carefully and comprehensively explain the complex dynamics at play in U.S.-China nuclear relations and discuss the challenge of managing this incredibly important aspect of the bilateral relationship. Both the United States and China are nuclear powers, and the fact that nuclear weapons could be deployed in a hypothetical conflict scenario makes this strategic domain one of critical importance. Given the range of irritants in the relationship that could spark conflict—such as disputes over the status of Taiwan, North Korean provocations, and territorial claims in the South and East China Seas—Washington and Beijing must work to find ways to cooperate and avoid miscalculations in this domain.

Nuclear weapons are not a bilateral issue but must be seen as part of both nations' broader global strategic policy. Today there are roughly 16,000 nuclear warheads across the globe, and the United States and China maintain a nuclear deterrent of desired size and scope. Thus, the nuclear dynamic between the two countries is relatively stable. However, the changing conventional military balance, heightened tensions in the region, and the existence of several potential flashpoints in U.S.-China relations make ensuring that this important component of the bilateral relationship remains stable and well-managed a key priority.

The authors argue that Beijing and Washington should begin a dialogue on nuclear strategic stability to address sensitive concerns on both sides, including mutual understanding of China's second-strike capability. The two presidents should also reaffirm their commitment to denuclearization on the Korean Peninsula.

oh well

The United States and China should impress on Pyongyang that a nuclear North Korea cannot be tolerated by the international community and take measures to actively head off the looming crisis. Both governments should also work toward breaking the stalemate and reviving the six-party talks.

Cyberspace. Adam Segal and Tang Lan skillfully describe the complex landscape of U.S.-China relations in cyberspace. While significant differences exist between how Washington and Beijing view and manage cyberattacks, Internet governance, and the security of information and communication equipment, policymakers on both sides have declared a commitment to prevent disagreement over cyber issues from permanently damaging the relationship.

declared commitment — save!

Hacking, cyberespionage, and the threat of cyberwarfare hold the capacity to not only severely derail the U.S.-China relationship but also upset global frameworks and unsettle geopolitical dynamics. Private and government actors in both countries invest significant resources to search the Internet, seeking to identify strengths and weaknesses on the other side. Fundamental disagreements exist between the United States and China over key questions such as how much control the government should have over the Internet.

to do list

In order to reduce tensions in this strategic domain, it is critical that both sides engage in joint projects and focused dialogue designed to establish common ground, norms, and mutual understanding. The two countries maintain concerns over issues ranging from threats to critical infrastructure, nonstate actors' capabilities to launch cyberattacks, and the security of global supply chains. Both the United States and China have shared interests in countering cybercrimes and cyberterrorism, and collaboration on these issues could become a stepping stone toward building and strengthening mutual trust and expanding cooperation in the cyber domain. In order to manage disagreements and avoid long-term conflict in cyberspace, the authors recommend that Beijing and Washington capitalize on the September 2015 agreement to fight cybercrime and commercial cyberespionage with specific and robust cooperation.

Top-level leaders should continue to discuss norms of behavior in cyberspace and avoid suspending these dialogues during times of heightened tension. Both states need to build intellectual and technical capacity by expanding research at universities and in civil society. Finally, it is key to identify and implement joint measures to prevent cyber capabilities from falling into the hands of nonstate actors that may have nefarious intentions and intentionally promote discord between the two nations and globally.

Space. Brian Weeden and Xiao He expertly address the emerging and increasingly important question of how the United States and China will manage relations in outer space. As a strategic domain critical to both nations' national and economic security, Beijing and Washington are highly focused on ensuring continued access to space and opportunities to capitalize on space capabilities for their own interests. Space presents an environment characterized by high risk of competition in which interests do not naturally overlap. Therefore, in order to expand opportunities for cooperation and mitigate against the worst-case scenario of armed conflict, proactive leadership by both nations is required.

The United States and China are two of the ten nations that maintain a significant presence in space. While a significant difference in capabilities exists between the United States and China, the tides are shifting. The United States holds a decades-long lead in many areas, but China is quickly making progress in the development of its space capabilities. Space is an important strategic domain that is emerging as an area in which the interests of both nations will increasingly develop and therefore an area in which steps to effectively engage should be taken today.

In order to control the strategic risks in space, the authors argue that the United States and China should put in place a range of transparency and confidence-building measures to guide the development and use of dual-use space technology. Furthermore, they should pursue bilateral and international cooperation on civil and scientific space projects. Such cooperation will require that both sides find the political will to consider actual cooperation in space that goes beyond crisis management. Finally, the two countries should consider cooperating in areas of mutual interest—space debris, for example—and establish regular dialogues and other forums for information exchange and notification.

Special modes of bilateral exchange

In addition to examining the aforementioned four strategic domains, the edited volume also includes studies on two special strategic domains—or modes of bilateral exchange at the P2P and mil-mil levels—and on how they can increase opportunities for cooperation and reduce tension and strategic mistrust.

People-to-people exchange. P2P exchange has become one of the fundamental pillars of the U.S.-China relationship. Though the benefits of P2P ties, specifically their effects on strategic domains, are still not fully understood, enhancing and elevating P2P exchange as a strategic mechanism could help reverse negative trends and address the trust deficit in the bilateral relationship.

Coordinated P2P exchange between the United States and China has been taking place for more than 40 years. These exchanges span interactions between students, scientists, artists, tourists, government leaders, business leaders, and athletes. In fact, over 10,000 U.S. and Chinese citizens cross the Pacific each day. Applying the goodwill and positive influence that these exchanges create toward the most challenging strategic issues facing the bilateral relationship presents a potentially valuable vehicle for boosting cooperation and strengthening U.S.-China relations.

Travis Tanner and Zhao Minghao assert that the U.S. and Chinese governments should develop a new high-level framework to orchestrate P2P activities focused on addressing key strategic issues. Track 1.5 and 2 dialogues should focus on specific global strategic challenges on which the United States and China can collaborate to find mutually beneficial solutions. Involving a wide range of interlocutors from a variety of fields, including the business, academic, policy, scientific, and media communities, will help enhance and broaden understanding of the other side's views. Furthermore, both countries should invest in more opportunities for student exchange in order to ensure that future leaders are equipped with the skills to collaborate with each other and manage the bilateral relationship in the decades ahead.

Military-military relations. The mil-mil component of the Sino-U.S. relationship has long been regarded as the weakest—with suspension of ties often being used to relay discontent with other elements of the bilateral relationship. While the mil-mil relationship has since matured and become more stable, sustaining and further enhancing mil-mil ties will remain a critical component of mitigating tensions and reducing the risk of miscalculations and conflict between the two sides.

This is ever more the case as leaders in Washington and Beijing navigate an increasingly complex bilateral relationship, the outcomes of which will have reverberations across the region and the world. The scope of the mil-mil relationship has expanded significantly since its inception during the Cold War. However, the United States and China could achieve more on this front through careful consideration of how to balance shared goals with conflicting interests.

Roy Kamphausen and Jessica Drun call for setting modest expectations when advancing the relationship, as acknowledgement of limitations allows for more productive and fruitful exchanges. The chapter's recommendations include determining an appropriate mix of mil-mil activities, fostering deeper cooperation between the two militaries outside the Asia-Pacific, increasing congressional involvement and highlighting the role of Congress accordingly, and pursuing trilateral security dialogues. These policy proposals aim to build on positive trends in the relationship to further develop ties, while addressing negative elements and working to mitigate their effects.

Xu Hui and Yu Ying argue that the development of bilateral military ties is a necessary component to building a U.S.-China relationship that is anchored in coordination, cooperation, and stability, and that this would lead to the maintenance of regional peace and stability. They suggest that the two militaries should adopt effective measures to expand communications, enhance mechanisms dedicated to crisis prevention and management, and thereby achieve the goal of developing a healthy and stable bilateral military relationship.

Key findings

There are a number of key findings discussed within the edited volume that span all domains and modes of exchange and that are important to highlight as ways to move forward in an effort to build a more stable and cooperative bilateral relationship. First, the United States and China need to set common definitions and parameters in each area. Mutual understanding of the central components of a strategic domain and mode of bilateral exchange is necessary for productive discussion on cooperation and trust building. Next, it is important for both countries to develop a better understanding of the broader dynamics of crisis stability and instability within the strategic domains. In the bilateral context, further discussion of red lines is essential to manage escalation and avoid miscalculations during crisis scenarios.

An important question addressed by the edited volume relates to the best structural approach to take in enhancing U.S.-China cooperation. Is a top-down or bottom-up approach, or perhaps a combination of both, the most conducive to achieving successful outcomes in these strategic domains and bilateral modes of exchange? Looking at the top-down approach, government leadership must be willing to spend significant political capital and keep up dialogue on key issues over a significant period of time. Moreover, because sensitive issues within the strategic domains are most commonly addressed through bilateral discussions, it is critical to not simply continue but expand Track 1.5 and 2 dialogues on these issues in order to help inform and guide the official process at the Track 1 level.

Finally, even though this edited volume has examined each strategic domain and mode of bilateral exchange independently, policymakers do not make decisions on issues in one domain or mode of exchange in isolation from others. It is therefore critical to examine how recommendations made for one area can affect issues in another. Fully and directly addressing the core issues raised in this study will help mitigate the signs of budding strategic rivalry between China and the United States, chart the roadmap for a new type of relationship, and anchor U.S.-China relations on more stable and durable ground in the years and decades to come.

Following Donald Trump's swearing in as 45th President of the United States, the degree of U.S.-China cooperation on strategic and various policy issues remains uncertain. The perceptions held by U.S. strategists and policy makers vis-à-vis China have undergone a fundamental shift. A new bipartisan consensus is emerging in the United States which holds that U.S. engagement with China as pursued by consecutive administrations since normalization of diplomatic relations in 1972 has failed. This consensus is predicated on the view that U.S.-China relations are at an inflection point, and that China's true strategic intention is to challenge U.S. hegemony and promote a China-dominated parallel order. A series of key U.S. official documents released since the advent of the Trump administration, such as the National Security Strategy Report, among others, have identified China as the major strategic competitor posing the greatest threat to the current U.S.-led liberal international order. Some American ultra-conservatives and super-hawks are even publicly advocating the decoupling of the Chinese and American economies and envisaging a new Cold War with China. Even former U.S. secretary of state Henry A. Kissinger has suggested that U.S.-China relations are now at "the foothills of a new Cold War" and that we can no longer go back to the old days. Does all this mean that China and the United States have already fallen into the so-called 'Thucydides Trap'?

We believe our study, a collective endeavor by dozens of leading experts from China and the United States, will add important perspectives to the ongoing debate on U.S.-China relations at a time when both countries are trying to find a new paradigm for bilateral relations. Our study will also serve as an important point of reference for strategists and policy makers in both countries. As this study shows, even in highly sensitive and complex strategic domains such as nuclear, space, maritime, cyber, and military-to-military relations, Chinese and American interests are not entirely conflictual or zero-sum. On the contrary, China and the United States still enjoy important mutual interests, and there is still immense potential for cooperation within these strategic domains. Indeed, what has changed since the Trump presidency is not the objective interests of China and the United States in these strategic domains but rather U.S. perceptions of China's intentions and interests. Our study also reminds strategic analysts and policy makers of the importance of avoiding zero-sum thinking, misperceptions, self-righteousness, and ideological prejudices. China and the United States are not necessarily destined for a new Cold War. Rather, it is possible for Beijing and Washington to avoid the 'Thucydides Trap' and forge a bilateral relationship that is characterized by coordination, cooperation, and stability. To do so, strategists and policy makers in both countries will have to avoid emotive decision making, fear, and ideological inclinations. U.S.-China relations should be approached rationally and pragmatically. The differences and commonalities in the strategic interests between these two great powers should be accurately assessed in an open and inclusive manner and not based on rigid orthodoxy. U.S.-China relations carry increasingly significant global implications. The evolution of the U.S.-China relationship will to a great extent determine the trajectory and modality of the global order in the decades to come. A pertinent question looms large in this early period of the 21st century: whether or not China and the United States can avoid the 'Thucydides Trap' and likewise whether they are able to jointly shape a peaceful, cooperative, and stable future. We hope our study serves as a sound intellectual basis for the ongoing debate on U.S.-China relations, and therefore makes a meaningful contribution to such a debate.

1 U.S.-China relations in the maritime security domain

Dong Wang and Christopher Yung

EXECUTIVE SUMMARY

This chapter examines the importance of the maritime domain to U.S. and Chinese national interests, discusses issues on which the two powers' interests diverge, identifies areas for cooperation, and proposes potential mechanisms to manage maritime tensions.

Main argument

The maritime domain is the most mature environment in which China and the U.S. interact and is an area where the two major powers repeatedly discuss key issues of contention and cooperation. Yet while this makes conceptualization of areas of agreement and disagreement easier than in other domains, the enormous interests involved and the potential for the two powers to confound one another make the task of arriving at cooperative measures no less daunting. Both countries have an interest in freedom of navigation, both recognize the tangible benefits from maritime-related economies, both have a vested interest in good order and stability at sea, and both view the sea as a means to foster and protect national security interests. At the same time, the two countries differ in how they define their respective national interests, what they believe to be appropriate means of displaying good and bad intentions, how they view the sea (either as a threat or as an opportunity), and how they interpret international law and the protection of maritime sovereignty. Yet despite these differences, the U.S. and China share enough overlapping interests in the maritime domain to warrant serious thought about deepening and strengthening cooperative programs already in existence.

Policy implications

- The U.S. and China should build on existing cooperative activities between their respective coast guards while sustaining and, if possible, extending cooperation between other government agencies related to anti-pollution measures, ocean observation, marine scientific research, and prevention of marine hazards.

- U.S. and Chinese efforts in the Gulf of Aden and the Indian Ocean to combat piracy are not presently coordinated. One ambitious option the two sides should consider is forming a quintilateral combined search and rescue agency (made up of the U.S., China, India, Australia, and ASEAN) to monitor the Indian Ocean region, detect and respond to crises, and provide rescue efforts for ships and aircraft transiting these waters.
- The two powers could expand on the military-to-military cooperation that has taken place within the maritime domain over the past few years. The Rim of the Pacific (RIMPAC) exercise should continue to serve as a platform for Chinese participation. Additionally, the U.S. should consider inviting China to exercises farther west, such as the Cooperation Afloat Readiness and Training (CARAT) exercise that it conducts annually with the Southeast Asian militaries.

Of all the strategic domains that China and the United States will interact in over the upcoming century, the domain with the greatest opportunity for cooperation and mutual benefit also happens to be the one that poses some of the greatest perils to the relationship: the maritime domain. This may be so because it is through the maritime domain that the two powers derive a substantial share of their economic prosperity; at the same time, it is in this domain that the two countries are likely to rub up against one another in a state of friction and could even clash with one another.

This chapter lays out the importance of the maritime domain to U.S. and Chinese national interests. It will present both Chinese and U.S. perspectives on the interests of the other country and will describe challenges in the maritime domain to U.S.-China relations. Additionally, the chapter will discuss the divergence in the two powers' interests and will conclude by considering areas of cooperation and identifying mechanisms to manage tension.

U.S. perspectives on U.S.-China relations in the maritime domain

The importance of the maritime domain for U.S. national interests

Since the inception of the United States, the sea has been a central element of the country's economic and commercial interests. In fact, even prior to U.S. independence from Great Britain, American fishermen and merchant traders were plying the waters of the Atlantic in search of livelihood.[1] Following the formation of the United States, American merchantmen made their way around the globe to conduct trade. Whalers of New England were commonplace, and a healthy share of the nation's GDP was derived from seagoing activities. It was in defense of the freedom to pursue these activities that the newly born United States first went to war. When Barbary pirates raided American merchantmen, the United States dispatched the newly created U.S. Marine Corps to North Africa to directly stop these activities.[2] And when British ships boarded U.S. merchant vessels and forced American sailors into servitude, the practice was so abhorrent to American sensibilities that the United States went to war with Great Britain over the issue.[3]

U.S. commercial and economic interests depend substantially on the maritime domain to this day. According to statistics from the National Oceanic and Atmospheric Administration in 2014, the ocean economy was responsible for the creation of close to three million jobs in the United States.[4] Beyond the narrow economic interests, Americans view secure sea lanes and open access to the maritime domain as the foundation for the modern international economic order. Freedom of navigation and the ability to ship goods intact anywhere on the globe with speed and at minimum expense is the basis for the U.S.-made trading order.

U.S. national interests benefiting from the sea extend beyond the commercial or economic, and U.S. strategic interests are also shaped by the maritime domain. Early in its inception, the United States had time to consolidate its domestic power and enhance its effectiveness at governance because it enjoyed an oceanic barrier between the continental United States and Europe.

Following the Louisiana Purchase and the acquisitions of the Florida, California, New Mexico, Arizona, and Texas territories, the United States had relatively secure land borders, with its neighbors to the north (Canada) and south (Mexico) not posing significant strategic threats. That two oceans now stood between a fledgling continent and potential predatory powers in Europe and Asia was a blessing few newly born nations enjoy.[5] The first strategic benefit of the maritime domain to U.S. national security interests is that it has served and continues to serve as a natural barrier, a moat, against national security threats.

As U.S. military power grew and as the United States took on increasing responsibilities in the international system, the maritime domain took on additional strategic significance. Throughout its later history, the United States has found itself in the role of balancer or police officer, in which it has had to either react militarily to the rise of a threat to its national interests or serve as a deterrent to further threats to its interests. In World War I, following Germany's pursuit of unrestricted submarine warfare, the United States found itself siding with the Grand Alliance—Great Britain, France, and Russia—against Germany, the Ottoman Empire, and the Austro-Hungarian Empire. Although the United States went to war under the banner of "the war to end all wars," the trigger for U.S. entry into the conflict was an attempt by another power not only to restrict the freedom of navigation of U.S. shipping in the Atlantic but also to strategically dominate Western Europe.[6] During World War II, the United States found itself in a position where access to the sea and the ability to project power to distant lands through the sea was essential to U.S. victory and Allied survival.[7] It was through the military necessity of ensuring access to the maritime arena in war that the U.S. military invented and perfected such techniques as carrier aviation, amphibious doctrine, submarine and antisubmarine warfare, antiair warfare, and seaborne logistics.[8]

For the United States, the importance of a secure maritime domain was again demonstrated during the Cold War. U.S. naval superiority over the Soviet Union enabled U.S. Navy submarines to track and monitor Soviet nuclear-missile-bearing submarines, and sound surveillance system arrays displayed in strategic locations across the oceans helped track and monitor subsurface threats to the U.S. homeland. U.S. naval superiority also ensured the ability to dispatch convoys of supplies and troops to Europe in case of a Soviet land invasion against the United States' NATO allies.[9] Just as importantly, U.S. maritime superiority ensured the ability to dispatch expeditionary forces to "hot spots" around the globe. The United States dispatched troops to the Korean Peninsula, Vietnam, Grenada, and Lebanon during the Cold War, and in the post–Cold War era troops were sent to Iraq (twice) and Afghanistan, to name but a few major crisis responses.[10]

The maritime domain is therefore a vital element of U.S. national security strategy. First, this space serves as an initial barrier to threats to the homeland. Second, it is seen as a highway for the United States to strategically respond to crises and threats abroad. Finally, because the United States sees the prevention of hegemonic powers dominating their respective continents or regions as vital to its own national security interests, the maritime domain has been seen as one in which the United States is able to take action to balance that emerging threat or, if necessary, defeat it. Thus, the United States uses the domain to project power abroad to affect the balance of power in important regions and, when necessary, to fight in world wars or regional conflicts. Secure access to sea lanes is especially important because the United States sees the deterrence of emerging threats as an important component of its national security strategy—and deterring threats in part depends on the ability of the United States to be seen as capable of rapidly deploying forces anywhere in the world.

U.S. views of Chinese interests in the maritime domain

U.S. strategists and observers of U.S.-China relations believe that China has an intrinsic interest in a secure maritime domain. It has become a mantra among China specialists in the United States that China has benefited from secure seas as much as, if not more than, almost any other nation in the globalized world economy.[11] To function effectively and efficiently, a globalized economy relies on freedom of navigation and secure sea lines of communication (SLOC). For China, secure SLOCs ensure that goods shipped from China reach their destination safely and that raw materials and petroleum from such places as the Middle East and Africa arrive in China. Chinese leaders themselves have voiced this point: for instance, former president Hu Jintao took note of China's vulnerability to the blockage of strategic chokepoints when he made reference to a "Malacca dilemma."[12]

However, U.S. observers also argue that while China has enjoyed the fruits of freedom of navigation and secure SLOCs, it has put in a minimally acceptable level of effort to ensure freedom of navigation and SLOC protection. Chinese analysts point to China's naval counterpiracy flotilla as evidence of the country's consistent contribution,[13] which is true, but U.S. observers note that China could certainly do a lot more, given its increasing military capability and the size of its economy.[14] Additionally, they note that while China makes contributions to securing the maritime domain, it appears to do so only when its economic interests are affected.[15] Hence, those U.S. observers argue that China is willing to put counterpiracy flotillas in the Gulf of Aden but is reluctant to cooperate with the United States and India to provide SLOC protection for ships transiting the Indian Ocean.

U.S. observers have also commented that it is in China's interest to establish norms and rules of behavior at sea and then obey them. The more China operates farther from its "near seas," and the more it interacts with the navies, coast guards, and official vessels of other countries, as well as with their fishermen and other merchant ships, the more it will be in China's interests to operate under a common set of principles that regulates how it interacts with other interested mariners. But the U.S. view is that China is selectively adhering to these maritime rules and norms of behavior.[16] For instance, U.S. observers believe that China's placement of an oil rig in waters disputed by Vietnam and the subsequent collisions between Chinese and Vietnamese vessels—or China's island reclamation activities beginning in 2014—are arguably a violation of the Declaration on the Conduct of Parties in the South China Sea.

The U.S. perspective on Chinese interests is that China values international law as a means to maintain a peaceful and stable international environment; however, it is also the U.S. view that China selectively adheres to international law or stretches the interpretation of international law to suit its narrow interests. Therefore, U.S. strategic analysts believe that China was relatively quick to sign the United Nations Convention on Law of Sea (UNCLOS) but will strictly interpret specific aspects of the law in order to reserve for itself a more restrictive definition of access to its own exclusive economic zone (EEZ).[17] Thus, the U.S. view is that in contradiction to most countries' interpretations of the roles, responsibilities, and rights of states operating outside another country's territorial waters and adjacent contiguous zone but within that country's 200-nautical-mile EEZ, China has asserted that no other country has the right to militarily operate within that EEZ (for exercises, scientific experiments, intelligence collection, surveillance, or even transiting) without the permission of that coastal state.[18] U.S. strategic analysts argue that most other countries, and the international courts as well, interpret UNCLOS differently. Most view the EEZ outside a coastal state's territorial waters as international waters, in which a visiting ship—military or civilian—may conduct whatever type of operation it so chooses.

Additionally, the U.S. view is that China has selectively ignored international law when it refuses to follow several legal precedents set by a range of other countries resolving their maritime territorial disputes through the courts. Hence, were China to go against its own past practices and simply submit its territorial disputes with the other South China Sea or East China Sea claimants to the International Court of Justice, these maritime disputes would no longer serve as a point of friction in the region. The maritime dispute between Nicaragua and Colombia was resolved this way, as was the recent Bay of Bengal arbitration between India and Bangladesh.[19]

Finally, some U.S. observers assert that such a list of grievances reflects, at best, a difference between the two powers' interpretation of international law or operational norms of behavior and, at worst, benign neglect on China's part of its obligations to be a responsible stakeholder. Some conservative U.S. strategists and analysts actually hold a significantly more pessimistic view of Beijing's motives. For them, China's ultimate interests involve the following: excluding the United States from East Asia, establishing China as a dominant maritime and hegemonic power in the region, and compelling rival claimants to recognize China's claims as a *fait accompli*.[20]

Chinese perspectives on U.S.-China relations in the maritime domain

Chinese interests in the maritime domain

China's interests and intent in the maritime domain can be understood as follows: (1) to safeguard the national unity and territorial integrity of the PRC as well as to defend maritime rights and benefits, (2) to keep SLOCs open and thus to support the free flow of goods and services, (3) to be able to deny or deter during wartime other powers' ability to pose threats within strategic maritime zones or layers of defense that are defined by the first and second island chains, and (4) to protect China's rapidly expanding overseas interests.

Traditionally regarded as a land power, contemporary China is nevertheless highly dependent on the oceans. The five coastal provinces in East China—Shandong, Jiangsu, Zhejiang, Fujian, and Guangdong—account for 27.8% of China's population and two-fifths of national GDP.[21] In coastal regions alone, there are more than 55 million people relying on the jobs created by foreign trade. The dependence on foreign trade in these provinces is as high as 97.5%.[22] In the energy sector, until 2014, China imported 60% of its oil. It is estimated that by the end of 2014, 53.6%, 69.0%, and 52.9% of minerals, copper, and aluminum, respectively, will need to be imported from abroad.[23] In addition, in 2014, 85% of China's imported oil and 55% of its imported natural gas transited the South China Sea and the Strait of Malacca.[24] The security of SLOCs is therefore critical to the economic growth of China. In other words, the country has a vital interest in ensuring freedom of navigation around the world, including in the western Pacific, the Indian Ocean, and the Persian Gulf.

Chinese military scholars emphasize the importance of "maritime strategic access" (*haishang zhanlue tongdao*).[25] Seeing maritime strategic access as a "focal point for great powers' competition for interests," as well as an important factor in "influencing China's security and development," Liang Fang of China's National Defense University argues that the People's Liberation Army Navy (PLAN) should enhance "core strategic capacity building" (*hexin zhanlue nengli jianshe*), including the development of "open seas protection" (*yuanhai fangwei*) operation capability, power projection capability, and maritime mobile logistics support capability.[26]

The idea of maritime security, however, followed a long trajectory in China. Repeated incursions by Western imperialist powers in Chinese modern history, beginning with the First Opium War of 1840, have left an indelible mark on the nation's ideational legacy of maritime security. As a result, the country places a high premium on sovereignty and the traditional military dimension of security. It was not until the end of the Cold War that China's concept of security expanded to include nontraditional security dimensions. Consequently, Chinese discourse on maritime security has also only gradually come to include issues such as energy, human trafficking, drug trafficking, environmental protection, and fishery disputes.[27]

Meanwhile, as China's overseas interests (*haiwai liyi*)—defined as investments, assets, and personnel abroad—have been rapidly expanding in the past decade, the protection of these interests has become an important part of China's maritime strategy. Between 2002 and 2014, China's annual overseas investments increased 45.6 times, from $2.70 billion to $123.12 billion.[28] In 2015 alone, it is estimated that more than 1.27 million Chinese citizens traveled abroad.[29] Several major incidents and turning points called Chinese leaders' attention to the myriad nontraditional threats to the country's overseas interests. Amid the rising piracy threat in the waters off the Gulf of Aden, China joined the international efforts to patrol the Gulf of Aden and the coast of Somalia in December 2008. By December 2015, China had sent 22 fleets for escort missions. Over 14,000 navy officers and sailors have taken part in the missions, and the PLAN fleets have conducted 900 missions and escorted more than 6,100 commercial ships, including chartered ships of the UN World Food Programme.[30] The Libyan civil war, and the evacuation missions of Chinese citizens and assets associated with it, alerted the Chinese public and leaders of the importance of protecting China's overseas interests.

It is therefore not surprising that the most recent white paper on China's military strategy stated the following:

> With the growth of China's national interests, its national security is more vulnerable to international and regional turmoil, terrorism, piracy, serious natural disasters and epidemics, and the security of overseas interests concerning energy and resources, strategic sea lines of communication (SLOCs), as well as institutions, personnel, and assets abroad, has become an imminent issue.[31]

For most of the time since 1949, however, China's strategy of military development was predominantly army oriented. From the 1950s to the early 1980s, China's naval strategy can be defined as one of "coastal defense" (*jin'an fangyu*). In 1985 the commander of the PLAN, Admiral Liu Huaqing, formally proposed "offshore waters (near sea) defense" (*jinhai fangyu*) as China's naval strategy. Admiral Liu, who is now widely regarded as the "father of China's modern navy," defined the near seas as Chinese sea areas to the west of the first island chain, defined by a line through the Kuril Islands, Japan and the Ryukyu Islands, Taiwan, the Philippines, Borneo, and Natuna Besar. Areas beyond the near seas were defined as the "medium and far seas" (*zhongyuan hai*). According to Admiral Liu's naval strategy, the maritime operational zones of the PLAN would encompass the first island chain, including the Yellow Sea, the East China Sea, and the South China Sea. As China's economy continues to grow and the strength of the PLAN increases, the PLAN should gradually expand its maritime operational zones to the northern Pacific, or the second island chain, a line stretching from the Kuril Islands through Japan, the Bonin Islands, the Mariana Islands, and the Caroline Islands.[32] The concept of an island chain, first discussed and elaborated by Liu in the Chinese strategic literature, remains active in Chinese thinking about naval strategy, with Taiwan as one of the key points in the chain. By the mid-2000s, Chinese military analysts had begun using the concept of "counterintervention" (*fan jieru*) in various writings, which was labeled as an anti-access/area-denial (A2/AD) strategy by U.S. policy planners and analysts.[33] The counterintervention strategy, arguably, serves to deter an adversary's military deployment in the western Pacific and limit or disrupt access to maritime operational zones along Taiwan or the South China Sea.[34]

China's participation in the international counterpiracy operations in the Gulf of Aden since December 2008 proved to be a turning point in the country's naval strategic thinking. The counterpiracy operations not only greatly improved the PLAN's ocean-going operational capabilities, but they also marked the gradual shift from an offshore waters defense strategy to an open seas protection strategy. In March 2009 the *People's Liberation Army Daily* stated that "as China's national interests extend, our maritime forces are moving from 'offshore waters defense' to 'open seas protection,' and assume the historical duty of carrying out diversified military tasks."[35] In March 2010, Rear Admiral Zhang Huacheng, commander of the East China Fleet, stated in an interview with the Xinhua News Agency that "the naval strategy is now undergoing change, transitioning from one of offshore waters defense to the direction of open seas protection."[36] Maintaining national unity and defending territorial as well as maritime integrity have from the very beginning been at the core of China's maritime strategy. The white paper *China's Military Strategy*, released in May 2015, lists the following objectives among China's strategic guidelines: "strike a balance between rights protection and stability maintenance, and make overall planning for both, safeguard national territorial sovereignty and maritime rights and interests, and maintain security and stability along China's periphery."[37]

China's views of U.S. interests in the maritime domain[38]

As the U.S. implements its strategy of "rebalancing to Asia," China heatedly debates the nature and implications of this strategy. Whereas policymakers in China largely remain sober-minded and stress the importance of cooperative, non-adversarial relations with the United States, the U.S. rebalancing strategy has nevertheless increased the sentiments of insecurity and being threatened among elites and the public in China. As a result, the rebalance has contributed to the emerging security dilemma between China and the United States.

Chinese strategic analysts' interpretations of U.S. intentions for rebalancing generally fall into a realist paradigm that has been dominant in China's strategic circles.[39] For Chinese analysts who tend to observe U.S.-China relations from the perspectives of hardcore realism and traditional geopolitics, the United States' high-profile strategy is a manifestation of the logic of classical power politics; that is, the United States is bent on maintaining its hegemony in East Asia.

These analysts tend to interpret the Obama administration's "returning to Asia" policy through the lens of a zero-sum game, and their classic realist reading of U.S. policy is also reflected in their policy prescriptions. In fact, American views about checking China before it becomes too powerful—offered by prominent offensive realists such as John Mearsheimer—were picked up by those Chinese analysts as *prima facie* evidence that the U.S. rebalance is indeed a part of efforts to contain China.[40]

Specifically, Chinese military scholars see that the United States has, since the September 11 terrorist attacks, "gradually shifted its strategic focus to the Asia-Pacific," "deployed massive forces" along the first and second island chains, and transformed Guam into "a central base and power projection center" in the western Pacific. Moreover, the United States, by controlling maritime chokepoints such as the Strait of Malacca and the Strait of Hormuz, has strengthened its "strategic containment" against China and posed a potential threat to the security of China's maritime strategic access.[41]

Within days of Secretary of State Hillary Clinton's declaration at the July 2009 Association of Southeast Asian Nations (ASEAN) Summit that "the United States is back,"[42] the *Global Times*, a popular international affairs newspaper in China, published an op-ed piece that interpreted Clinton's statement as "a declaration that the United States is prepared to compete with China for influence in East Asia." The article suggested that the United States would exert pressures of "encirclement and blockage" (*weidu*) through enhancing alliance relations with Japan and South Korea and that it would try to "consume" (*xiaohao*) China's power through "manipulating" Southeast Asian countries to engage in territorial disputes with China.[43]

Numerous moves by the Obama administration have been perceived in China as evidence of U.S. hostility toward Beijing. These moves have included deploying U.S. Marines to Darwin, Australia; asserting U.S. interests in freedom of navigation in the South China Sea; taking the sides of China's rivals in the territorial disputes in the East and South China Seas; bolstering military alliances with the Philippines, Japan, and Australia; enhancing security cooperation with Vietnam and India; improving bilateral relations with Myanmar; and beefing up the United States' ballistic missile defense systems in East Asia. This more assertive U.S. posture in rebalancing to Asia increased both the Chinese public's and the Chinese elite's perceptions of a U.S. bent on containing China.

At an interagency conference on maritime security in February 2013, Lieutenant General Qi Jianguo, deputy chief of the General Staff of the People's Liberation Army (PLA), remarked that "China's security threats as well as the focal point for development mainly come from the maritime domain." He added that "maritime struggle (*haishang douzheng*) is concerned about state sovereignty and security, but also state construction and development." Qi declared that China would never provoke maritime dispute and conflict, nor would it ever undermine freedom of navigation permitted by international law; instead, China would "steadfastly defend state sovereignty, territorial integrity as well as maritime right and benefits."[44]

The white paper *China's Military Strategy* also observes that

> on the issues concerning China's territorial sovereignty and maritime rights and interests, some of its offshore neighbors take provocative actions and reinforce their military presence on China's reefs and islands that they have

illegally occupied. Some external countries are also busy meddling in South China Sea affairs; a tiny few maintain constant close-in air and sea surveillance and reconnaissance against China. It is thus a long-standing task for China to safeguard its maritime rights and interests.[45]

In line with the changing strategic environment, the white paper stipulates that the PLAN will "gradually shift its focus from 'offshore waters defense' to the combination of 'offshore waters defense' with 'open seas protection'" and "build a combined, multifunctional, and efficient marine combat force structure." To fulfill such goals, the PLAN should "enhance its capabilities for strategic deterrence and counterattack, maritime maneuvers, joint operations at sea, comprehensive defense, and comprehensive support."[46]

The convergence of interests and challenges to U.S.-China maritime relations

The convergence of interests

The United States and China enjoy a significant convergence of interests in the maritime domain. Both countries value free and open trade and view security of the domain as important to this goal. As a consequence, they view secure sea lanes as absolutely necessary for national security. Both countries believe in safety and order at sea and act to enforce rules set down by interested countries to maintain that safety and order.

Both countries believe that military forces can be used and force structure can be developed to protect a nation's maritime security, even though the two countries differ on how military force should be used and how transparent the militaries should be to assure one another. On the issue of how militaries can be used in the maritime domain, both countries have an existing or growing network of interests abroad and believe that overseas interests need to be protected and that therefore the use of force to protect overseas interests is valid. Additionally, both countries believe that military forces can be used to help nations that have experienced natural and man-made disasters.

Finally, both countries have extensive economic interests in the maritime domain and have a substantial interest in policies designed to protect those economic interests. Some of those policies have been discussed earlier—for example, in the case of Chinese counterpiracy task forces. However, the protection of economic interests also extends to common policies against driftnet fishing, ocean pollution, and terrorist threats to major ports, as well as providing an effective search and rescue process to aid in shipping and aviation commerce.

Challenges to the U.S.-China relationship within the maritime domain

While the maritime domain remains one of the areas of greatest potential for cooperation between the United States and China, it also has some of the greatest potential for conflict between the two powers. First, almost all the potential hot spots or crisis points between the two powers are in the maritime arena. Although the Korean Peninsula remains one of the potential areas of major-power rivalry, the current scenarios of greatest concern are those related to Taiwan and the South and East China Seas. Most U.S. and Chinese analysts who focus on security issues and U.S.-China relations believe that it is possible for the two powers to coordinate and work with each other on the Korean Peninsula should the security situation there deteriorate.[47] These are all issues that Washington and Beijing can work out, discuss, and come to an agreement on—albeit one that requires a large dose of sensitivity to allies.

By contrast, the sovereignty issues associated with Taiwan, the South China Sea, and the East China Sea are all "hot button" issues for both major powers, and it remains unclear if the two sides can resolve these issues through dialogue. For China, the issue of Taiwan and its sovereignty over the island is nonnegotiable. When it comes to territorial disputes over the Diaoyu Islands (called the Senkaku Islands in Japan) in the East China Sea or over the Nansha (or Spratly) Islands in the South China Sea, China, while maintaining that its sovereignty is unquestion-able, nevertheless has put forward proposals of "shelving differences, and joint development."[48] For the United States, the issues pertaining to Taiwan and the South and East China Seas extend to questions of the value of democracy, alliance credibility, freedom of navigation, and the peaceful resolution to disputes. There is no consensus among either American or Chinese analysts that any of these hot spots can be easily resolved by the two sides talking to one another. In fact, China argues that the United States has no business in these issues—especially with regard to Taiwan—and indeed regards U.S. behavior as "interference into Chi-na's internal affairs" and "infringement upon China's sovereignty."[49] As a result, there remains the possibility that China and the United States could tangle with each other over a crisis emerging from a Taiwan, a South China Sea, or an East China Sea scenario. All three scenarios involve military capabilities substantially operating in the maritime domain, and the likelihood of military success rests on military capabilities that are partially air-based but primarily maritime in nature. Consequently, because these issues are of great political importance to both coun-tries, we can expect both militaries to be continually developing capabilities that can better operate in the maritime domain to the detriment and possible destruc-tion of units of the other.

Second, the maritime domain serves as the medium through which one country has the capability to most frustrate the political objectives of the other. As alluded to earlier, both China and the United States are expected to develop military capa-bilities that will deter, frustrate, and possibly destroy the capabilities of the other in a Taiwan contingency. Additionally, in relation to a Taiwan contingency, but pos-sibly relevant to other conflict scenarios, the United States could choke off the eco-nomic growth of China by using its navy to blockade and strangulate China's access to petroleum and raw materials—the so-called Malacca dilemma. China could use any number of developing military technologies to prevent the United States from operating freely in the Asia-Pacific maritime sphere—the operational concept of

A2/AD or counter-intervention. The United States could provide amphibious lift to Japanese forces during a Diaoyu/Senkaku scenario, or China could complicate U.S. military responses to a Taiwan contingency by threatening U.S. naval forces with Chinese surface and subsurface forces and anti-ship ballistic missiles.

Third, dominance over the maritime arena serves as a symbol for great-power status. Every nation that has been labeled a great power has had a powerful navy to both advance and protect its commercial interests overseas.[50] However, in attaining this status through the development of a powerful navy, many of these nations necessarily grow in power relative to already powerful countries with strong navies themselves. Thus, if major powers are not careful, the maritime domain will become the medium through which a zero-sum game is played out with the possibility of major systemic war.

A perfect illustration of this dynamic is China's acquisition of an aircraft carrier. Arguably, China needs at least several carrier battle groups to protect its maritime interests; however, other observers have noted that a considerable factor in the Chinese decision to acquire the carrier was to represent China's rise in a tangible way, portray its great-power status, and symbolize its changing international status both abroad and at home.[51] To be sure, operationally a single carrier does not diminish U.S. maritime supremacy in the western Pacific. Additionally, the United States is not standing still as China adds to its naval order of battle. The United States is projected to add another aircraft carrier (the USS *Ford*) to its inventory along with additional Arleigh Burke–class destroyers, Virginia-class submarines, and large-deck amphibious ships.[52] On the other hand, prior to China's acquisition of carrier groups, and barring Thailand and India with their smaller carriers, the United States was the only power in the western Pacific to display its might through carrier operations. China's acquisition of the *Liaoning* changes that equation, if only slightly. The possible arrival of a second, third, or even fourth carrier over the next few decades necessarily means that U.S. maritime might is weaker than it had been when the United States had a monopoly on carrier operations in the western Pacific.

The same can be said of China's acquisition of expeditionary capabilities. The procurement of Chinese landing platform docks, each capable of carrying troops, landing craft, and helicopters to distant locations (in China's case to the Gulf of Aden area), has meant that the United States no longer has a monopoly on long-distance expeditionary operations. Prior to the arrival of this capability, only the United States could embark large numbers of marines on amphibious ships and send them to distant lands for amphibious landings and other expeditionary operations. Other countries in Asia have marines and expeditionary ground forces, but none of these countries, including even Australia, could embark a sizable number of these forces and send them off to conduct missions. China's acquisition of modern L-class ships, and the report that it is likely to procure the larger L-class ships—the landing helicopter dock—takes away the U.S. monopoly on this kind of military capability.[53]

Conceivably, this gradual yet undeniably upward trajectory of Chinese naval power could in the long term pose a direct challenge to U.S. national interests in the maritime domain. A worst-case scenario could involve China's long-term ability to project military power not just out of the area but globally, thereby eventually challenging the United States' global leadership position. Of course, a best-case scenario would involve the possibility of U.S.-China "joint patrol" of SLOCs in the future, an idea that has been endorsed by former senior U.S. policy-makers such as the former national security advisor Stephen Hadley. Speaking at a forum in Beijing in June 2014, Hadley noted that the United States was "ready to accept a growing Chinese open sea naval capability to defend the sea lanes" and that allowing China to share the responsibility of sea-lane protection would be "of significant benefit" to the United States.[54]

As stated previously, the maritime sphere serves as a perfect stage on which countries can demonstrate their great-power status. However, that display of status might come at the expense of existing great powers. If the United States and China are not careful, this maritime stage could become not only a place that China uses to demonstrate how far it has come but also a place where the two countries overtly display the strategic competition between them.

Finally, U.S.-China relations are challenged by the maritime domain because the two countries have fundamentally different philosophies about the nature and meaning of the sea. Historically for modern China, the sea is first and foremost a means of access by enemies to threaten and humiliate the country. It was through the sea that the British dominated China and began its 150 years of humiliation. The sea is thus seen as a domain that requires China to impose zones or belts of defenses to prevent hostile powers from gaining access to the country and taking advantage of it. While the United States also views the sea as a potential pathway for threats to the homeland, it is more often conceptually seen as a means for the United States to push out and advance its own interests. Thus, one power largely sees the domain as a potential threat, while the other power sees the domain largely as an opportunity; one sees its maritime strategy as mostly defensive in nature, while the other naturally exhibits a more offensive way of thinking. This fundamental difference in philosophies shapes how the two powers look at a range of maritime issues, some of which could be incompatible if they are not creative in their strategic thinking.

This dynamic is most easily seen in the tensions existing between the two countries over U.S. Navy surveillance and reconnaissance operations (SRO). The United States regards as its right the ability to fly surveillance aircraft or sail sur-veillance ships within China's EEZ but outside China's territorial waters. From the U.S. perspective, this right accords with international law, represents prudent military and strategic planning insofar as there is a potential conflict with China over Taiwan or the East or South China Sea, and importantly represents the U.S. mindset that national security is best served by operating forward and monitoring and dealing with threats before they grow beyond U.S. capabilities. The U.S.-termed freedom of navigation operations conducted by the USS *Lassen* in October 2015 and USS *Wilbur* in January 2016 in waters near or within 12 nautical miles of the China-controlled Nansha (Spratly) Islands are an illustration of such a dynamic.

By stark contrast, China sees U.S. SROs as an affront to Chinese sovereignty, intrusive in nature, and potentially threatening to China's security. It is therefore no surprise that Beijing lashed out at Washington's freedom of navigation operations and harshly criticized the U.S. moves as "illegal," "muscle-flexing," and "intimidating China with U.S. military power."[55] Moreover, the United States could pass the operational intelligence it acquires through these activities to regional allies, thus negatively affecting the operational capability of the PLA and potentially posing a threat to China's security interests. In strategic dialogues between the U.S. and Chinese militaries, often the Chinese side will say that, first of all, the act of operating this way betrays what Americans think of the relationship. The existence of SROs strongly suggests that the United States sees China as an enemy. Second, the Chinese will often suggest that perhaps the SROs would not be so offensive were they farther out and not undertaken with such intensity. Finally, they will acknowledge that the two countries do have a difference of opinion on what is permissible within a country's EEZ. All of the remarks attributable to the Chinese position on SROs reflect the mindset that the sea is a domain where threats need to be kept at bay and that there are zones or layers of space in the sea that represent acceptable distances for foreign navies to operate, as well as those in which they should not be permitted to operate. China's interpretation of international law is that it should reflect this mindset of zones and layers of defense.

Areas of cooperation and mechanisms to manage tensions

Given the substantial areas of interest convergence, there are opportunities for the United States and China to cooperate in major areas of maritime domain activities. First, in the area of economic interests, the China and U.S. Coast Guards already have in place a number of cooperative activities that can be built upon. At present, both coast guards cooperate to combat driftnet fishing in the northern Pacific. The cooperation is so extensive that teams from China's Fisheries Law Enforcement Command are embarked on U.S. Coast Guard cutters patrolling the northern Pacific to deter illegal activities, monitor the area, and if necessary intercept, arrest, and place into custody Chinese and other Asian violators of this international ban.[56] The two countries' coast guards already have a substantial cooperative relationship. The momentum of this cooperation should be sustained and possibly even deepened.

Economic interests are also satisfied by sound environmental and anti-pollution efforts. The two countries have in place cooperation by China's State Oceanic Administration and the United States' National Oceanic and Atmospheric Administration on ocean observation and marine scientific research.[57] They also have developed cooperative programs in marine hazards prevention. All these current efforts need to be sustained and, if possible, expanded.

A second major area of interest convergence is sea-lane security. China has taken initial steps to address part of this problem through the frequent deployment of its counterpiracy task force.

U.S. participation in the European Union's cooperative counterpiracy program does not involve a significant coordination of effort with the PLAN. This needs to change. Better coordination and cooperation between the Shared Awareness and Deconfliction (SHADE) initiative and China's counterpiracy task force would be helpful. Additionally, a more ambitious and possibly controversial recommendation would be to form a quintilateral (made up of the United States, China, India, Australia, and ASEAN) combined search and rescue agency to monitor the Indian Ocean region, detect and respond to crises, and conduct rescue efforts for mariners and aircraft transiting these waters. Such a combined effort might have led to better coordination of the search and rescue operations for Malaysia Airlines Flight 370. This recommendation specifically builds on the 2013 International Search and Rescue Advisory Group exercise in Malaysia, in which disaster-rescue teams from the East Asia Summit countries were invited to participate in a multilateral search and rescue exercise.[58]

Finally, the two powers could expand on the military-to-military cooperation that has already taken place within the maritime domain over the past four years. The PLAN was for the first time invited to participate in the Rim of the Pacific (RIMPAC) exercise in summer 2014.[59] RIMPAC should continue to serve as a platform for PLAN participation. The United States should also consider inviting the PLAN to exercises farther west in the Pacific. For instance, China could first serve as an observer for the Cooperation Afloat Readiness and Training (CARAT) exercise that the United States conducts annually with the Southeast Asian militaries, and then at a subsequent date the PLAN could be invited to participate as a full partner in an extension of the exercise. Maritime military cooperation could expand to include enhanced cooperative programs such as a tabletop noncombatant evacuation operation or a humanitarian assistance and disaster relief exercise with the two navies. Although formal staff talks are usually reserved for allies, the PLAN could be invited to engage in such talks with the U.S. Navy staff on a range of security issues. At present the two navies do not engage in staff talks as the U.S. Navy does with allies such as Japan and South Korea. Yet even though China is not an ally of the United States, the two navies could still engage in formal staff discussions to develop the habit of cooperation and coordination. A good argument can also be made that navy-to-navy staff talks, through facilitating repeated interaction, can help prevent miscommunication and avert the buildup of unintended tension. Finally, the two navies could cooperate to provide SLOC protection in the Indian Ocean or work together near the Gulf of Aden to provide antipiracy protection to ships operating in the area.

Areas of divergence and recommended mechanisms to manage tensions

Areas of divergence

One of the most worrisome areas of divergence between China and the United States in maritime security is that the United States believes in unfettered military access in international waters and EEZs, whereas China believes in conditional military access. Such a divergence has added stress to U.S.-China relations as so-called close-in surveillance—U.S. SROs within China's EEZ—has repeatedly heightened tensions and caused frequent confrontations between Chinese and U.S. forces. The divergence partly stems from the two states' different interpretations of UNCLOS. While both the United States and China agree that maritime territorial issues and access rights to maritime resources need to be governed by international law (e.g., UNCLOS), they disagree over some interpretations of UNCLOS (especially over whether surveillance within EEZs is permitted).

The difference is often framed as a freedom of navigation issue. Apparently, the United States and China have different understandings of Article 58 of UNCLOS, which states the following:

> In the exclusive economic zone, all States, whether coastal or land-locked, enjoy, subject to the relevant provisions of this Convention, the freedoms referred to in article 87 of navigation and overflight and of the laying of submarine cables and pipelines, and other internationally lawful uses of the sea related to these freedoms, such as those associated with the operation of ships, aircraft and submarine cables and pipelines, and compatible with the other provisions of this Convention.[60]

The inherent ambiguity in the article leads to different interpretations between the United States and China. According to the official U.S. interpretation, freedom of military operations is part of the freedom of navigation and overflight. By contrast, the official Chinese position is that "China always respects and safeguards the freedom of navigation and overflight in the South China Sea all countries are entitled to under international law, but firmly opposes any country or person undermining the sovereignty and security of littoral countries under the pretext of 'freedom of navigation and overflight.'"[61] Consequently, both the United States and China accuse the other of abusing UNCLOS and thus violating international law.

Another major difference lies in China's "nine-dash line" claim in the South China Sea. The United States insists that the nine-dash line is "inconsistent with international law" and urges China to clarify its claims. For instance, in February 2014 testimony before the House Subcommittee on Asia and the Pacific, Assistant Secretary of State Daniel Russel alleged that the nine-dash line "limits the prospect for achieving a mutually agreeable resolution or equitable joint development arrangements among the claimants" and suggested that "the international community would welcome China to clarify or adjust its nine-dash line claim to bring it in accordance with the international law of the sea."[62] On the contrary, China believes that its claims are based on history and international law, that the nine-dash line is legitimate, and that "historical rights" (*lishixing quanli*) should be considered in resolving maritime territorial disputes.[63]

The United States argues that the sustainment of U.S. power and continuing military access to the region is the key to regional peace and security.[64] This is so because the U.S.-led alliance system depends on assured U.S. access to the region, and the U.S.-led international trade and economic order is also dependent on the peace and stability that the United States provides through its forward military presence. Other factors include the U.S. ability to react not only to direct strategic threats to the U.S. homeland but also to international threats to U.S. friends and allies and to broadly conceived international security; and, some would argue, the U.S. has the ability to hedge against the possibility that a rising China does not act benignly as its military power becomes commensurate with its growing economic power. However, in stark contrast with these views, China believes that U.S. freedom of navigation operations, as well as the reinforcement of the U.S.-led alliance system in Asia, add tension to regional stability.[65]

The United States, which already is capable of power projection, has an interest in modernizing and economizing these capabilities. China, which has a rudimentary power-projection capability, seeks to build those capabilities and assume greater access for its navy to operate both within and outside the Asia-Pacific and for the purpose of protecting national interests as well as providing international public goods. Power projection is one of the five main capabilities of U.S. sea power and the basis of all-domain access. The United States will project power in a more distributed fashion and in littoral environments, including using forward deployment and expeditionary forces.[66] China will develop its power-projection capability with the aim of influencing conflicts beyond its immediate area, relying on both conventional and nonconventional means.[67]

The United States believes that all nations have a right to build military maritime capabilities but that those capabilities need to be combined with transparency and reassurances about how they are to be used. The United States has repeatedly called on China to exhibit greater transparency about its military capabilities, activities, and intentions.[68] China, however, believes that it is reasonable for the weaker of two competitors to shield some of its capabilities from the stronger country. In other words, ambiguity, rather than transparency, should be valued. Unfiltered transparency is not in China's interests.

One final complication to U.S.-China maritime cooperation is the "third-party factor" (*disanfang yinsu*). Some of the specific maritime territorial disputes in the Asia-Pacific involve countries that either are formally allied to the United States or are developing close relationships with the United States. Japan and the Philippines are immediate examples of the former, while Vietnam is an example of the latter. The third-party factor is a complication and a challenge because, from the Chinese point of view, a maritime territorial dispute between China and another country should be handled through bilateral negotiations, but instead the dispute becomes internationalized and immediately involves the United States because of its alliance commitment or evolving relationship with one of the disputants. Additionally, for China this factor is a complication because, taken as a whole, the United States and these countries effectively form a united front against China. Obviously from the U.S. point of view, alliance commitments are not seen as a complication but as a foundation for stability in the region. There is definitely a difference in perspective on the role of U.S. relationships with regional countries in either helping or hindering maritime security cooperation in Asia.

Tension management mechanisms

to list

- During President Barack Obama's visit to China and summit with President Xi Jinping in November 2014, the two sides signed memoranda of understanding on encounters at sea. The annex on air-to-air encounters was signed during President Xi's state visit to the United States in September 2015. Now both sides should ensure that all parties adhere to the agreements. They should consider conducting either joint or separate training sessions for sailors and pilots from both sides.
- Think tanks from China and the United States should start Track 2 and 1.5 dialogues over legal interpretations of maritime territorial claims.
- China and the United States should work to establish a working group at ASEAN to discuss maritime security cooperation and dialogue.
- China and the United States should establish a bilateral exercise and training program that focuses on managing or even averting unexpected encounters at sea.
- The two sides should strengthen the Military Maritime Consultative Agreement and ensure that operational discussions are central to the meetings rather than political or larger strategic issues.
- The United States and China should begin minilateral Track 2 dialogues, such as China-U.S.-Japan dialogues, and expand minilateral joint maritime exercises that help reduce strategic distrust between China, on the one hand, and the United States and some of its regional allies, on the other.

Conclusion

The maritime arena serves as the most mature environment in which China and the United States have repeatedly discussed key issues of contention and cooperation. Compared with other strategic domains in which the two major powers interact, such as space and cyber, both countries are well aware of the specifics of their respective national interests, and government representatives in numerous dialogues have exchanged these views for several years. Yet while this makes conceptualization of areas of agreement and disagreement easier than in the other domains, the enormous interests involved and the potential for the two powers to confound one another in the maritime domain make the task of arriving at cooperative measures no less daunting.

As stated previously by both authors of this chapter, there is a significant convergence of interests in the maritime domain. Both countries have an interest in freedom of navigation, the tangible benefits from maritime-related economies, good order and stability at sea, and the use of the sea to foster and protect national security interests. Both countries are also in fundamental agreement that the buildup of a military, especially a navy, is well within reason if it is used to protect legitimate national security interests.

Where Chinese and U.S. interests and perspectives diverge lies in how the two countries define their respective national interests, what they believe to be appropriate means of displaying good and bad intentions, how the two sides view the sea (either as a threat or as an opportunity), and how they interpret international law and the protection of maritime sovereignty.

Complicating this divergence of interests and perspectives is the complex reality involved when a hegemon or superpower is confronted by a rising challenger—the so-called Thucydides Trap—and the security dilemmas that emerge from this trap. An additional complication is the vexing fact that all the present hot spots or potential conflict scenarios between the two countries reside in the maritime domain. Consequently, both countries are in the delicate position of being able to frustrate the other's political objectives through actions of their own or through the development of specific military capabilities and weapon systems designed to counter the capabilities of the other. Finally, the complication that some of China's rival claimants to maritime territorial disputes also happen to be allies or evolving partners of the United States—the so-called third-party factor—is a significant challenge to the prospects for improved maritime security cooperation between China and the United States.

Despite these challenges and complications, there are enough overlapping interests in the maritime domain to warrant serious thought about deepening and strengthening cooperative programs between agencies and military services already in existence. Furthermore, the convergence of interests is substantial enough that new programs that can foster habits of cooperation and reduce tensions and automatic suspicions deserve consideration.

Prior to 2016, U.S.-China relations in the maritime domain were characterized by a number of differences, but many opportunities for cooperation existed as well. Cooperation based on a gradual and steady improvement in military-to-military relations had been apparent, as well as considerable progress in reaching agreements on maritime and air encounters within the maritime domain. To some degree the interactions between China and the United States in the maritime environment were conducted in the midst of an already well-known backdrop, namely the "Rebalance to Asia" as a new guiding policy of the United States, or as China viewed it, a "New Model of Major-Country Relationship." The election of Donald Trump as President of the United States in November 2016 has upended this relatively stable state of affairs between the two countries. Arguably, the Trump administration's "Indo-Pacific" strategy is an updated version of what was termed the Rebalance to Asia during the Obama administration. Against the new backdrop of the Indo-Pacific strategy, we can surmise with some confidence that U.S. interests in the maritime domain would remain relatively constant; that is, the United States will likely continue to adhere to the principle of freedom of navigation, the use of the sea as both a bulwark to threats and as an offensive area from which to project power abroad, as well as viewing the maritime domain more generally as a vital feature for the continued growth of the global economy. However, as opposed to previous administrations, the Trump administration has appeared far less willing to cooperate with China on a range of issues in which there are clearly overlapping interests, instead designating China as its principle "strategic competitor." The Trump administration seems to be far more interested in confronting China, as ample evidence shows that the U.S. Navy has intensified FONOPs in the South China Sea. Ironically, as "strategic competition" between China and the United States increases and spills over from trade into technology, policymakers in Washington and Beijing seem eager to stem confrontation in the maritime domain. Senior military leaders on both sides agree that the U.S.-China military-to-military relationship should serve as a "stabilizer" in bilateral relations. Lastly, it is still unclear as to what extent the Trump administration will attempt to implement its Indo-Pacific strategy or whether it will exert influence in the region largely through the military means as opposed to the previous administration's reliance on other elements of national power—economic, diplomatic, and legal. These new developments will have a powerful effect on the U.S.-China relationship and will, in no small measure, affect the likelihood of the two countries working together on pressing issues in the maritime security domain.

Notes

1 Edward Mead Earle, "Adam Smith, Alexander Hamilton, Friedrich List: The Economic Foundations of Military Power," in *Makers of Modern Strategy: From Machiavelli to the Nuclear Age*, ed. Peter Paret (Princeton: Princeton University Press, 1986), 240.
2 Allan R. Millet, *Semper Fidelis: The History of the United States Marine Corps* (New York: Free Press, 1991), 27–28, 43–44.
3 Ibid., 27.
4 National Oceanic and Atmospheric Administration, "NOAA Report on the U.S. Ocean and Great Lakes Economy," 2015, 4, https://coast.noaa.gov/data/docs/digitalcoast/econreport.pdf.
5 Colin S. Gray, "Seapower and Western Defense," in *Seapower and Strategy*, ed. Colin S. Gray and Roger W. Barnett (Annapolis: Naval Institute Press, 1989), 277.
6 Williamson Murray, "Naval Power in World War I," in Gray and Barnett, *Seapower and Strategy*, 201–03.
7 Jeffrey G. Barlow, "World War II: U.S. and Japanese Naval Strategies," in Gray and Barnett, *Seapower and Strategy*, 267–70.
8 Ibid.
9 Gray, "Seapower and Western Defense," 286.c.
10 Roger W. Barnett and Jeffrey G. Barlow, "The Maritime Strategy of the U.S. Navy: Reading Excerpts," in Gray and Barnett, *Seapower and Strategy*, 344–47.
11 Dale C. Rielage, "Multipolarity and the Future of Sea Lane Security," in *Beyond the Wall: Chinese Far Seas Operations*, ed. Peter Dutton and Ryan Martinson (Newport: Naval War College, 2015), 8; and Jonathan G. Odom, "Freedom of the 'Far Seas'? A Maritime Dilemma for China," in Dutton and Martinson, *Beyond the Wall*, 80–85.
12 Shi Hongtao, "Nengyuan anquan zaoyu 'Maliujia kunjing': Zhong Ri Han nengfou xieshou?" [Energy Security Runs Up against the 'Malacca Dilemma': Will China, Japan, and Korea Cooperate?], *Zhongguo qingnian bao* [China Youth Daily], June 13, 2004.
13 Zhang Junshe, "Chinese/U.S. Naval Cooperation in Counterpiracy and Escort Missions," in Dutton and Martinson, *Beyond the Wall*, 80–85.
14 Odom, "Freedom of the 'Far Seas'?" 82–84.
15 Robert G. Sutter, "Dialogues and Their Implications in Sino-American Relations," in *Conflict and Cooperation in Sino-U.S. Relations: Change and Continuity, Causes and Cures*, ed. Jean-Marc F. Blanchard and Simon Shen (New York: Routledge Press, 2015), 190.
16 Odom, "Freedom of the 'Far Seas'?" 75–80.
17 Ibid.
18 Ibid., 77–78.

19 D.H. Anderson, "Bay of Bengal Maritime Boundary (Bangladesh v. India)," *American Journal of International Law* 109, no. 1 (2015): 146–54; and Nienke Grossman, "Territorial and Maritime Disputes (Nicaragua v. Colombia)," *American Journal of International Law* 107, no. 2 (2013): 396–403.

20 For more on such viewpoints, see Aaron L. Friedberg, "A New China Strategy," John Hay Initiative, www.choosingtolead.net/a-new-china-strategy; and Dan Blumenthal, "The Power Projection Balance in Asia," in *Competitive Strategies for the 21st Century: Theory, History, and Practice*, ed. Thomas G. Mahnken (Stanford: Stanford University Press, 2012).

21 Data has been compiled from National Bureau of Statistics of China, "Diliuci quanguo renkou pucha shuju" [The Sixth National Demographic Census], 2010, www.stats.gov. cn/tjsj/pcsj/rkpc/6rp/indexch.htm; and National Bureau of Statistics of China, "Disanci quanguo jingji pucha" [The Third National Economic Census], 2014, http://data.stats. gov.cn/ifnormal.htm?u=/census3/visual/main/base. html?macro&h=900.

22 "Guangdongsheng 2014 nian jingji yunxing qingkuang" [Economic Performance of Guangdong Province in 2014], Statistics Bureau of Guangdong Province, May 2015, www.gdstats.gov.cn/ydzt/jjxsxwfbh/201505/t20150506_296435.html.

23 Zhu Min, "Nengyuan ziyuan duiwaiyicundu guogao de fengxian ji duice" [The Risks and Solutions of the Overdependence on Foreign Trade of Chinese Energy and Resources], *China Economic Times*, December 12, 2014, 6.

24 U.S. Department of Defense, *Military and Security Developments Involving the People's Republic of China 2015* (Washington, DC, 2015), 24, 86, www.defense.gov/Portals/ 1/Documents/pubs/2015_China_Military_Power_Report.pdf.

25 Wang Wenrong, ed., *Zhanlue xue* [The Science of Military Strategy] (Beijing: National Defense University Press, 2011), 276.

26 Liang Fang, *Haishang zhanlue tongdao lun* [On Maritime Strategic Access] (Beijing: Current Affairs Press, 2011), 251, 310, 314–15.

27 For an excellent collection of Chinese scholars' studies on nontraditional security issues, see Zha Daojiong, ed., *Zhongguo xuezhe kanshijie: feichuantong anquan juan* [Chinese Scholars Eye the World: Volume of Nontraditional Security] (Beijing: Xinshijie chubanshe, 2007).

28 Ministry of Commerce of the People's Republic of China (PRC) et al., "2014 niandu Zhongguo duiwai zhijie touzi tongji gongbao" [2014 Annual Statistical Bulletin of China's Outward Foreign Direct Investment], September 2015, 6, http://fec.mofcom. gov.cn/article/tjsj/tjgb/201512/20151201223579.shtml.

29 China Tourism Academy, "Zhongguo chujing lvyou fazhan niandu baobao 2015" [Annual Report of China's Outbound Growth of Overseas Tourism in China], August 31, 2015, www.ctaweb.org/html/2015-8/2015-8-31-11-46-62356.html.

30 Ministry of Defense (PRC), "Wo haijun huhang biandui leiji wancheng 900pi zhongwai chuanbo" [The PLAN Escort Fleets Have Accomplished 900 Escort Missions of Chinese and Foreign Ships], December 18, 2015, http://news.mod.gov.cn/action/2015-12/18/ content_4633157.htm.

31 Information Office of the State Council of the PRC, *China's Military Strategy* (Beijing, May 2015), http://china.org.cn/china/2015-05/26/content_35661433.htm.

32 Liu Huaqing, *Liu Huaqing huiyilu* [Memoirs of Liu Huaqing] (Beijing: People's Liberation Army Press, 2011), 432–37.

33 Roger Cliff, Mark Burles, Michael S. Chase, Derek Eaton, and Kevin L. Pollpeter, *Entering the Dragon's Lair: China's Antiaccess Strategies and Their Implications for the United States* (Santa Monica: RAND Corporation, 2007).

34 For a critique of the use of the term "counter-intervention" to characterize China's strategy, see Taylor Fravel and Christopher P. Twomey, "Projecting Strategy: The Myth of Chinese Counter-Intervention," *Washington Quarterly* 37, no. 4 (2015): 171–87.

35 Dong Guozheng, "Zouxiang shenlan ting haixiao" [Going Toward Blue Water and Listening to the Tsunami], *People's Liberation Army Daily*, March 26, 2009, 4.

36 Tao Hongxiang, Chen Xin, and Mu Lianglong, "Zhang Huacheng daibiao: haijun yaoxiang daxinghua, xinxihua, zonghehua fazhan" [Representative Zhang Huacheng: Navy Has to Develop into One That Is Characterized as Large-Scale, Informationized, and Comprehensive], *Xinhua*, March 8, 2010, http://news.xinhuanet.com/mil/2010-03/08/content_13124149.htm.

37 Information Office of the State Council of the PRC, *China's Military Strategy*.

38 This section partly draws on Dong Wang's work in "Mainland China Debates U.S. Pivot/Rebalancing to Asia," *Issues and Studies* 50, no. 3 (2014): 57–101.

39 Yong Deng, "Conception of National Interests: Realpolitik, Liberal Dilemma, and the Possibility of Change," in *In the Eyes of the Dragon: China Views the World*, ed. Yong Deng and Fei-ling Wang (Lanham: Rowman & Littlefield, 1999), 47–72.

40 For Mearsheimer's views, see John J. Mearsheimer, *The Tragedy of Great Power Politics* (New York: W.W. Norton, 2001); Zbigniew Brzezinski and John J. Mearsheimer, "Debate: Clash of the Titans," *Foreign Policy*, January–February 2005, 46–49; and John Mearsheimer, "'Peaceful Rise' Will Meet U.S. Containment," *Global Times*, November 6, 2013, www.globaltimes.cn/content/823045.shtml.

41 Liang Fang, *Haishang zhanlue tongdao lun*, 277–78.

42 "U.S. 'Is Back' in Asia, U.S. Secretary of State Hillary Clinton Declares," *Associated Press*, July 21, 2009.

43 Dai Qingcheng, "Gaodu jingjue Meiguo 'chongfan' yazhou" [Highly Vigilant against U.S. 'Returning' to Asia], *Global Times*, July 24, 2009, 14.

44 "Jiefangjun fu zongcanmouzhang: Zhongguo anquan weixie zhuyao laizi haishang" [Deputy Chief of the General Staff of the PLA: China's Security Threats Mainly Come from the Maritime Domain], *Renmin wang* [People.cn], February 5, 2013, http://politics. people.com. cn/n/2013/0205/c1026-20431056.html.

45 Information Office of the State Council of the PRC, *China's Military Strategy*.

46 Ibid.

47 Bonnie Glaser and Yun Sun, "Chinese Attitudes toward Korean Unification," *International Journal of Korean Unification Studies* 24, no. 2 (2015): 83–95.

48 "Chinese FM: Confrontation Not Conducive to Solving South China Sea Issues," *Xinhua*, June 27, 2013, http://news.xinhuanet.com/english/china/2013-06/27/c_132492885.htm.

49 Chen Qimao, "The Taiwan Issue and Sino-U.S. Relations: A PRC View," *Asian Survey* 27, no. 11 (1987): 1161–75.

50 Peter M. Swartz, "Rising Powers and Naval Power," in *The Chinese Navy: Expanding Capabilities, Evolving Roles*, ed. Phillip C. Saunders, Christopher D. Yung, Michael Swaine, and Andrew Nien-Dzu Yang (Washington, DC: National Defense University Press, 2011), 12–16.

51 Robert S. Ross, "China's Naval Nationalism: Sources, Prospects, and U.S. Response," *International Security* 34, no. 2 (2009): 61–72.

52 Ronald O'Rourke, "Navy Force Structure and Shipbuilding Plans: Background and Issues for Congress," Congressional Research Service, CRS Report for Congress, RL32665, January 8, 2016, 7.

53 Ronald O'Rourke, "China's Naval Modernization: Implications for U.S. Navy Capabilities," Congressional Research Service, CRS Report for Congress, RL33153, September 21, 2015.

54 Both Wang Jisi and Susan Shirk have mentioned such a possibility in author conversations. See also Stephen Hadley, "Asia-Pacific Major Power Relations and Regional Security," remarks at World Peace Forum, June 21, 2014, Beijing.

55 Hua Yisheng, "U.S. Muscle-Flexing in South China Sea Is Unprofitable," *People's Daily*, November 11, 2015, http://en.people.cn/n/2015/1111/c98649-8974557.html.

56 "U.S. and China Coast Guards Interdict Vessel for Illegally Fishing on the High Seas," *U.S. Coast Guard Newsroom*, News Release, June 3, 2014, www.uscgnews.com/go/doc/4007/2173349/Multimedia-Release-United-States-and-China-Coast-Guards-interdict-vessel-for-illegally-fishing-on-the-high-seas.

57 "U.S. and China Agree to Increase Cooperation in Greenhouse Gas and Fisheries and Ocean Management," *National Oceanic and Atmospheric Administration*, May 11, 2011, www.noaanews.noaa.gov/stories2011/20110511_china.html.

58 "Malaysia's Rescue Team Equipped to Handle Disaster," *Borneo Post*, November 8, 2013, 36–37, www.theborneopost.com/2013/11/08/malaysias-rescue-team-equipped-to-handle-disaster; and "List of U.S.-China Cooperative Projects," *U.S. State Department*, January 22, 2014, www.state.gov/r/pa/prs/ps/2014/01/220530.htm.

59 Christopher D. Yung, "Continuity and Change in Sino-U.S. Military-to-Military Relations," in Blanchard and Shen, *Conflict and Cooperation in Sino-U.S. Relations*, 218.

60 The entire UNCLOS agreement, including Article 58, can be found at www.un.org/Depts/los/convention_agreements/texts/unclos/closindx.htm.

61 "Foreign Ministry Spokesperson Hua Chunying's Remarks on the US Warships' Entry into the Neighboring Waters of China's Islands and Reefs in the South China Sea," March 24, 2018, www.fmprc.gov.cn/mfa_eng/xwfw_665399/s2510_665401/2535_665405/t15 45150.shtml.

62 Daniel R. Russel, "Maritime Disputes in East Asia," *Testimony Before the House Committee on Foreign Affairs Subcommittee on the Asia Pacific*, Washington, DC, February 5, 2014, www.state.gov/p/eap/rls/rm/2014/02/221293.htm.

63 Gao Zhiguo and Jia Bingbing, *Lun Nanhai jiuduanxian de lishi, diwei he zuoyong* [The Nine-Dash Line in the South China Sea: History, Status, and Implications] (Beijing: Ocean Press, 2014); and Zhang Lei, "Dui jiuduanxian zhengyi jiejue tujing de zaisikao" [Rethinking the Ways to Solve the Dispute Over Nine-Dash Line], *Taipingyang xuebao* [Pacific Journal], no. 12 (2013): 50–61.

64 "Subcommittee Hearing: America's Security Role in the South China Sea," House Committee on Foreign Affairs, July 23, 2015, http://foreignaffairs.house.gov/hearing/subcommittee-hearing-america-s-security-role-south-china-sea.

65 Zhou Fangyin, "Meiguo de yatai tongmeng tixi yu Zhongguo de yingdui" [The U.S. Asia-Pacific Alliance System and China's Responses], *Shijie jingji yu zhengzhi* [World Economic and Politics], no. 11 (2013): 4–24.

66 U.S. Navy, *A Cooperative Strategy for 21st Century Seapower: Forward, Engaged, Ready* (Washington, DC, March 2015), 32, www.navy.mil/local/maritime/150227-CS21R-Final.pdf.

67 Thomas Kane, "China's Power Projection Capabilities," *Parameters* 44, no. 4 (2014–15), www.strategicstudiesinstitute.army.mil/pubs/Parameters/Issues/Winter_2014-15/6_KaneThomas_ChinasPowerProjectionCapabilities.pdf.

68 Michael Kiselycznyk and Phillip C. Saunders, "Assessing Chinese Military Transparency," *National Defense University, Institute for National Strategic Studies*, China Strategic Perspectives, no. 1, 2–5, http://ndupress.ndu.edu/Portals/68/Documents/stratperspective/china/ChinaPerspectives-1.pdf.

2 Seeking strategic stability for U.S.-China relations in the nuclear domain*

Elbridge A. Colby and Wu Riqiang

EXECUTIVE SUMMARY

This chapter lays out U.S. and Chinese views on and interests in the nuclear weapons domain, describes how the stability model could serve as an appropriate framework for bilateral engagement, proposes specific collaborative initiatives the two nations could profitably pursue, and identifies remaining disagreements that will need to be managed.

Main argument

Nuclear weapons play an important role in Sino-U.S. relations. In light of changing strategic dynamics and the potential for deeper competition between China and the U.S., that role could grow. While the two sides differ on a range of issues and in their perspectives on the appropriate role of strategic forces, both countries profit from intelligent and constructive interaction on strategic matters and would benefit from deeper and more focused engagement grounded in a stability model. In particular, such engagement could help diminish the chances that relations deteriorate or even of crisis or conflict due to essentially mistaken, misperceived, or accidental causes. Given the consequences of a substantial deterioration in relations, let alone the outbreak of war, it is important and of common benefit for the two states to pursue such initiatives.

Policy implications

- The U.S. and China should base their relations in the nuclear weapons domain on the concept of strategic stability.
- The U.S. and China should focus dialogue on eliciting greater insight into how the other thinks about the role and potential use of nuclear weapons, its red lines, its perception of vital interests, its conception of escalation, and related topics.
- The U.S. and China should pursue a range of specific initiatives focused on developing agreed-upon concepts of and frameworks for strategic stability, enabling the two sides to demonstrate that their military programs are

consistent with such frameworks, and generating mechanisms to help avoid accidental escalation and de-escalate crises if they arise.

Nuclear weapons are a crucial element in Sino-U.S. relations for the simple reason that they could be brandished in a crisis or even used in a conflict between the two most important nations in the world. The fact is that there are significant sources of tension and disagreement between the United States and the People's Republic of China (PRC), and some of these disputes appear to be, if anything, worsening. These include the status and future of Taiwan, how to handle Pyongyang and the potential collapse of North Korea and reunification of the Korean Peninsula, and territorial disputes between China and U.S. ally Japan in the East China Sea and between China and several Southeast Asian states, including U.S. ally the Philippines, in the South China Sea.

Beyond specific disputes and exacerbating factors, tensions between the United States and China are likely to persist because of the security consequences of a rising China. The study of international relations has long suggested that such power transitions are especially fraught with the danger of conflict for reasons having to do with concrete calculations of power and wealth, as well as more ineffable factors of honor and pride.[1] A rising nation usually expects to be granted greater influence and respect in accordance with its growing stature, but nations that already possess that influence are generally reluctant to part with it, especially if they do not trust the rising state. Hence, tensions can grow. The ideological incompatibility between Beijing and Washington further intensifies the pressures generated by the basic structural problems of how China's rise can be squared with both the United States' established position and the existing regional order Washington has underwritten.

At the same time, there is also a danger that the emerging structural dynamics between the United States and China could generate elements of a classic security dilemma, in which the actions one side takes to increase its defensive strength are interpreted as hostile or threatening by the other side, thus eliciting a defensive response that the first side views as hostile or threatening. Some argue that this dynamic already exists to an extent in the arena of conventional military competition—for instance, China's conventional ballistic and cruise missile program, undertaken at least in part in response to improved U.S. conventional capabilities, is now leading to a countervailing U.S. response—but such a dynamic has thus far had a limited effect on U.S.-China nuclear dynamics.[2] This is fortunate, as a security dilemma in the nuclear realm would be destabilizing, intensify suspicions, and potentially raise the danger of conflict escalation. Some observers contend, however, that the conditions do exist for such a dynamic to develop.[3] Chinese voices already claim that the expansion of China's nuclear missile force is designed to compensate for advances in U.S. ballistic missile defense (BMD), conventional prompt global strike, and strategic strike capabilities.[4] Some U.S. experts, meanwhile, point to China's expansion of its nuclear and missile forces as proof of hostile intent and the need for improved U.S. capabilities.[5]

These factors do not need to lead to conflict—conventional or nuclear—between the United States and China. In fact, several economic and security factors may mitigate the possibility of a general conflict. But, singly and especially together, these exacerbating tensions might lead to such a result. Any war between the United States and China would be incredibly dangerous and likely tremendously damaging, and nuclear war between the two would be even more so. Even though the day-to-day likelihood of major war between the two nations appears to be low—and the probability of nuclear war is even lower—its appallingly high costs, dangers, and risks demand that active steps be taken to make armed conflict more unlikely and less dangerous. For while the fact that China and the United States could come to blows does not mean that any conflict would result in the use of nuclear weapons, neither could nuclear use be confidently ruled out, especially given that even conflicts over apparently marginal issues can—in ways that are not entirely predictable—escalate into conflicts over core interests. A war between the two states would implicate broader considerations of prestige, alliance commitments, and broader interests, and thus would be subject to strong escalatory impetuses. Moreover, military-technological developments could further heighten the risk of escalation—for instance, due to the increasing interconnectedness of the full range of military forces with cyber, space, and unmanned systems.

For these reasons, it is incumbent on the United States and China to work to mitigate the threat of such a conflict breaking out. This chapter hopes to contribute to this effort. It first diagnoses the current state of Sino-U.S. nuclear relations, beginning with assessments of this issue from the standpoints of both the United States and China. It then identifies potential areas of cooperation and agreement between the United States and China, proposes recommendations for how the two sides can promote stability in mutually advantageous ways, and identifies persisting points of disagreement.

The United States' perspective on Sino-U.S. nuclear relations[6]

U.S. interests in the nuclear domain

For the United States, dealing with China in the context of nuclear weapons must be framed within the broader U.S. approach to the international order in general and to the Asia-Pacific region in particular. From the U.S. perspective, nuclear issues between Washington and Beijing are not purely a bilateral matter, nor can they be divorced from other geopolitical considerations. Instead, these issues must be seen as a constituent part of the United States' broader strategy for the Asia-Pacific and for the integration of China into a changing world.

U.S. policy toward the Asia-Pacific has been notably consistent for almost half a century. Though its strategy and posture have evolved, Washington has sought to uphold and defend an order in the region favorable to the interests of the United States and its allies and partners, while also reaching out to and seeking to integrate into the existing international system those not aligned with Washington, above all Beijing. This approach has been rooted in a strong U.S. presence in the Asia-Pacific, taking the form of alliances with a number of regional countries as well as deep but less formal ties with other Asian nations. This approach has in turn rested on the continued ability of U.S. military forces to project power effectively throughout the western Pacific, thereby ensuring the United States access to protect its own territory, defend its allies and partners, and sustain the security of the global commons.

The U.S. government believes that this basic approach to the Asia-Pacific remains well suited to protecting broad U.S. interests and fostering a favorable international political and economic order, and such a view is likely to continue to predominate in future administrations of either political party. Thus the United States continues to see its alliance relationships in Asia, as well as the military capabilities needed to effectively undergird those commitments, as necessary guarantors of regional stability and prosperity, which are in turn conducive both to its own interests and to those of the entire region.[7]

The United States has long seen the PRC as a central factor in its strategy in Asia—originally as an adversary, then as a counterweight against Soviet power, and now as a key player in the region and the international community. Since the 1970s, U.S. policy has sought to encourage and contribute to China's economic reforms and development in order to integrate the country into the existing international political and economic order. While still hopeful that China will develop into a constructive stakeholder, the United States and much of the Asia-Pacific share deepening concerns about major elements of China's military posture and policies that they fear could undermine regional stability, challenge U.S. and allied interests, and, if left unchecked or unbalanced, enable Beijing to exercise a dominant role in the region.[8] As a result, in the last decade, the United States has pursued a policy of strategic hedging, in which it has engaged China to try to capitalize on areas of agreement while also maintaining a potent capability to deter, deny, and (if needed) defeat Chinese aggression against the United States and its allies.

China's growing assertiveness and strength in recent years, however, has begun to prompt Washington to reassess the advisability of this hedging approach and has increasingly pushed the policy discussion in the United States toward the balancing end of the traditional dual approach to China's rise.[9] U.S. government policy has reflected this shift. Washington, for instance, has become more diplomatically active in strengthening U.S. relationships in Asia and seeking to push back on Chinese assertiveness in the South and East China Seas. The United States is also increasingly focused on adapting its military to deal with the PRC's growingly formidable armed forces. There is a heightened sense among U.S. defense leaders and experts that the rise of China requires a serious and sustained investment in high-end military capabilities if the United States hopes to maintain a favorable conventional balance in the western Pacific, and this recognition is increasingly being translated into concrete programmatic and deployment activities.[10]

Going forward, the rise of China is thus very likely to play a central, if not defining, role in U.S. defense planning, procurement, and diplomacy.[11]

China's rise could also have a significant impact on U.S. nuclear policy. Following the collapse of the Soviet Union, technological advances in U.S. military capabilities, and a diminishment of highly charged ideological hostility, conventional forces for the last several decades have constituted the primary focus of U.S. defense planning and posture in East Asia.[12] While U.S. nuclear weapons currently play a relatively limited role in U.S. strategy for the Asia-Pacific—largely reserved for deterrence of adversary nuclear use, extreme scenarios, and assurance of allies—the scale and scope of their role could change. The central factor in determining the degree of salience of nuclear weapons in the U.S. strategic posture pertaining to the Asia-Pacific is China, and more specifically how significant a military challenge China poses to U.S. security interests, including its extended deterrence commitments.[13] If China's military modernization effort were to slow or if the United States is able to sustain a reliable conventional military preeminence over China, such that the PRC could not credibly threaten U.S. or allied security with its conventional forces, U.S. nuclear forces are likely to continue to play a relatively recessed role. Alternatively, nuclear weapons are likely to become more salient to U.S. strategy in the Asia-Pacific if the regional balance of conventional military power were to shift toward China.[14] Avoiding this eventuality is one of the reasons that the United States is investing so heavily in the modernization of its conventional forces.

Substantial changes in China's nuclear policy or posture could also drive a significant revision of U.S. nuclear strategy. China has long made known its commitment to a "no first use" policy, to a strategic force sized to be "lean and effective," and to avoiding arms racing.[15] The PRC has been essentially consistent, with some modifications, in its enunciation of these principles since the initiation of its nuclear weapons program under Mao Zedong.[16] China has regularly signaled that these policies represent evidence that it is a responsible and constructive force in international politics and that its rise does not portend danger to other states.

In light of this, Washington, in addition to states throughout Asia and beyond, has regarded Beijing's continued commitment and adherence to these policies as indicators not only of the nature and ambition of the PRC's defense strategy but also of its broader strategic approach as a rising power. Thus, while there is substantial and sometimes heated debate in the United States about whether and to what degree the PRC is building up its nuclear force and modifying its nuclear strategy and how much of such change should be seen as innocent rather than menacing, there is generally broad consensus that a materially significant expansion of China's nuclear arsenal and a shift away from its legacy nuclear policies and strategies would signal a dangerous change in China's approach not only to the nuclear domain but to international politics more generally.

The United States, therefore, has viewed with growing disquiet the substantial modernization and expansion of China's nuclear forces, and U.S. analysts have observed closely reports and rumors that the PRC has considered shifting away from some of its cardinal policies.[17] This attention is likely to increase as China grows in strength and its military power waxes. Should such growth not taper off,

Washington's concern could shift to alarm, with substantial implications for U.S. strategic, defense, and nuclear policy.

For all these reasons, the United States is keenly interested in the evolving nuclear dynamics with China and is likely to become more so. In light of these factors, the United States has a particularly significant interest in pursuing bilateral engagement on nuclear weapons issues with China. The United States and its allies benefit in numerous ways from the relative restraint that China has exhibited in its nuclear policy, both in terms of how Beijing states that it would employ its nuclear forces and in terms of their size, sophistication, and diversity. Yet as China's economy continues to grow and its military continues to modernize, Beijing will increasingly have the choice of greatly expanding its nuclear forces, improving their capability, and broadening their role in the PRC's national security strategy. The United States ultimately cannot realistically prevent Beijing from pursuing such a course should it decide to do so, but in cooperation with its allies, the United States may be able to persuade Beijing that it is not in China's interests to markedly expand its nuclear forces or broaden the role of nuclear weapons in its planning and strategy. The United States also benefits from engagement with China (and vice versa), as such engagement can help improve understanding of the other side's red lines, understandings of escalation, and the like, thereby mitigating the possibility of inadvertent escalation or miscalculation.

Enhancing constructive cooperation with China on bilateral nuclear weapons issues is therefore a significant security interest of the United States over the long term. As China's strategic options expand and some of its strategists consider a shift away from its legacy approach to nuclear policy and strategy—such as the no-first-use policy—the United States should encourage China's continued restraint vis-à-vis nuclear force size, posture, strategy, and policy. U.S. acts of restraint that could plausibly contribute to Chinese restraint should therefore be seriously considered by Washington if they contribute to this goal. Conversely, actions that prompt China to build up its forces, especially without a compensatory strategic gain in other respects, should be viewed more skeptically. Needless to say, the United States will need to make decisions about its strategic capabilities based on the totality of considerations and will indubitably need to make, and indeed should make, decisions that aggravate Beijing. To the extent possible, however, the United States should seek at least to minimize policies, particularly those without substantial strategic benefit, that would inflame Chinese anxieties and drive Beijing to adopt a more expansionist and destabilizing approach to its nuclear posture.

U.S. policies will play an important role in Beijing's decisions on these issues because China's nuclear strategy and policy have been and will be shaped by the United States. Indeed, although other countries such as India and Russia play a role, Chinese strategists regularly cite U.S. strategic capabilities and authoritative U.S. government statements as a prime motivator for the qualitative and quantitative expansion of China's nuclear force.[18] It is therefore in the U.S. interest to pursue an agenda for engagement on nuclear weapons issues with

China that reinforces Beijing's continued adherence to a nuclear policy of relative restraint.

A strategic basis for U.S. engagement with China on nuclear weapons

The stability approach

Meaningful engagement on bilateral nuclear weapons issues between the United States and China requires a coherent intellectual basis, lest it lapse into mere expressions of goodwill that may lack credibility on both sides. The United States needs to be able to adjudicate which potential steps are helpful and which are not, and this requires a strategic logic with which to examine its relations with the PRC in the nuclear weapons domain.

The United States is likely to continue applying to China the well-established policy of pursuing the twin objectives of maintaining a strong deterrent while reducing the dangers associated with nuclear weapons through the pursuit of appropriate cooperative measures.[19] Beyond this, however, there is currently no explicitly agreed-upon analytical framework for how to deal with China's nuclear forces. The Obama administration stipulated early in its tenure that it was prepared to engage with China on the basis of the concept of "strategic stability" but did not define the concept further.[20] Some experts, meanwhile, argue that the United States should seek to retain or reacquire a position of nuclear dominance, whereby it could plausibly disarm China's strategic forces without the PRC being able to strike back.[21] Alternatively, some wish to place disarmament as the foremost goal and take steps designed to encourage builddowns.[22]

While this debate remains fairly active, practical policy discussion appears to be increasingly internalizing a set of pregnant realities (or probabilities). With China now approaching the United States in economic size and with the PRC's military modernization increasingly clear and formidable in its scale and sophistication, the prospect that the United States could wholly disarm China's strategic forces appears decreasingly plausible. This realization is shifting U.S. discussion about China's nuclear forces toward a settled, if often tacit, acceptance that the United States is very unlikely to be able to deny China some level of retaliatory capability.[23] At the same time, however, intensifying tensions with China, the persistence and scale of its military buildup, and the general sense of the implausibility and probable inadvisability of major reductions in light of a worsening global security situation have markedly reduced the appeal of disarmament as the lodestar of U.S. policy toward China on nuclear weapons issues.

As a consequence of these trends, policy discussion in the United States is tending to converge on something like a combination of effective deterrence and stability or strategic stability as the appropriate basis for relations in the nuclear weapons domain with China. While the 2010 Nuclear Posture Review signaling U.S. preparedness to deal with Beijing on the basis of strategic stability did not provide much specificity about what that would entail, a panoply of non- and semi-official engagements at the Track 1.5 and Track 2 levels have also been using stability as a basis for engagement, and there has been an active discussion of the applicability of the concept in the expert literature.[24] Stability thus appears to be the policy approach to which the United States is increasingly gravitating with respect to China's nuclear weapons.

History of nuclear weapons engagement

Historically, engagement on bilateral nuclear issues between the United States and China has been limited. Both countries have pursued strategic nuclear dialogues at various levels since the late 1980s, with occasional periods of increased engagement as well as periods of disengagement often linked to downturns in broader Sino-U.S. relations. In the last decade, the United States has sought to directly engage the PRC in official discussions regarding nuclear weapons and other strategic capabilities. During the George W. Bush and Obama administrations, Washington has repeatedly sought to open channels for dialogue with Beijing to demonstrate that U.S. nuclear and missile defense forces should not be construed by the PRC as an attempt to upend the balance between the two nations. Neither administration's initiatives have met with much success, however, owing to China's apparent reluctance to participate in such a dialogue.[25] A formal dialogue on nuclear strategy, for example, was held in Beijing in April 2008, but no successor meeting has been held. This is true even despite the fact that in recent years bilateral engagement has generally intensified, particularly through the Strategic and Economic Dialogue, the Defense Consultative Talks, and the Strategic Security Dialogue, which touch to a degree on nuclear issues, although reportedly not in any depth.

In the multilateral realm, in 2009 the permanent members of the UN Security Council held the first Conference on Confidence Building Measures towards Nuclear Disarmament and Non-Proliferation. They later met in Paris in 2011 to discuss nuclear transparency issues and methods of verifying potential additional arms reductions. In total, the permanent members have so far held six meetings. Overall, however, Sino-U.S. engagement on nuclear issues has thus far not resulted in direct practical steps for official bilateral cooperation on nuclear confidence-building measures.[26]

Despite these difficulties, the United States should actively pursue both informal and formal means to reinforce restraint in China's nuclear decision-making and promote strategic stability through bilateral and unilateral initiatives, while putting the United States in an improved strategic position even if Beijing is reluctant to pursue enhanced engagement on nuclear weapons issues. In this vein, the United States should pursue a substantial but realistically tailored program of engagement and dialogue on nuclear issues that reinforces Chinese nuclear restraint and advances U.S. interests in stability, dialogue, transparency, and progress toward arms control. Recognizing, however, the limited success that attempts at dialogue and cooperation have thus far yielded and Beijing's consistent unwillingness to engage meaningfully on these issues, the United States should pursue this approach in a way that, should Beijing refuse to engage, Washington would be left with a powerful strategic capability and in the strong international political position of having proffered a serious and fair-minded path forward in bilateral nuclear weapons relations that China had rebuffed.

The PRC's perspective on Sino-U.S. nuclear relations[27]

Chinese interests in the nuclear domain

The sole purpose of Chinese nuclear weapons is to deter nuclear attacks or nuclear coercion.[28] China's decision to build nuclear weapons originated from and was shaped by the humiliating memories of being "blackmailed" by the United States in the 1950s and by the Soviet Union in 1969.[29] Chinese leaders believe that because of the taboo against nuclear weapons use, actual use of nuclear weapons is unlikely. Therefore, political use of nuclear weapons—in other words, nuclear coercion—is a more realistic threat than nuclear attack.[30]

Consistent with this nuclear philosophy, China maintains a unique nuclear posture. As summarized by Gregory Kulacki, the Chinese strategic capability is constituted in "a small force kept off alert and used only for retaliation."[31] First, China maintains a small nuclear arsenal. One estimate holds that China has 45 intercontinental ballistic missiles (ICBM) capable of targeting the continental United States. The number of total Chinese nuclear warheads is estimated to be 260.[32] Second, China's nuclear warheads have traditionally been separated from delivery systems and stored in different bases in peacetime.[33] Third, China has insisted on maintaining an unconditional no-first-use policy since the day it detonated its first nuclear bomb.[34]

For the foreseeable future, the biggest challenge confronting China's nuclear deterrent will be U.S. missile defense systems. Missile defense might neutralize China's nuclear retaliatory capability. The United States argues that its homeland missile defense system is designed to defend against North Korea rather than China. But a missile defense system designed against North Korea naturally has an intercept capability against Chinese strategic missiles due to proximity. Given China's small nuclear arsenal, even a small-scale missile defense system has the potential to neutralize China's deterrent in the context of a hypothesized U.S. first strike. The effectiveness of current missile defense architecture is believed to be limited because of the difficulty of identifying real warheads from decoys. It is the unpredictable future of missile defense capabilities that concerns Beijing. However, Washington refuses to accept any limits on missile defense, despite its frequent expressions of willingness to discuss this issue with China.[35]

To resolve this dispute and maintain strategic stability, China and the United States both have a clear interest in reaching a common understanding on strategic offensive and defensive capabilities. For example, the United States could commit to maintaining a low level of BMD effectiveness, which is sufficient to counter North Korea's unsophisticated missiles without threatening China's more advanced strategic missiles. In return, China could agree to refrain from expanding its nuclear arsenal.[36] If Washington's declaration that homeland missile defense is not directed at China is sincere, this solution is in the United States' interest. China has maintained a small nuclear arsenal for several decades, and the only reason it would have to increase its stockpile of weapons is to compensate for its nuclear deterrent being undermined by improvements in the United States' missile defense system. This solution would therefore also be in Beijing's interest.

Besides missile defense, technologies that contribute to the U.S. ability to detect, identify, track, and strike mobile missiles also have the potential to undermine the Chinese nuclear deterrent. Such technologies include prompt precision-strike capabilities, stealth unmanned aerial vehicles, unattended ground sensors, automatic target recognition, and hyperspectral imaging.[37] It is generally believed that mobile ICBMs are still quite survivable, although some American scholars do argue that technological advancements could offer the United States the capability to neutralize other countries' nuclear deterrents.[38] China must observe relevant technological developments very carefully.

In order to maintain its nuclear deterrent, China has been modernizing its nuclear arsenal to improve survivability and penetrability. China began to deploy solid-propellant road-mobile ICBMs, the DF-31 and DF-31A, in 2006–7[39] and is flight-testing the next-generation DF-41 ICBM.[40] China is also building the Type 094 nuclear-powered ballistic missile submarine (SSBN) (Jin-class) and its associated JL-2 submarine-launched ballistic missiles (SLBM).[41] The Type 094 is expected to begin conducting deterrent patrols soon.[42] However, given the high noise level of the Type 094 and China's lack of experience with running a SSBN fleet, China is unlikely to put it into combat duty in the near future.[43]

The number of total Chinese nuclear warheads is believed to have increased slightly in recent years.[44] The expansion is not significant, however, and can be attributed to the deployment of new strategic missiles without phasing out old liquid-propellant missiles. In the foreseeable future, China could continue to maintain the effectiveness of its nuclear deterrent through modernization without an expansion of its nuclear arsenal. However, if the United States significantly improves the scale or effectiveness of its missile defense, China might have to build more nuclear warheads. It should be noted that China has no interest in pursuing nuclear parity with the United States.

China might have to build more nuclear warheads to restore strategic stability undermined by U.S. BMD, but this does not mean it is preparing to "sprint to parity." As previously mentioned, the sole purpose of its nuclear arsenal is to deter nuclear attack or coercion. In order to do that, nuclear parity is not necessary. As long as China has a secure second-strike capability and could inflict unacceptable damage on an adversary, its nuclear deterrent remains effective.

From the Chinese perspective, the nuclear dynamics between China and the United States will lead to two possible outcomes. If both sides can constrain the development of their strategic capabilities, then the United States' strategic missile defense system would remain small and have a low effectiveness, while the Chinese nuclear arsenal would also remain small.[45] If not, the world will probably see a highly effective and large-scale U.S. missile defense system facing off against a bigger Chinese nuclear arsenal. Needless to say, the first outcome is in both sides' interests, but the likelihood it will come to pass will be determined by China-U.S. interactions and cooperation. Currently, both the Chinese and U.S. militaries are engaged in discussion about setting up a new dialogue on strategic stability, which would certainly cover nuclear relations. This is great progress, but strategic dialogues are not enough. In order to maintain strategic stability and avoid arms buildup, mutual constraints of strategic defensive and offensive capabilities are critical. Given that Washington has repeatedly expressed a willingness to talk but an unwillingness to accept any limit, the prospect for greater cooperation in the nuclear domain seems dim.

Chinese views of U.S. interests

The United States is opposed to the possibility of mutual vulnerability with respect to China, which is understandable because every superpower hates vulnerability. However, given the force structures of the opposing sides, U.S. leaders will have to face the reality of being mutually vulnerable. Although Beijing cannot ask Washington to recognize mutual vulnerability, it can build better (and more, if necessary) nuclear weapons so that mutual vulnerability becomes a strategic fact for the United States, not a policy choice.[46] The 2010 Nuclear Posture Review report stated that the United States would maintain strategic stability with Russia and China, but Washington still cannot acknowledge mutual vulnerability with China publicly.[47]

Therefore, Washington will maintain the option of achieving nuclear primacy over China. The U.S. technological advantages in missile defense, precision strike, surveillance, and reconnaissance provide the United States the means to keep that option open. However, China's capability to improve its nuclear weapons qualitatively and quantitatively will probably offset such efforts. It seems unlikely that the United States will be able to achieve lasting nuclear primacy over China, even if Washington attempts to keep this option on the table.

Regarding missile defense, U.S. domestic politics makes negotiated constraints extremely unlikely. Because of prevailing attitudes in the United States, missile defense is likely to improve as fast as technology advances and will be constrained only by budgets. As former senator Sam Nunn observed, "National missile defense has become a theology in the United States, not a technology."[48] Even if North Korean and Iranian nuclear and missile threats were to disappear in the future, the United States would not dismantle its homeland missile defense system.

Areas of convergence and recommendations for cooperative initiatives

A logic for engagement: strategic stability

While Chinese and U.S. interests do not mirror one another, both nations nonetheless have an interest in finding ways to cooperate so as to reduce misunderstanding, the likelihood of miscalculation, and ultimately the risk of war. In particular, the United States and China would benefit from applying some of the concepts associated with the idea of strategic stability as a framework for U.S.-China engagement on nuclear weapons issues.[49] Based on this concept, stability can emerge between the United States and China if they each field forces that are capable of surviving a first strike and are able to credibly demonstrate to one another that their current and future capabilities cannot deny the other side a viable strategic deterrent. As a result, fear of preemption and the need to launch weapons early become irrelevant, either as irritants in a crisis or as dangers in conflict. In this way, the benefits of deterrence can be retained while minimizing the chances of nuclear escalation.

The premise of arms control and stability-oriented measures is that even potential adversaries can achieve the twin goals of sustaining effective nuclear deterrence and mitigating the possibility of conflict.[50] This is relevant because nuclear forces themselves can intensify, if not cause, competition and even conflict—but they need not. Nuclear deterrence is not simply a unilateral action that takes place in a vacuum; rather, it is a relationship shaped by perceptions. Indeed, the ways in which a country procures, postures, and operates its nuclear forces have a major interactive effect on how other countries procure, posture, and operate their forces. Potential adversaries can allay, and possibly even remove, these exacerbating factors through unilateral and cooperative measures that effectively demonstrate that each side's strategic forces are not capable of conducting a disarming first strike or of defeating a retaliatory strike. Although such measures do not solve more fundamental political and strategic disputes, they can help lessen tensions and mistrust due to essentially ancillary technical features of interstate relations.

Both sides could derive value from cooperation on nuclear weapons grounded in the stability concept. The United States worries about the composition of the Chinese nuclear force, Chinese views on escalation and plans for nuclear use, and the future trajectory of the Chinese strategic posture. China, meanwhile, worries about the United States' potential ability to deny it a second-strike capability, the scope and sophistication of future U.S. programs, and U.S. unwillingness to acknowledge a condition of mutual vulnerability between the two nations. A stability-grounded model could help address these anxieties—on the U.S. side by providing deeper insight into China's nuclear strategy and its current and future force structure, and on the Chinese side by providing similar insight into U.S. developments and a greater degree of assurance about U.S. acknowledgement of the survivability of the Chinese force. Concurrently, such an approach would have the added benefit of building confidence on both sides.

In summary, maintaining stability in U.S.-China nuclear relations will be critical to both Chinese and U.S. interests in the coming years. The stability concept provides that such risks can be decreased if the two nuclear powers structure, posture, and acquire their forces in such ways that neither is able to launch an effective disarming strike nor is vulnerable to one. Within this framework, both sides could continue to derive deterrent value from their nuclear forces, while understanding that any decision to use nuclear weapons would be extremely dangerous and fraught with unpredictable consequences.[51]

Areas of agreement

In line with an approach grounded in strategic stability, the United States and China could reasonably agree on the following propositions about their relations in the nuclear weapons domain.

- Major war, including major conventional war, would be exceedingly dangerous and possibly disastrous for both sides. Both China and the United States therefore share strong interests in minimizing the chances of war while seeking to defend their interests.
- The current Sino-U.S. relationship in the nuclear weapons domain is relatively stable.
- Mutual restraint is important to maintaining strategic stability. Both sides should seek areas where their restraint can contribute to stability in the relationship.
- The United States is not orienting or designing its national ballistic missile defenses against China. Rather, they are motivated with respect to the Asia-Pacific by North Korea's long-range ballistic missile and nuclear weapons programs.
- Nonetheless, missile defense programs designed against intercontinental-range systems have the potential to undermine the viability of the other side's second-strike capability. Measures designed to validate that such BMD systems do not threaten to negate the other party's second-strike capability are therefore to be encouraged.
- The deployment of theater-range missile defense systems is understandable and need not undermine strategic stability. Because components of such systems can potentially threaten strategic-range missiles, or may be perceived to do so, each side should strive to differentiate its theater-range defense systems from its national defense systems. Steps that can validate to the other party that theater missile defense systems do not have capabilities against long-range systems should be encouraged.
- Efforts to differentiate both sides' nuclear (especially strategic nuclear) forces, bases, networks, and other assets from their conventional analogs should be encouraged.
- Because North Korea's advancing missile and nuclear programs are driving U.S. national missile defense developments with respect to the Asia-Pacific, satisfactorily addressing these programs is crucial for stability in East Asia. North Korea's nuclear program, in particular, is a grave and worsening challenge for regional stability.
- A conventional conflict between China and the United States would involve serious risks of escalation, and a major conventional conflict would involve risks of escalating to the nuclear level. Both sides should therefore focus on ensuring that their military plans, capabilities, doctrines, and postures seek to avoid encouraging nuclear escalation on the part of the other.
- Both sides would benefit from a clearer understanding of the other's nuclear doctrine, red lines, and conceptions of escalation, thereby lessening the risk

of conflict arising or of one that has already broken out escalating due to a preventable misunderstanding. Engagements that illuminate each side's perspectives on these issues should therefore be encouraged.

- Crisis management cooperation should be encouraged to enable both countries to stem or stop inadvertent or accidental escalation.

Engagement and policy initiatives

Dialogues on doctrine and concepts of escalation

The United States and China should engage in dialogues designed to elicit greater insight into how the other thinks about the role and potential use of nuclear weapons, its red lines and perception of its vital interests, its conception of escalation, and related topics. Both sides could gain a firmer understanding of the other's views on these subjects, which could help minimize the possibility of escalation, especially inadvertent escalation, in a crisis or conflict. For instance, a working group could be tasked to agree on channels of communication, the relative authoritativeness of these channels, and the meaning of military actions. It could also help both sides understand the other's standard operating procedures, which could be misinterpreted in a crisis.[52] In addition, responsible officials would have the opportunity to explain directly to their counterparts their government's official thinking on these matters.

Given that miscalculation or misunderstanding of the other country's red lines is regarded as a more plausible pathway toward Sino-U.S. conflict, such dialogue would be highly constructive for minimizing the chances of such a disastrous outcome.

The two countries should also focus on exploring mechanisms for information exchange. While such exchanges can be structured through formal mechanisms such as the Strategic Arms Reduction Treaties (START and New START) between the United States and Russia, information can be productively exchanged through less formal dialogues. The U.S. side has delivered briefings on why it views U.S. BMD as not posing a genuine threat to China's strategic deterrent, for instance. The United States could continue to provide briefings on this topic, as well as on the implications of its ongoing efforts to modernize its nuclear arsenal and develop conventional prompt global strike programs. China, meanwhile, could provide a fuller explanation of its nuclear strategy and its approach to escalation and could deliver briefings on some of its systems that pose concerns to the United States, such as anti-satellite weapons capabilities.

Beyond holding discussions, China and the United States should pursue concrete steps that would contribute to these goals that would also be worthwhile for both sides. Such measures should be oriented toward developing agreed-upon concepts of and frameworks for strategic stability, enabling the two sides to demonstrate that their military programs are consistent with such frameworks, and generating mechanisms to help avoid accidental escalation and de-escalate such crises if they arise. Some such measures that the two sides could consider include:

Reciprocal visits to national missile defense sites

Through this measure, each side would be given the opportunity, with appropriate security precautions to protect classified information, to visit the other side's national missile defense facilities. These visits would be designed to give each side a greater degree of confidence in its assessment of the nature and scale of the other's national missile defenses. Such visits could include, again with appropriate security precautions, exhibitions of interceptors, tours of facilities, and observation of radars and other installations.[53]

Reciprocal notification of BMD and hypersonic weapon test launches

As in the U.S.-Russia context, missile launch notifications can be an important confidence-building and stability-oriented measure that can alleviate concerns on both sides about accidental launch and help pave the way for more ambitious arrangements.[54] An agreement on launch notifications could be the next entry in the series of annexes to the memorandum of understanding signed by Presidents Barack Obama and Xi Jinping in November 2014 on confidence-building measures for major military activities.[55]

Observation of national BMD exercises and/or tests

As appropriate in light of security considerations, another concrete step the United States and China should take is inviting each other to send observers to attend exercises and tests of designated BMD capabilities.[56] The sides could, for instance, explore the possibility of sharing burnout velocity data in order to demonstrate the limits of interceptor capability. The United States has previously, for instance, offered to allow Russia to observe missile defense tests and measure parameters with its own equipment. A similar offer could be made to the PRC.

Mutual visits to military reactors, enrichment, and reprocessing facilities

The United States has ceased all production of fissile material for weapons and has made detailed, public declarations of the quantities of fissile material it has produced. China is believed to have ceased production but has not declared an official moratorium or given any information on its stockpile. For the United States, visits to Chinese facilities would confirm that China has indeed ceased production and help refine estimates of the quantity of material it has produced. For China, visits to U.S. facilities would build Chinese confidence in the United States' declaration.

Chinese participation in New START practice inspections

On a number of occasions Chinese experts have expressed an interest in gaining firsthand knowledge of what arms control inspections involve. Since Russia is very unlikely to consent to Chinese observers at an actual New START inspection, the United States could invite China to send observers to a practice inspection conducted in the United States.[57] Ideally, such observers would be both high-level and technically competent so that they could effectively contribute to debates within the PRC government about China's participation in confidence-building measures.

Exchanges on verification techniques

Technical discussions on the merits, utility, and appropriateness of verification techniques could be a useful topic for discussions and other efforts between the two sides, including eventually laying the groundwork for verification-based agreements. In recent years, China has shown an increased interest in this area and indicated that the People's Liberation Army (PLA) may be more willing than in the past to discuss this topic.[58]

Discussions on submarine security issues

As China's SSBN program advances and the PLA Navy likely moves toward regular patrolling, the two sides could engage on nonsensitive best practices and/or rules of the road for security. For instance, the PLA Navy and U.S. Navy could engage in discussions regarding how to protect against the possibility of a rogue commander. They could also discuss protocols for preventing and managing accidents or incidents involving submarines at sea.[59]

Common concept of strategic stability

U.S. and Chinese scholars, with input from their respective governments, should develop a public joint statement on U.S.-China nuclear dynamics that includes areas of collaboration and engagement. The statement could also reaffirm the utility of the crisis hotline and non-targeting accord to build on existing agreements. Such a project could eventually include government officials and culminate in an official government-to-government agreement.[60]

Joint studies on key issues

Another promising avenue would be for the two sides, particularly through nonofficial or semiofficial bodies, to engage in joint studies of key areas of concern—for instance, the future trajectory of ballistic missile defenses, anti-satellite weapons, nuclear forces, and crisis management.[61] Such studies could help elucidate and clarify both sides' perspectives and views of escalation and de-escalation as well as identify areas of possible cooperation.[62]

Laying the groundwork for formal arms control

While a formal arms control agreement between the United States and China seems unlikely in the near term, and thus should not be a focus of attention in that time frame, the two sides can begin to lay the groundwork for such a compact. Many of the concrete steps described here will help to do so. In addition, both countries should issue official statements expressing their commitment to creating the conditions for such an agreement.

Areas of divergence and recommendations for mechanisms to manage tension and crises

Despite these opportunities for constructive engagement, several areas of concern and disagreement in the strategic domain remain. This section presents perspectives from China and the United States.

Chinese perspective[63]

U.S. refusal to adopt a no-first-use policy

The 2010 Nuclear Posture Review made great progress in reducing the role of nuclear weapons. However, Washington still cannot accept a no-first-use policy or statement such as "deterring nuclear attack is the sole purpose of U.S. nuclear weapons." From the Chinese perspective, U.S. refusal of a no-first-use policy means that Washington wants to maintain the option of nuclear coercion. If the United States enjoys nuclear superiority over its adversary, Washington could transform this superiority into coercive power. The United States could also use nuclear weapons in a limited and discriminated way to offset conventional inferiority or to signal resolve. Such doctrines would blur the line between conventional and nuclear war and carry serious risks of escalation.

U.S. tactical nuclear weapons

The United States has operated a tactical nuclear arsenal and is working to modernize it.[64] Furthermore, some American scholars argue that the United States should develop limited nuclear strike capabilities to give Washington "employable nuclear options at all rungs of the nuclear escalation ladder."[65] The Obama administration maintained a policy that the United States will not develop new nuclear warheads.[66] However, the B61 Life Extension Program has caused serious concerns in the strategic community that the upgrade increases the targeting capability of nuclear weapons by "allowing some targets that previously would not have been attacked because of too much collateral damage to be attacked anyway."[67] More importantly, lower yield and higher accuracy reduce the nuclear threshold and make the weapon more thinkable and usable in a conflict.[68]

Regional BMD with strategic implications

The missile defense debate between China and the United States recently has focused on the United States' potential deployment of the Terminal High Altitude

Area Defense (THAAD) system in South Korea. The THAAD radar (TPY-2), rather than the system's interceptors, is what concerns China. Besides serving as the fire-control radar of the THAAD system, TPY-2 could also be deployed in a forward-based mode, tracking Chinese strategic missiles during their boost phase of flight and observing the deploying process of decoys and real warheads. The U.S. missile defense system would easily be able to discriminate real warheads from decoys because decoys are much lighter and therefore generate much smaller velocity changes. If deployed, the THAAD radar would pose a big threat to the penetrability of Chinese strategic missiles.

Another component of regional missile defense systems that is worrisome to China is the SM-3 IIA missile. Jointly developed by the United States and Japan, the SM-3 IIA was deployed in 2018. With a burnout speed of roughly 4.5 kilometers per second, this missile is capable of engaging Chinese strategic missiles. Deployed off the U.S. coast, two SM-3 IIA systems could protect the whole continental United States from China's ICBMs and SLBMs. If deployed close to Japan—for example, off the coast of Hokkaido—the SM-3 IIA would have a limited capability to intercept Chinese SLBMs.[69] Given the system's capability to engage Chinese strategic missiles, China will consider the SM-3 IIA as a strategic interceptor in the same category as ground-based interceptors.

Evaluation of the North Korean missile threat

From the Chinese perspective, the United States overestimates the North Korean missile threat. North Korea is unlikely to be able to build an operational ICBM in the foreseeable future for two reasons. First, it has yet to master the advanced R-27/SS-N-6 rocket engine technology acquired from Russia, and building an ICBM based on Scud technology is impossible. Second and foremost, the heat-protection technology in reentry vehicles for ICBMs is very challenging to develop and cannot be tested in space launches. North Korea will have to flight test its prototype reentry vehicles to gain reasonable confidence in their viability. However, North Korea is too small a country to conduct an ICBM flight test (full-range or depressed-trajectory) within its own territory; the missile would have to be launched into the open sea. In order to do that, a group of ships should be sent out to the impact zone for recovery and telemetry purposes, which is a highly challenging task for the North Korean navy. It seems unlikely that North Korea will be able to build an operational ICBM in the foreseeable future.[70]

U.S. intelligence does not have a good record in assessing the North Korean threat. In 1998 the Rumsfeld Commission maintained that "emerging ballistic missile powers" such as North Korea and Iran are capable of developing ICBMs "within about five years of a decision to acquire such a capability."[71] In December 2001 the U.S. intelligence community stated that North Korea would have ICBMs before 2015.[72] The then U.S. secretary of defense Robert Gates also said in 2011 that North Korea was within five years of developing ICBMs.[73] Today, we can say that all these estimates seriously exaggerated the threat. In June 2014, Dean Wilkening, a physicist at Lawrence Livermore National Laboratory, observed that "either you conclude that North Korea did not have an intent to build [intercontinental ballistic missiles], or it's more difficult than people were led to believe. I think it's the latter."[74]

U.S. perspective[75]

Future evolution of China's nuclear forces

The continuing lack of transparency regarding the development of China's nuclear and strategic forces, including with respect to future plans, the doctrine and strategy for employment of nuclear weapons in crisis and conflict, the role of SSBNs, the role of hypersonic weapons, and other issues, are a source of significant concern for the United States. There are particular questions about the possible increased role of nuclear weapons in China's national and military strategies, which would be a major destabilizing force in the bilateral relationship, the Asia-Pacific region, and even globally.[76] The United States is also concerned that some aspects of China's nuclear modernization program detract from more than they contribute to stability.

Uncertainty about China's nuclear forces

While official estimates of China's nuclear forces continue to size them at a relatively modest level compared with those of the United States, there is growing concern in the United States and throughout the region about the imperfect and partial underpinnings of these estimates in light of China's growing military power.[77] The United States will become more and more intent to establish reliable estimates of China's nuclear forces as the PRC grows in power, the PLA advances in capability, and Chinese nuclear forces expand and modernize. The United States is particularly concerned about the potential for China to expand its nuclear forces substantially and rapidly.[78]

Chinese activities in other strategic domains

China's activities in space/counter-space, cyber, missile defense, and precision strike are increasingly raising questions in the United States about the future of strategic stability between China and the United States, including as these issues touch on nuclear weapons matters.[79]

China's conventional military buildup

If China's military buildup continues at the pace of the last decade and China continues to act in an assertive fashion in the region, the United States will need to reassess its broad defense posture and strategy. This will have implications for relations regarding nuclear forces, not least because the United States is likely to rely more on its nuclear arsenal for extended deterrence in Asia if the conventional military balance shifts in China's favor.[80]

North Korea

The United States is resolved to protect itself and its allies against North Korean attack, especially nuclear attack.[81] While the United States will attempt to take into account Beijing's reasonable concerns about Washington's response to North Korea's provocations and continued development of a nuclear and missile arsenal, the United States will do what is necessary to achieve its objectives, even if this means discomfiting Beijing.[82] In point of fact, the United States will seek to ensure that Beijing shares the discomfort and burden caused by Pyongyang's irresponsible and dangerous behavior.

Missile defense

The United States is also resolved to develop effective theater missile defenses to protect its forces and allies and to enable effective power projection.[83] In pursuing these objectives, the United States will not bear an unreasonably large burden of establishing that its missile defense capabilities, often designed to defend against China's very large arsenal of conventional missiles, are not destabilizing.

Conclusion

The relationship between the United States and China will be of tremendous geopolitical consequence for the 21st century, and no issue in that relationship will be more important for both sides than adequately protecting their interests while maintaining peace. Although major conflict appears unlikely at this point, it cannot be ruled out and could be becoming more plausible. With both sides possessing and looking set to retain formidable nuclear weapons arsenals, any conflict between them would be exceedingly dangerous and quite possibly devastating. Finding ways to minimize the probability of war and of nuclear use is therefore a primary obligation of political leaders on both sides of the Pacific. This chapter is an effort to provide a flexible joint roadmap that U.S. and Chinese leaders can use in working to fulfill this responsibility.

Notes

* The joint and U.S. sections of this chapter are substantially derived from the working group report of 14 U.S. experts on U.S.-China relations in the nuclear weapons domain. This report represented a year-long effort to develop a consensus position among the group, which was composed of leading experts on the topic and reflected a variety of backgrounds, viewpoints, and political affiliations. The report therefore provides a solid basis for understanding U.S. views on these issues. See Elbridge A. Colby and Abraham M. Denmark, "Nuclear Weapons and U.S. China Relations: A

Way Forward," Center for Strategic and International Studies (CSIS), report of the PONI Working Group on U.S.-China Nuclear Dynamics, 2013, http://csis.org/files/publication/130307_Colby_USChinaNuclear_Web.pdf. The authors are grateful to CSIS for its permission to draw from this report.

Disclaimer: Two sections of this chapter in the original English language text, which was published by the National Bureau of Asian Research in April 2016, were updated for this version by Chinese author Professor Wu Riqiang. These revisions were made unilaterally by Professor Wu to reflect recent developments and are intended to solely convey his viewpoint. His American co-author, Mr. Elbridge Colby, neither endorsed nor contributed to these updates, and they do not necessarily represent his views nor the views of the U.S. government in which he now serves.

1 See, for instance, A.F.K. Organski, *World Politics* (New York: Knopf, 1968); and Robert Gilpin, *War and Change in World Politics* (Cambridge: Cambridge University Press, 1981).

2 Chinese adaptation to U.S. capabilities is discussed in John Wilson Lewis and Xue Litai, *Imagined Enemies: China Prepares for Uncertain War* (Stanford: Stanford University Press, 2006), 39, 188–90, 212; Thomas G. Mahnken, "China's Anti-Access Strategy in Historical and Theoretical Perspective," *Journal of Strategic Studies* 34, no. 3 (2011): 317; Michael S. Chase and Andrew S. Erickson, "The Conventional Missile Capabilities of China's Second Artillery Force: Cornerstone of Deterrence and Warfighting," *Asian Security* 8, no. 2 (2012): 120–22; and Frank Miller, "People's Liberation Army Lessons Learned from Recent Pacific Command Operations and Contingencies," in *Chinese Lessons from Other Peoples' Wars*, ed. Andrew Scobell, David Lai, and Roy Kamphausen (Carlisle: Strategic Studies Institute, 2011): 214–24. An emerging U.S. response to expanding Chinese capabilities is outlined in Thomas Rowden and Peter Fanta, "Distributed Lethality," Proceedings, January 2015.

3 James M. Acton, "The Dragon Dance: U.S.-China Security Cooperation," in *Global Ten: Challenges and Opportunities for the President in 2013*, ed. Jessica T. Matthews (Washington, DC: Carnegie Endowment for International Peace, 2012), 121–23.

4 Yao Yunzhu, "Chinese Nuclear Policy and the Future of Minimum Deterrence," *Strategic Insights*, September 2005.

5 Keith B. Payne and Thomas Scheber, "Appendix E: An Adaptable Nuclear Force for the 2030+ Security Environment," in *Project Atom: A Competitive Strategies Approach to Defining U.S. Nuclear Strategy and Posture for 2025–2050*, ed. Clark Murdock et al. (Washington, DC: CSIS, 2015), 71–88.

6 This section is authored by Elbridge A. Colby.

7 U.S. Department of Defense, *Sustaining U.S. Global Leadership: Priorities for 21st Century Defense* (Washington, DC, 2012), 2.

8 U.S. Department of Defense, *Military and Security Developments Involving the People's Republic of China 2015* (Washington, DC, 2015), 21–23; and *U.S.-China Economic and Security Review Commission, 2014 Annual Report to Congress* (Washington, DC, 2014), 328.

9 For an analysis of China's growing activism, see Ely Ratner, Elbridge Colby, Andrew Erickson, Zachary Hosford, and Alexander Sullivan, "More Willing & Able: Charting China's International Security Activism," *Center for a New American Security*, 2015, 11–28. For an important example of the changing view of how to deal with China, see Robert D. Blackwill and Ashley J. Tellis, "Revising U.S. Grand Strategy Toward China," *Council on Foreign Relations*, Special Report, no. 72, March 2015. For a description of the evolving policy discussion, see Geoff Dyer, "U.S.-China: Shifting Sands," *Financial Times*, June 21, 2015; and Andrew Browne, "Can China Be Contained?" *Wall Street Journal*, June 12, 2015.

10 See, for instance, Robert O. Work, "The Third U.S. Offset Strategy and Its Implications for Partners and Allies" (speech at the Willard Hotel, Washington, DC, January 28, 2015),

www.defense.gov/News/Speeches/Speech-View/Article/606641/the-third-us-offset-strategy-and-its-implications-for-partners-and-allies.

11 For an indication of the increasing willingness that the U.S. military has displayed in highlighting the challenge of Chinese capabilities, note copious references in the bibliography of U.S. Department of Defense, *Joint Operational Access Concept* (Washington, DC, 2012).

12 For a more detailed history, see Elbridge Colby, "U.S. Nuclear Weapons Policy and Policymaking: The Asian Experience," in *Tactical Nuclear Weapons and NATO*, ed. Tom Nichols et al. (Carlisle: Strategic Studies Institute, 2012), 75–105.

13 For an analysis of this point, see Elbridge Colby, "Asia Goes Nuclear," *National Interest*, January/February 2015. See also Paul Bracken, *The Second Nuclear Age: Strategy, Danger, and the New Power Politics* (New York: Henry Holt and Co., 2012), 189–213. Of course, political assessments of how assertive the PRC is in its strategic and geopolitical actions and how ambitious it appears to be in advancing and expanding those interests will also be crucial factors. U.S. nuclear and broader defense policy, however, are likely to be driven by an assessment of China's actual capabilities rather than of its inherently changeable intent, especially given that Washington and Beijing are, at the very least, likely to be competitors in the region.

14 For a sobering, rigorous assessment of the shifting conventional military balance, see Eric Heginbotham et al., *The U.S.-China Military Scorecard: Forces, Geography, and the Evolving Balance of Power, 1996–2017* (Santa Monica: RAND Corporation, 2015).

15 For China's most recent defense white paper reiterating the no-first-use policy, see Information Office of the State Council of the PRC, *China's Military Strategy* (Beijing, May 2015), http://eng.mod.gov.cn/Database/WhitePapers/2014.htm. China's 2008 defense white paper uses the term "lean and effective" to describe its nuclear force. See State Council Information Office of the PRC, *China's Military Strategy* (Beijing, 2008), http://eng.mod.gov.cn/Database/WhitePapers/2008.htm.

16 M. Taylor Fravel and Evan S. Medeiros, "China's Search for Assured Retaliation: The Evolution of Chinese Nuclear Strategy and Force Structure," *International Security* 35, no. 2 (2010): 48–87; and Fiona S. Cunningham and M. Taylor Fravel, "Assuring Assured Retaliation: China's Nuclear Posture and the Future of U.S.-China Strategic Stability," *International Security* 40, no. 2 (2015): 7–50.

17 See, for instance, James Acton, "Is China Changing Its Position on Nuclear Weapons?" *New York Times*, April 18, 2013; and Bill Gertz, "First Strike: China Omission of No-First-Use Nuclear Doctrine in Defense White Paper Signals Policy Shift," *Washington Free Beacon*, April 26, 2013, http://freebeacon.com/national-security/first-strike.

18 Yao Yunzhu, "Chinese Nuclear Policy and the Future of Minimum Deterrence," in *Perspectives on Sino-American Strategic Nuclear Issues*, ed. Christopher P. Twomey (New York: Palgrave Macmillan, 2008), 111–24. Yao is currently a major general and an expert on nuclear issues at the PLA's Academy of Military Science.

19 See, for instance, Congressional Commission on the Strategic Posture of the United States, *America's Strategic Posture: The Final Report of the Congressional Commission on the Strategic Posture of the United States* (Washington, DC, 2009), 9.

20 U.S. Department of Defense, *Nuclear Posture Review Report* (Washington, DC, April 2010), www.defense.gov/Portals/1/features/defenseReviews/NPR/2010_Nuclear_Posture_Review_Report.pdf.

21 Keir A. Lieber and Daryl G. Press, "The Rise of U.S. Nuclear Primacy," *Foreign Affairs*, March/April 2006, www.foreignaffairs.com/articles/united-states/2006-03-01/rise-us-nuclear-primacy.

22 George P. Shultz, William J. Perry, Henry A. Kissinger, and Sam Nunn, "Next Steps in Reducing Nuclear Risks," *Wall Street Journal*, March 5, 2013, www.wsj.com/articles/SB10001424127887324338604578325912939001772.

23 See, for instance, the comments of former secretary of defense James R. Schlesinger during testimony before the U.S. Senate Subcommittee on Foreign Relations on "The Historical and Modern Context for U.S.-Russian Arms Control," Washington, DC, April 29, 2010, 25. For similar assessments, see William J. Perry, Brent Scowcrot, and Charles D. Ferguson, "U.S. Nuclear Weapons Policy," Council on Foreign Relations, Independent Task Force Report, no. 62, 2009, 45; Elbridge A. Colby and Abraham M. Denmark, "Nuclear Weapons and U.S. China Relations: A Way Forward," *CSIS*, Report of the PONI Working Group on U.S.-China Nuclear Dynamics, 2013, 18–20; Charles L. Glaser and Steve Fetter, "Should the United States Pursue a Damage-Limitation Capability against China's Strategic Nuclear Force?" (panel discussion at the U.S. Strategic Nuclear Policy toward China Conference, Washington, DC, September 11, 2015); and International Security Advisory Board, U.S. Department of State, "Report on Maintaining U.S.-China Strategic Stability," October 26, 2012, www.state.gov/documents/organization/200473.pdf.

24 Lora Saalman, "Placing a Renminbi Sign on Strategic Stability and Nuclear Reductions," in *Strategic Stability: Contending Interpretations*, ed. Elbridge A. Colby and Michael S. Gerson (Carlisle: Strategic Studies Institute, 2013), 350–55; James M. Acton, "Reclaiming Strategic Stability," in Colby and Gerson, *Strategic Stability*, 117–46; Elbridge Colby, "Defining Strategic Stability: Reconciling Stability and Deterrence," in Colby and Gerson, *Strategic Stability*, 47–83; Michael Glosny, Christopher Twomey, and Ryan Jacobs, "U.S.-China Strategic Dialogue, Phase VIII Report," Naval Postgraduate School, Report, no. 2014–008, December 2014; Ralph Cossa, Brad Glosserman, and Matt Pottinger, "Progress Despite Disagreements," Pacific Forum CSIS, Issues and Insights, November 2011, http://csis.org/files/publication/issuesinsights_vol12no05.pdf; and Ralph A. Cossa and David Santoro, "Paving the Way for a 'New Type of Major Country Relations': The Eighth China-US Dialogue on Strategic Nuclear Dynamics," Pacific Forum CSIS, Issues and Insights, November 2013, http://csis.org/files/publication/issuesinsights_vol14no9.pdf.

25 Outside of formal government channels, a Track 2 (or so-called 1.5) strategic dialogue between the United States and China—which includes participants from academia and think tanks, as well as members of government as observers—has made considerable strides toward promoting an understanding of each side's strategic concerns that contribute to reducing the prospect for mutual misunderstanding. These dialogues offer the admittedly more modest benefits deriving from regularized personal contact, accumulated expertise, and information exchange on terminology, capabilities, strategy, and policy. Yet while Track 1.5 and 2 dialogues can be helpful, they do have limitations. Participants are largely not government officials and are therefore unable to speak authoritatively, and those government officials who do participate are limited in what they are able to do in these venues. Thus, while these meetings are useful, they are no substitute for a genuine dialogue at the official level. For recent U.S. frustration on this, see Ralph A. Cossa and John K. Warden, "The Time is Right for U.S.-China Nuclear Dialogue," Pacific Forum CSIS, PacNet, no. 14, March 4, 2015, http://csis.org/files/publication/Pac1514.pdf.

26 The one partial exception is progress toward a potential launch notification agreement. See "President Xi Jinping's State Visit to the United States," Fact Sheet, Office of the White House Press Secretary, September 25, 2015, www.whitehouse.gov/the-press-office/2015/09/25/fact-sheet-president-xi-jinpings-state-visit-united-states.

27 This section is authored by Wu Riqiang.

28 Information Office of the State Council of the PRC, *China's Military Strategy*; Yao, "Chinese Nuclear Policy and the Future of Minimum Deterrence," 111–24; and Fravel and Medeiros, "China's Search for Assured Retaliation."

29 Rosemary J. Foot, "Nuclear Coercion and the Ending of the Korean Conflict," *International Security* 13, no. 3 (1988): 92–112; and Lyle J. Goldstein, "Do Nascent WMD Arsenals Deter? The Sino-Soviet Crisis of 1969," *Political Science Quarterly* 118, no. 1 (2003): 53–79.

30 Li Bin, "China's Potential to Contribute to Multilateral Nuclear Disarmament," *Arms Control Today*, March 3, 2011, www.armscontrol. org/act/2011_03/LiBin.
31 Gregory Kulacki, "Chickens Talking with Ducks: The U.S.-Chinese Nuclear Dialogue," *Arms Control Today*, September 30, 2011, www.armscontrol.org/act/2011_10/U.S._Chinese_Nuclear_Dialogue.
32 Hans M. Kristensen and Robert S. Norris, "Chinese Nuclear Forces, 2015," *Bulletin of the Atomic Scientists* 71, no. 4 (2015): 77–84.
33 Mark A. Stokes, "China's Nuclear Warhead Storage and Handling System," Project 2049 Institute, March 12, 2010, http://project2049.net/documents/chinas_nuclear_warhead_storage_and_handling_system.pdf.
34 Information Office of the State Council of the PRC, *China's Military Strategy*.
35 Ellen Tauscher, "Missile Defense: Road to Cooperation" (remarks at the Missile Defense Conference, Russia, May 3, 2012), www.state. gov/t/avc/rls/189281.htm.
36 Wu Riqiang, "China's Anxiety about U.S. Missile Defence: A Solution," *Survival* 55, no. 5 (2013): 29–52. See also Hui Zhang, "How U.S. Restraint Can Keep China's Nuclear Arsenal Small," *Bulletin of the Atomic Scientists* 68, no. 4 (2012): 73–82.
37 Alan Vick et al., *Aerospace Operations Against Elusive Ground Targets* (Santa Monica: RAND Corporation, 2001).
38 Austin Long and Brendan Rittenhouse Green, "Stalking the Secure Second Strike: Intelligence, Counterforce, and Nuclear Strategy," *Journal of Strategic Studies* 38, no. 1–2 (2015): 38–73; and Keir A. Lieber and Daryl G. Press, "The End of MAD? The Nuclear Dimension of U.S. Primacy," *International Security* 30, no. 4 (2006): 7–44.
39 U.S. Department of Defense, *Military Power of the People's Republic of China 2008* (Washington, DC, March 2008).
40 Bill Gertz, "China Tests ICBM with Multiple Warheads," *Washington Free Beacon*, December 18, 2014, http://freebeacon.com/national-security/china-tests-icbm-with-multiple-warheads.
41 Bill Gertz, "China Conducts Flight Test of JL-2 Sub-Launched Missile," *Washington Free Beacon*, February 19, 2015, http://freebeacon.com/national-security/inside-the-ring-china-conducts-flight-test-of-jl-2-sub-launched-missile; and Wu Riqiang, "Survivability of China's Sea-based Nuclear Forces," *Science & Global Security* 19, no. 2 (2011): 91–120.
42 U.S. Department of Defense, *Military and Security Developments Involving the People's Republic of China 2015*, 9.
43 Wu Riqiang, "Zhongguo zhanlue heqianting kaishi zhanbei xunhang le ma?" [Did China's Strategic Nuclear Submarines Begin to Conduct Deterrence Patrols?], *Xiandai jianchuan*, no. 2 (2016): 32–36.
44 Kristensen and Norris, "Chinese Nuclear Forces, 2015."
45 Wu, "China's Anxiety about U.S. Missile Defence," 29–52. See also Zhang, "How U.S. Restraint Can Keep China's Nuclear Arsenal Small," 73–82.
46 James M. Acton, "Managing Vulnerability," *Foreign Affairs*, March/April 2010, 145–53; and Linton Brooks, "The Sino-American Nuclear Balance: Its Future and Implications," in *China's Arrival: A Strategic Framework for a Global Relationship*, ed. Abraham Denmark and Nirav Patel (Washington, DC: Center for a New American Security, 2009), 60–76.
47 U.S. Department of Defense, *Nuclear Posture Review Report*, 28–29; and Jeffrey Lewis, "Challenges for U.S.-China Strategic Stability in the Obama Administration," in *Getting to Zero: The Path to Nuclear Disarmament*, ed. Catherine M. Kelleher and Judith Reppy (Stanford: Stanford University Press, 2011), 149–63.
48 Philip E. Coyle, "Ask McCain and Obama about Missile Defense," *Nieman Watchdog*, September 10, 2008, www.niemanwatchdog.org/index.cfm?fuseaction=ask_this.view&askthisid=365.
49 For a contemporary examination of this concept, see Colby and Gerson, *Strategic Stability*. For the American coauthor's view of this concept, see Colby, "Defining Strategic Stability," 47–83.

50 For the classic statement, see Thomas C. Schelling and Morton H. Halperin, *Strategy and Arms Control* (New York: Twentieth Century Fund, 1961).

51 For a discussion of these and related issues, see David C. Gompert and Philip C. Saunders, *The Paradox of Power: Sino-American Strategic Restraint in an Age of Vulnerability* (Washington, DC: National Defense University Press, 2011).

52 See, for instance, Cossa and Santoro, "Paving the Way"; and Cossa, Glosserman, and Santoro, "Progress Continues, But Disagreements Remain," Pacific Forum CSIS, Issues and Insights, January 2013, 15, 16.

53 It is worth recalling that the George W. Bush administration offered Russia formal inspections of missile defense sites in Europe.

54 See, for instance, M. Elaine Bunn and Vincent A. Manzo, "Conventional Prompt Global Strike: Strategic Asset or Unusable Liability?" National Defense University, Institute for Strategic Studies, 2011, 16; and Nicholas Cosmas, Meicen Sun, and John K. Warden, "U.S.-China Need a Missile Launch Notification Deal," *Diplomat*, October 27, 2014, http://thediplomat.com/2014/10/us-china-need-a-missile-launch-notification-deal.

55 "President Xi Jinping's State Visit to the United States."

56 See, for instance, Linton Brooks, "Building Habits of Cooperation in Pursuit of the Vision: Elements and Roles of Enhanced Dialogue for Strategic Reassurance," in *Building Toward a Stable and Cooperative Long-Term U.S.-China Strategic Relationship*, ed. Lewis A. Dunn (Pacific Forum CSIS, December 31, 2012), 47–48.

57 This is a suggestion of Linton Brooks. See Colby and Denmark, "Nuclear Weapons and U.S. China Relations," 25.

58 Cossa and Santoro, "Paving the Way," 11.

59 See Cossa, Glosserman, and Pottinger, "Progress Despite Disagreements," 15.

60 For a discussion of the idea of a Joint Statement for Strategic Stability, see Jeffrey Lewis, "Strengthening U.S.-China Dialogue on Strategic Stability (unpublished working paper), October 1, 2012.

61 See, for instance, the proposals of Linton Brooks in Michael O. Wheeler, "Track 1.5/2 Security Dialogues with China: Nuclear Lessons Learned," Institute for Defense Analyses, IDA Paper, no. P-5135, September 2014, 23–24, www.ida.org/~/media/Corporate/Files/Publications/IDA_Documents/SFRD/2014/P-5135.ashx; and Cossa, Glosserman, and Pottinger, "Progress Despite Disagreements," vii–viii.

62 See, for instance, Cossa, Glosserman, and Santoro, "Progress Continues," viii.

63 This subsection is authored by Wu.

64 William J. Perry and Andy Weber, "Mr. President, Kill the New Cruise Missile," *Washington Post*, October 15, 2015, www.washingtonpost.com/opinions/mr-president-kill-the-new-cruise-missile/2015/10/15/e3e2807c-6ecd-11e5-9bfe-e59f5e244f92_story.html.

65 "2025–2050: Recommended U.S. Nuclear Strategy," in Murdoch et al., *Project Atom*, 13. See also Colby, "Defining Strategic Stability"; and Keir A. Lieber and Daryl G. Press, "The Nukes We Need: Preserving the American Deterrent," *Foreign Affairs*, November/December 2009, 39–51.

66 U.S. Department of Defense, *Nuclear Posture Review Report*, 39.

67 Hans M. Kristensen, "B61 LEP: Increasing NATO Nuclear Capability and Precision Low-Yield Strikes," Federation of American Scientists, Strategic Security, June 15, 2011, http://fas.org/blogs/security/2011/06/b61-12.

68 William J. Broad and David E. Sanger, "As U.S. Modernizes Nuclear Weapons, 'Smaller' Leaves Some Uneasy," *New York Times*, January 11, 2016.

69 Wu, "China's Anxiety about U.S. Missile Defence."

70 John Schilling, "Why North Korea Won't Have Its ICBM Anytime Soon," *Diplomat*, March 16, 2015, http://thediplomat.com/2015/03/why-north-korea-wont-have-its-icbm-anytime-soon.

71 "Executive Summary of the Report of the Commission to Assess the Ballistic Missile Threat to the United States," July 15, 1998, http://fas.org/irp/threat/bm-threat.htm.

72 U.S. National Intelligence Council, "Foreign Missile Developments and the Ballistic Missile Threat through 2015," December 2001, http://fas.org/irp/nic/bmthreat-2015.htm.

73 Larry Shaughnessy, "Gates: North Korea Could Have Long-Range Missile within 5 Years," *CNN*, January 12, 2011, http://edition.cnn.com/2011/WORLD/asiapcf/01/11/china.us.north.korea/index.html.

74 Dean Wilkening, "U.S. Missile Defense Developments: How Far? How Fast?" (speech at Brookings Institution workshop, Washington, DC, June 4, 2014), www.brookings.edu/events/2014/06/04-us-missile-defense-developments.

75 This subsection is authored by Colby.

76 Concerns discussed, but not necessarily shared, are in Thomas J. Christensen, "The Meaning of the Nuclear Evolution: China's Strategic Modernization and U.S.-China Security Relations," *Journal of Strategic Studies* 35, no. 4 (2012): 478; Michael Chase, Andrew Erickson, and Christopher Yeaw, "Chinese Theater and Strategic Missile Force Modernization," *Journal of Strategic Studies* 32, no. 1 (2009): 87–98; Fravel and Medeiros, "China's Search for Assured Retaliation"; and Fravel and Cunningham, "Assuring Assured Retaliation."

77 Widely cited estimates of China's nuclear arsenal use leaked U.S. intelligence estimates from the 1990s as a baseline, putting a cap on the total number of likely Chinese warheads by estimating the number that could be built with plutonium produced before production was halted in 1991. Compare the estimates and methodologies compiled in Anthony H. Cordesman, Steven Colley, and Michael Wang, *Chinese Strategy and Military Modernization in 2015: A Comparative Analysis* (Washington, DC: CSIS, 2015), 374–87, http://csis.org/files/publication/151215_Cordesman_ChineseStrategyMilitary Mod_Web.pdf.

78 Brad Roberts, "On Order, Stability, and Nuclear Abolition," in *Abolishing Nuclear Weapons: A Debate*, ed. George Perkovich and James M. Acton (Washington, DC: Carnegie Endowment for Peace, 2009), 167; and Michael O. Wheeler, "Nuclear Parity with China?" Institute for Defense Analyses, 2012, 13–16. The highest estimates have been offered by Phil Karber, who argues that China could have as many as 3,000 nuclear weapons. See William Wan, "Digging Up China's Nuclear Secret," *Washington Post*, November 30, 2011.

79 See, for instance, James M. Acton, "The Arms Race Goes Hypersonic," *Foreign Policy*, January 30, 2014, http://foreignpolicy.com/2014/01/30/the-arms-race-goes-hypersonic; and Bruce W. MacDonald and Charles D. Ferguson, "Understanding the Dragon Shield: Likelihood and Implications of Chinese Strategic Ballistic Missile Defense," Federation of American Scientists, Special Report, September 2015, 32–35, https://fas.org/wp-content/uploads/2015/09/DragonShieldreport_FINAL.pdf.

80 Colby and Denmark, "Nuclear Weapons and U.S. China Relations," 2–3; and Colby, "Asia Goes Nuclear."

81 U.S. Department of Defense, *Quadrennial Defense Review 2014* (Washington, DC, 2014), 14, 20, 32; and Susan E. Rice, "America's Future in Asia," (remarks prepared for delivery at Georgetown University, Washington, DC, November 20, 2013), www.white house.gov/the-press-office/2013/11/21/remarks-prepared-delivery-national-security-advisor-susan-e-rice.

82 See "U.S. Official Dismisses China's Concern Over Missile Defense System in S. Korea," *Japan Times*, March 17, 2015, www.japantimes.co.jp/news/2015/03/17/asia-pacific/u-s-official-dismisses-chinas-concern-over-missile-defense-system-in-s-korea/#.Vh_0LU3lumy.

83 U.S. Department of Defense, *Sustaining U.S. Global Leadership*; and Karen DeYoung, "U.S. to Deploy Anti-Missile System to Guam," *Washington Post*, April 3, 2013.

3 Reducing and managing

U.S.-China conflict in cyberspace

Adam Segal and Tang Lan

EXECUTIVE SUMMARY

This chapter examines the increasing importance of cyberspace in the U.S.-China relationship and assesses the significant differences between Beijing and Washington over cyberattacks, Internet governance, and the security of supply chains and information and communications equipment.

Main argument

Despite the gaps in their views on Internet governance, cyberattacks, cyberespionage, and how to secure supply chains and information and telecommunications equipment, as well as the hyperbolic rhetoric that often shows up in the media in both countries about cyberwar, Chinese and U.S. policymakers appear committed to not letting cyber issues derail the U.S-China relationship or interfere with cooperation on other high-profile issues. Beijing and Washington seem to agree that continued cooperation on other issues such as economic growth, regional stability, and climate change should not be held hostage to cyber issues and that there is still a realistic prospect that the two sides can build greater collaboration. Both countries share a number of concerns, including addressing threats to critical infrastructure, stopping the proliferation of cyberattack capabilities to nonstate actors, and securing global supply chains. While the two governments have vowed to clarify responsible behaviors through bilateral and multilateral discussions, identifying common ground and cooperative projects is necessary to reduce tensions in cyberspace.

Policy implications

In order to manage conflict in cyberspace, China and the United States should pursue the following actions:

- Follow up on the September 2015 agreement on fighting cybercrime and cyber-enabled theft of intellectual property with concrete cooperation;
- Ensure that discussions on norms of behavior in cyberspace continue at the highest level and are not suspended during times of tension;

- Discuss joint measures such as intelligence exchanges to prevent the proliferation of cyber capabilities to nonstate actors;
- Build cybersecurity capacity and expand cooperative research in universities and civil society.

Although cyberspace is an issue of increasing importance to the U.S.-China relationship, Beijing and Washington still have significant differences over the free flow of information and the openness of the Internet, cyberattacks and norms of behavior in cyberspace, Internet governance, and the security of supply chains and information and communications equipment. As a result, each country is likely to see the other as an important, if not the main, competitor to the pursuit of its interests in cyberspace.

Yet despite the gaps in their positions, and the hyperbolic rhetoric that often shows up in the media in both countries about cyberwar, policymakers in Zhongnanhai and the White House appear committed to not letting cyber issues derail the relationship. The September 2015 summit between Presidents Barack Obama and Xi Jinping produced breakthrough agreements on several important cybersecurity measures. Both sides pledged that "neither country's government will conduct or knowingly support cyber-enabled theft of intellectual property, including trade secrets or other confidential business information, with the intent of providing competitive advantages to companies or commercial sectors."[1] Washington and Beijing also agreed to identify and endorse norms of behavior in cyberspace and establish two high-level working groups and a hotline between the two sides.

However, as President Obama acknowledged following the summit in September, "Our work is not yet done. I believe we can expand our cooperation in this area."[2] The U.S.-China cyber agreement could be a model for future international discussions. China and the United Kingdom, for example, reached a similar agreement, and in November 2015, China, Brazil, Russia, the United States, and other members of the Group of Twenty (G-20) accepted the norm against conducting or supporting the cyber-enabled theft of intellectual property.[3]

After a year of ups and downs in the Sino-U.S. cybersecurity relationship, the agreement signed by the two presidents may provide a mechanism to mediate conflict in the future. Failure to build on the agreement, however, could generate greater mistrust that spills over into other aspects of the relationship. U.S. and People's Republic of China (PRC) forces, for example, are in close contact in the South China Sea, and cyberattacks could quickly escalate a stand-off and, through misperception or miscalculation, lead to military conflict. Defense planners in both countries appear to assume that offense dominates in cyberspace, and so there are strong incentives to strike first, further heightening the risk that a crisis could quickly escalate. A cyberattack that causes damage or destruction could create domestic demand for immediate action that both leaderships would have a hard time ignoring.

Finding some common ground and developing cooperative projects are necessary first steps to reducing tensions in cyberspace. Both sides increasingly depend on digital infrastructure for economic and national security and share a number of concerns. Globally, cyberattacks are growing in frequency, scale, sophistication, and severity of impact. Cybercrime continues to rise—McAfee estimates that it cost the global economy more than $400 billion in 2014—and terrorists groups appear to be seeking the ability to launch destructive cyberattacks.[4] The proliferation of cyberattack capabilities to nonstate actors that are not easily deterred puts critical infrastructure in both China and the United States at risk. There are also strong economic incentives for greater cooperation. The Chinese and U.S. information and communications technology (ICT) markets are tightly linked, and both economies rely on the security, integrity, and availability of global supply chains. While avoiding greater mistrust and preventing virtual events from escalating into physical conflicts are essential, Beijing and Washington should not stop there. They should also work together to identify positive goals. The growth of the Internet has brought immense economic, political, social, and cultural benefits to both sides. Strategic cooperation in cyberspace could result in further gains for China, the United States, and the rest of the world.

The first section of this chapter examines U.S. interests in cyberspace and U.S. perceptions of Chinese interests. The next section shifts the frame, discussing Chinese motives and objectives and Chinese views of U.S. interests. After laying out each side's interests, the chapter identifies areas of convergence between China and the United States and recommends cooperative initiatives. It then describes areas of divergence between the two countries and considers mechanisms to manage tension.

U.S. perspectives on cyberspace

U.S. interests in cyberspace

The White House's 2011 International Strategy on Cyberspace declares that the United States has a national interest in an "open, interoperable, secure and reliable" Internet that fosters international trade, economic development, and innovation; strengthens international security; and promotes free expression.[5] As a 2013 Council on Foreign Relations task force concluded, "A global Internet increasingly fragmented into national Internets is not in the interest of the United States."[6]

The United States has an economic and political interest in the flow of information across borders, with the requisite framework for respecting intellectual property rights and the privacy of individuals. According to the Internet Association, a trade group representing some of the biggest Internet companies, the Internet generates 6% of the domestic economy.[7] U.S. technology companies dominate the global Internet economy, with the United States accounting for 25% of global telecom revenue in 2015 and capturing close to 25% of the G-20's Internet economy.[8] In India, nine of the top ten websites are U.S.-based sites such as Google, Facebook, Twitter, and LinkedIn; seven of the top ten sites in Brazil are run by U.S. companies.[9] Google is the leader in search engines, and its Android operating system is on over three-quarters of the smartphones being made in the world.[10]

In May 2015, Deputy U.S. Trade Representative Robert Holleyman warned that existing trade agreements were being battered by rising digital protectionism—

regulations requiring data localization or censoring. In response, the United States developed the "dirty dozen," 12 principles for digital trade that U.S. negotiators had been working to incorporate into the Trans-Pacific Partnership. The principles include that the Internet should remain free and open so consumers can access online services and that countries should be prevented from requiring companies to transfer technology or localize their computing services.[11]

The United States also has a stated interest in the free flow of information. In three speeches over 2010 and 2011, then secretary of state Hillary Clinton identified information networks as a "new nervous system for our planet" and asserted that users must be assured freedom of expression and religion online, as well as the right to access the Internet and thereby connect to websites and other people.[12] The U.S. State Department spent approximately $100 million between 2008 and 2012 to fund activities such as training digital activists in hostile environments and developing circumvention tools to bypass state-sponsored Internet filters. In September 2015, U.S. ambassador to the United Nations Samantha Power announced a $10 million venture capital–like fund for the development of new circumvention technologies as part of an increase of the annual budget for Internet freedom to $33 million.[13]

While the Internet is seen as a powerful diplomatic and economic tool, it is also viewed as creating dangerous and unforeseen vulnerabilities. The United States has described a cyberthreat to its national and economic security that is, in the words of the director of national intelligence's 2015 Worldwide Threat Assessment, "increasing in frequency, scale, sophistication, and severity of impact." The assessment continues that the range of actors and methods of attacks is expanding and, as a result, "the unclassified information and communication technology (ICT) networks that support U.S. government, military, commercial, and social activities remain vulnerable to espionage and/or disruption."[14]

U.S. military strength is intertwined with and dependent on the current structure of the Internet. Because the Pentagon relies on secure networks and data to carry out its missions, much of the emphasis has been on its vulnerability to cyberattacks from potential adversaries. The Defense Science Board, for example, warned in a January 2013 report that the "benefits to an attacker using cyber exploits are potentially spectacular." "U.S. guns, missiles, and bombs may not fire, or may be directed against our own troops," the report stated: "Resupply, including food, water, ammunition, and fuel may not arrive when or where needed. Military Commanders may rapidly lose trust in the information and ability to control U.S. systems and forces. Once lost, that trust is very difficult to regain."[15]

A global Internet, and the dependence of others on it, creates targets for the United States. While the Department of Defense's 2015 cyber strategy emphasizes the defensive nature of U.S. Cyber Command, it also recognizes offensive missions. "If directed by the President or the Secretary of Defense," states the strategy, the Department of Defense "must be able to provide integrated cyber capabilities to support military operations and contingency plans."[16]

Moreover, the disclosures by Edward Snowden suggest that the National Security Agency (NSA) has taken advantage of the dominant position of U.S.

technology companies and exploited the U.S. position at the center of the Internet for intelligence gains. Through legal and other means, the United States can access the data of millions of Google, Facebook, Twitter, YouTube, and other social media users around the world. A small number of Internet providers carry the bulk of data over the backbone, and a majority of Internet data is drawn in and routed through the United States, even if it makes little geographic sense. Fiber-optic cables can be tapped and data collected, analyzed, and stored.[17] Former NSA director Michael Hayden put it bluntly when justifying some of the agency's activities by telling the *National Journal*, "This is a home game for us. Are we not going to take advantage that so much of it goes through Redmond, Washington? Why would we not turn the most powerful telecommunications and computing management structure on the planet to our use?"[18]

The United States would like to preserve this ability to spy on others, while limiting the type of spying countries conduct. Washington has tried to create a norm against the cyber-enabled theft of intellectual property, trade secrets, and business strategies. In the U.S. view, however, there is a distinction between espionage conducted for political-military reasons and hacks in support of industrial competitiveness.

Maintaining this distinction occasionally placed Obama administration officials in the strange position of praising the tradecraft of Chinese hackers. According to a *Washington Post* report and numerous others studies, People's Liberation Army (PLA) hackers and other groups stole information from over two dozen Defense Department weapons programs, including the Patriot missile system and the U.S. Navy's new littoral combat ship.[19] In July 2014, media reported that Chinese hackers had gained access to the servers of the Office of Personnel Management, which contained the personal information of tens of thousands of federal employees. The hackers compromised 22 million records, including security background checks and data on intelligence and military personnel, as well as close to 5 million fingerprint records. These records would allow Chinese counterintelligence agencies to identify spies working undercover at U.S. embassies around the world. The director of national intelligence James Clapper told an audience in June 2015, "You have to kind of salute the Chinese for what they did, you know? If we had the opportunity to do that, I don't think we'd hesitate for a minute."[20]

The objectives of these hacks were political and military and would in effect be seen from the U.S. perspective as legitimate tools to promote national interests. The Chinese government has denounced claims that China was behind the Office of Personnel Management hack and presented evidence at a bilateral meeting that the motives of the hack were commercial rather than espionage. Although the Chinese press reported that the U.S. side accepted this evidence, the U.S. government has not confirmed these reports.

From the U.S. perspective, the hacking of companies to steal intellectual property, however, is seen as illegitimate. As President Obama told the Business Roundtable, "We have repeatedly said to the Chinese government that we understand traditional intelligence-gathering functions that all states, including us, engage in." He continued, "That is fundamentally different from your government or its proxies engaging directly in industrial espionage and stealing trade secrets, stealing proprietary information from companies."[21]

While there is no accepted measure of the size of cyber-enabled theft, it is assumed to significantly affect U.S. competitiveness. Former NSA head General Keith Alexander estimated the actual cost to U.S. companies at $250 billion in stolen information and another $114 billion in related expenses. The 2013 Commission on the Theft of American Intellectual Property, a private commission chaired by Dennis Blair, former director of national intelligence, and Jon Huntsman, former ambassador to China, argued that the annual "losses are likely to be comparable to the current annual level of U.S. exports to Asia—over $300 billion."[22]

U.S. perspective on Chinese interests

From the moment Chinese users first went online, Chinese policymakers and analysts conceived of the Internet as a double-edged sword—essential to economic growth and good governance but also the source of threats to domestic stability and regime legitimacy. As early as 2006, James R. Keith, senior adviser for China and Mongolia in the U.S. Department of State, described Chinese Internet regulations as trying "to ensure that ideas that do not have the government's imprimatur or that challenge its authority do not take root in China."[23]

China's first Internet white paper in 2010 declared that Chinese citizens enjoy full freedom of speech on the Internet but also stated that the exercise of those rights must not "jeopardize state security, the public interest or the legitimate rights and interests of other people."[24] To prevent these threats, the Chinese government has built an Internet management system that has an external and domestic face. Offending material from outside China is filtered and blocked by a number of technologies colloquially known as the "great firewall."

The challenge for Chinese leaders is how to get the balance between control and openness right. Beijing wants to ensure that the Internet does not destabilize the country while still playing a critical role in driving innovation and growth. The 2010 white paper described the Internet's "irreplaceable role in accelerating the development of the national economy."[25] According to McKinsey, China's Internet economy in 2013 as a share of GDP was 4.4% higher than in Germany and the United States, and the total value by revenue of China's Internet market was 637.73 billion renminbi ($104.15 billion) in 2014.[26] A number of Chinese technology and Internet companies, including Alibaba, Tencent, Baidu, and Xiaomi, are expanding into global markets. Huawei and ZTE have a strong presence in Europe and emerging markets, and the smartphone messaging application WeChat (*Weixin*) has tens of millions of users in Southeast Asia. New uses in the domestic market, such as wearables and the "Internet of things," could be responsible for 7%–22% of China's incremental GDP growth through 2025, depending on technology adoption rates.[27]

While the Chinese leadership has been optimistic about China's ability to compete in developing Internet technology, there has been a long-held concern about the country's dependence on Europe, Japan, and the United States for advanced technologies. When the leadership hears U.S. technology companies speak of global standards, what they hear is "U.S." technologies. Chinese industries need to move out of labor-intensive, high-energy, highly polluting manufacturing sectors to more technology-intensive ones, and policymakers fear being caught in a technology trap in which China is dependent on U.S., Japanese, and European firms for core technologies.

The dependence is particularly acute in network security. According to an April 2012 article in *Outlook Weekly*, 90% of China's microchips, components, network equipment, and communications standards and protocols and 65% of firewalls, encryption technology, and ten other types of information security products rely on imported technology. Foreign producers also dominate the market for programmable logic controllers, which are devices used to control manufacturing and other industrial processes.

The efforts to raise China's technological capabilities are both overt and covert. Beijing has committed significant resources to science and technology. The 20-year plan for science and technology development envisions China becoming an "innovative nation" by 2020 and a "global scientific power" by 2050. Scientific R&D funding has increased by 12%–20% annually for each of the last 20 years, and China passed Japan in 2010 as the world's second-largest spender on R&D.[28] Beijing has also relied on regulation and industrial policy. The desire to spur indigenous innovation and make it harder for the NSA to gain access to Chinese networks has fostered a focus on technology that is "secure and controllable" and has motivated a number of recent regulations, including banking provisions, the national security law, and the cybersecurity law. In September 2015 the *New York Times* reported that the Chinese government sent letters to U.S. technology companies requesting that they sign a pledge to not harm Chinese national security and to store user data locally, as well as pledging to make their products secure and controllable.[29] In December 2015, China passed a new antiterrorism law that did not require foreign companies to provide backdoors or store their data locally. While the Chinese government has insisted that it will follow international standards and implement transparent procedures, the law does mandate, however, that companies provide "technical interfaces, decryption and other technical support assistance to public security organs and state security organs."[30]

The covert efforts have involved cyber- and industrial espionage. The Office of the National Counterintelligence Executive names France, Israel, and Russia, among others, as states collecting economic information and technology from U.S. companies but places China in a category all its own. The office notes: "Chinese actors are the world's most active and persistent perpetrators of economic espionage."[31] Larry Wortzel, a commissioner on the U.S.-China Economic and Security Review Commission, argues that "Chinese entities engaging in cyber and other forms of economic espionage likely conclude that stealing intellectual property and proprietary information is much more cost-effective than investing in lengthy R&D programs." He adds that "these thefts support national science and technology development plans that are centrally managed and directed by the PRC government."[32]

Chinese leaders have denied such accusations that China hacks U.S. companies. Noting the vulnerability of domestic networks to disruptive and destructive attacks, Chinese officials have argued that in fact China is the "world's biggest victim" of cyberattacks, with the majority of attacks conducted via Internet protocol addresses in Japan, the United States, and South Korea. According to Huang Chengqing, who is the director of the National Computer Network Emergency Response Technical Team/Coordination Center of China, Beijing has "mountains of data, if we wanted to accuse the U.S., but it's not helpful in solving the problem."[33]

Moreover, until the September 2015 summit, China had not accepted U.S. efforts to distinguish between legitimate political-military espionage and cyber-enabled theft of intellectual property. Chinese officials and academics have criticized this distinction as a unilateral attempt to define the rules of the road of cyberspace. As Wu Xinbo, director of the Center for American Studies at Fudan University, put it, "The U.S. has always adopted a double standard on cyber security. It accuses other countries, especially China, of industrial espionage or other cyber attacks while the U.S. monitors other countries' senior officials or political figures almost constantly."[34] In addition, the Chinese press has repeated allegations by Snowden that the NSA also targets Chinese universities and businesses. In a public statement, the director of national intelligence James Clapper insisted that these types of activities were designed to enhance security and protect national interests; the intelligence community does not steal "trade secrets of foreign companies on behalf of—or give intelligence we collect to—U.S. companies."[35] But there is little reason to believe that these avowals were accepted by Chinese policymakers.

An April 2015 executive order authorizes the U.S. Treasury Department to sanction individuals or companies that engage in cyber-enabled theft. Just eight days before a scheduled working dinner with President Xi, President Obama stated the following to a meeting of the Business Roundtable on September 16, 2015:

> We are preparing a number of measures that will indicate to the Chinese that this [the issue of cyberattacks] is not just a matter of us being mildly upset, but is something that will put significant strains on the bilateral relationship if not resolved, and that we are prepared to [do] some countervailing actions in order to get their attention.[36]

Although the summit removed the immediate threat of sanctions, Washington may still resort to them if there is not a notable decline in Chinese-based attacks on U.S. companies.

Much like their U.S. counterparts, Chinese defense analysts believe that cyber operations will be part of any future military campaigns. According to the Pentagon, "Developing cyber capabilities for warfare is consistent with authoritative PLA military writings, which identify information warfare as integral to achieving information superiority and an effective means for countering a stronger foe."[37] Chinese open-source writings discuss the importance of seizing information dominance early in a conflict through cyberattacks on command-and-control centers. Follow-up attacks would target transportation, communications, and logistics networks to slow down an adversary. Chinese military writings also suggest that cyber operations can have widespread destructive effects and thus are a strong deterrent. Chinese analysts believe that the United States is much more dependent on banking, telecommunications, and other critical networks than China is, and they thus argue that attacks on these networks could dramatically reduce the chances that the United States might get involved in a regional conflict.[38]

Chinese perspectives on cyberspace

China's interests in cyberspace

At the beginning of 2014, China's Central Network Security and Informatization Leading Group held its first meeting. At the meeting, President Xi stressed that "network and information security is a major strategic issue that relates to national security, development and the broad masses of working life" and that there can be "no national security without cybersecurity."[39] This was a milestone event for understanding China's cyber policy. Though not the first time that China put a high value on cybersecurity, it was the first time that the country put the issue at the highest level. Afterward, at the first meeting of the Central National Security Council, President Xi added cybersecurity to the national security system, creating an "overall national security" concept (*zong ti guo jia an quan guan*).

Looking back at the history of the development of the Internet in China, it is useful for outsiders to understand the country's cyber policy. As mentioned in a report entitled "Twenty Years of Internet Development in China," released at the World Internet Conference held in Wuzhen in December 2015, the development of the Internet occurred in four periods: (1) the start-up period, (2) the formation of industry, (3) rapid development and innovation, and (4) integration.[40] China was a major beneficiary at the first stage of the information revolution, while turning into a major contributor and constructor for global cyberspace in later stages. For now, the 13th five-year plan (2016–20) concluded that it is time to "build China into a great cyberpower, rise to the challenges and seize the valuable opportunity of development."[41] From now on, China vigorously implements its cyber great-power strategy, national big-data strategy, and "Internet plus" initiative, which aims at a digital China. In the view of the Chinese government, combating the risks caused by ICT and maintaining the stability, trust, openness, and safety of the digital environment are the priorities.

Driven by the profound evolution of ICT and the emergence of a real security threat, China's top leaders' perspectives on cybersecurity are deepening: "We are concerned about network security, including ideological security, data security, technical security, application security, capital security, channel security and others."[42] Cybersecurity not only means the security of traditional information infrastructure but now encompasses various types of networks, data, and equipment. In sum, from the view of top Chinese leaders, massive and sophisticated cyberattacks, especially sponsored by nation-states aiming to disrupt and destroy the function of critical infrastructure and services; various illegal online actions that harm public security and social stability and subvert the regime; cyberterrorism; and cyberwarfare are all on the list of cyberthreats. The first national security law, which was issued in July 2015, viewed cybersecurity as an imminent and severe security risk that requires China to "build an assurance system to protect network and information security, promote the defense capability, [and] safeguard sovereignty, security, and development benefits for the country in cyberspace."[43] It is the first time that China clarified the importance of cybersecurity by law.

China needs to leverage the security problems threatening the healthy growth of its digital economy. The Internet, along with various kinds of information systems, infrastructure, and data, is not simply a tool or platform anymore but is now a key catalyst of Chinese economic transformation and development. A Chinese report on e-commerce shows that in 2014 national information consumption reached 2.8 trillion renminbi.[44] According to the China Internet Network Information Center, by June 2019, the number of Chinese Internet users had reached 854 million, and the penetration rate of smartphones was over 99.1%. The amount of online transactions has rapidly increased from 1 trillion renminbi in 2004 to 31.3 trillion renminbi in 2018, and China has become the biggest online retail market in the world.[45] Recently, China released its Internet Plus Action Plan and Made in China 2025 Plan, which will help the country find new tools to reform the developing format and improve competitiveness. The security of cyberspace is a fundamental priority in China's digitalization and should be an integral part of national security strategy. In particular, protecting critical information infrastructure in the era of hyper-interconnectedness is a priority of the government. Due to the heavy reliance on key foreign technology, it is reasonable to take legal and administrative measures to change the situation and improve the capacity of cyberdefenses.

Combating cybercrime is also in China's interest. "Cybercrime is the greatest threat to every company in the world," said the president and CEO of IBM, Ginni Rometty.[46] Juniper Research has predicted that "the rapid digitization of consumers' lives and enterprise records will increase the cost of data breaches to \$2.1 trillion globally by 2019, increasing to almost four times the estimated cost of breaches in 2015."[47] The situation inside China will likely be worse. Profit-driven hackers build a huge black industrial chain and gray market, facilitating the shift of traditional criminals to the cyber domain. The situation is getting serious and rampant. According to a November 2015 Norton survey of Internet security, in 2014 approximately 240 million Chinese consumers were victims of cybercrime, totaling economic losses of up to 700 billion renminbi. Preventing the use of cyberspace for criminal activities such as terrorism, pornography, drug trafficking, money laundering, and gambling is a major task faced by law enforcement. Almost every year, the Ministry of Public Security and other involved departments launch multiple special operations against online piracy, telecommunications fraud, and hacking.

President Xi clearly defined the Chinese position on the issue of cybersecurity and Internet governance in his keynote speech in Wuzhen in December 2015.

For China, it is critical to balance security, domestic stability, and development. Cybersecurity and Internet development are just like two wings of a bird, while domestic stability is a precondition. Without social stability, both security and digitalization are out of the question. It is the same abroad. Incomplete rules and unreasonable order have a negative impact on the world's ability to fully enjoy the social benefits of the Internet, even increasing the possibility of potential tension among countries. President Xi argued that "all countries should work together to contain the abuse of information technology, oppose cyber surveillance and cyberattacks, and reject [an] arms race in cyberspace."[48] For this purpose, he also proposed four principles: respect for sovereignty in cyberspace, maintenance of peace and security, promotion of openness and cooperation, and cultivation of good order. As a big player in the cyber domain, China has the duty to play a major role in and contribute to the stability and peace of international cyberspace in accordance with its national interests and security. That is why President Xi urged all countries to jointly build a community based on the idea of a shared future in cyberspace, which he characterized as governed by all, explaining that "cyberspace should not become a battlefield for countries to wrestle one another," nor should it become "a hotbed for crime."[49] On March 1, 2017, the Chinese Foreign Ministry and State Internet Information Office jointly released "The International Strategy for Cooperation on Cyberspace," the first of its kind by the Chinese government. The document specifies six strategic goals of China's participation in international cyberspace cooperation: safeguarding sovereignty and security, developing a system of international rules, promoting the building of a rule-based order in cyberspace, promoting fair internet governance, protecting legitimate rights and interests of citizens, promoting cooperation on digital economy, and building a platform for cyber cultural exchange.[50]

Chinese views of U.S. interests

A few Chinese analysts believe that the United States has soaked itself in Cold War and hegemonic thinking and wants to compete with China in all aspects of cyberspace, even wanting to jeopardize the current regime. One of the intents of the United States advocating for Internet freedom and online human rights is targeting China. In the two addresses of then secretary of state Hillary Clinton about Internet freedom in 2010 and 2011, she vowed to invest more to develop advanced circumvention technology to bypass censorship by the Chinese government, which views such actions as an intervention into its internal affairs and as motivated by a desire to topple the current regime.[51] In the eyes of the Chinese government, the stability of the regime is the core security concern. Some scholars argue that Internet freedom is used as an excuse to intervene in China's internal affairs. China proposes that countries should respect other states' rights to choose their methods of cyber development, cyber administration, and related public policy.

At the same time, the United States and its allies carry out massive surveillance at the cost of people's privacy and even the security of other nation-states. This double standard is viewed as a form of cyber hegemony.[52] The Chinese government cannot accept the fact that one country is secure while others are not and that one state's chasing of absolute security could sacrifice another's security.[53]

The United States, for example, has a strict foreign investment review system and forbids Chinese information technology companies from entering the U.S. market for the sake of national security. Both Huawei and ZTE are victims of such a system. Meanwhile, U.S. companies like Cisco, Microsoft, and IBM became the biggest providers of Chinese telecommunications and critical information infrastructure, serving as the backbone of Internet service and gaining huge revenue over the last two decades. When China planned to implement tougher regulations referring to and modeled on international practice, including unveiling a cybersecurity evaluation system and drafting laws that emphasized the importance of ICT security and controllability, Beijing suffered numerous condemnations from the United States. China wants assurance that the United States, as the most powerful and technologically advanced country in the world in ICT, will not hurt China's interests with this advantage. Technologically speaking, the United States is much more powerful than China. The weaker state should be worried about the stronger one, not the other way around.[54] Facing significant risk and potential damage, China has no choice but to take action and try to balance the need for regulation and the forces of the free market while keeping procedures transparent and impartial. In an interview with the *Wall Street Journal*, President Xi assured foreign readers that the long-term policy of attracting foreign investment will not change and that China opposes protectionism and discriminatory policies in all forms.[55]

The United States appears to consider China a big source of cyberattacks and perhaps the greatest cyberthreat. In the perspective of a majority of Chinese academics, in order to guarantee the security and freedom of operations in cyberspace, the United States will continue its strategy of containment and deterrence by pursuing a strong offensive capacity in cyberspace and suppressing the rapid development of China's cyber power. The U.S. coordinator for cyber issues indicated in May 2015 that cyberthreats, especially from China, rank high on the list of worldwide threats to the United States: "We face significant and growing challenges, especially from China, Russia, and other authoritarian governments that seek increased sovereign control over the Internet and its content."[56] As discussed earlier, the United States distinguishes between cyberactivities for national security or intelligence purposes and cyberactivities against commercial secrets. This binary approach gives sufficient reason for the United States' intelligence activities in the cyber domain. Following the U.S. Office of Personnel Management's data breach, Clapper called China the "leading suspect" in the attack.[57] Stemming from this judgement, the White House outlined a whole-government deterrence strategy: reserve the right and capability of retaliation, impose a cost on the attacker, make cyber an option in conflict, and promote active defense.[58]

The Pentagon created the U.S. Cyber Command in 2010 and recently announced plans to expand it. In its new cyber strategy, the Department of Defense pledges to "build and maintain viable cyber options" and "to deter shared threats." The strategy mentions China three times and views the country as a key threat, while only mentioning the importance of dialogue with China at the end. These narratives and initiatives gave China the impression that the U.S. military has finished its war preparedness in cyberspace and raised concerns that China has become the first target. Meanwhile, all this activity has stirred up a fierce arms race in cyberspace, which is causing more and more countries to devote resources toward building a cyber army and developing cyberweapons.[59] The ultimate aim of the United States is to maintain a leading edge against China by controlling technology, resources, and information.[60]

Moreover, the United States worries that China will push to rewrite the rules of the global Internet by promoting "an alternative to the borderless Internet embraced by Americans."[61] Preventing Chinese challenges to the U.S.-led cyber order is now a major task for the White House. It seems to China that the United States does not always support its proposed norms of behavior in cyberspace. Thinking about the U.S. attitude toward the International Code of Conduct for Information Security, many Chinese scholars think that the United States wants to preserve its first-mover advantage by insisting that the existing system of international law provides a foundation for building norms in cyberspace.[62] The United States prefers to take cyberspace as a global commons to hedge the sovereign control strongly advised by China.

Contrary to the negative language mostly used by Chinese scholars, senior officials usually take a more rational and calm position. As President Xi has highlighted, steady and constructive cooperation in cyberspace will be beneficial to the whole bilateral relationship. Obviously, there is a structural difference of cyber awareness between China and the United States. The two countries are at different stages of technological development. All China does today is what the United States has already accomplished. China tends to learn and absorb U.S. best practices and lessons and has followed the U.S. model, which one might perhaps call a late-starting advantage. The United States, for its part, keeps a close eye on the measures China takes to improve its defense capabilities in the cyber domain and views these as a challenge. The root cause is absence of strategic trust between both sides. Undoubtedly, a cybersecurity agreement that includes a practical cooperative mechanism would be a crucial step in building trust in the two countries' future relationship in the cyber domain.

Areas of convergence and recommendations for cooperative initiatives

Despite the wide ideological gulf between the two sides, both China and the United States have identified cyberspace as an area that requires cooperation. As President Xi said in Washington in September 2015, "All in all, we have broad, common interest in the field of the cyber. But we need to strengthen cooperation and avoid leading to confrontation."[63] China and the United States have a shared interest in controlling cybercrime, reducing the likelihood of cyber conflict, limiting the proliferation of cyber capabilities, developing rules of supply-chain security, and building cybersecurity exchanges and expertise. The 2015 summit agreement begins to lay a foundation for cooperation on cybercrime, stating that the two sides will establish a "high-level joint dialogue mechanism" in order to "review the timeliness and quality" of requests for information and assistance in criminal investigations. On the U.S. side, the mechanism is led by the Departments of Homeland Security and Justice. Chinese participation includes the Ministries of Public Security, State Security, and Justice; and the State Internet Information Office.

For the goodwill created at the summit to endure, concrete cooperation in the investigation and exchange of evidence will be required. There was positive follow-up in the first round of talks between the Department of Homeland Security and the Ministry of Public Security in December 2015. The two sides agreed on guidelines for requesting assistance on cybercrimes or other malicious cyberactivities, as well as agreeing to conduct "tabletop exercises" in spring 2016 and to define procedures for use of a hotline. Washington said it would consider China's proposal for a seminar on combatting terrorist misuse of ICT, while Beijing agreed to study the United States' proposal on inviting experts to conduct network protection exchanges.[64] Future discussions involving participants from both countries' law-enforcement agencies and computer emergency response teams should identify the types of information that are necessary to attribute the nature and source of a cyberattack.

In a 2015 UN report, representatives from 20 countries, including the United States and China, known as the Group of Governmental Experts (GGE), agreed to three norms of peacetime behavior in cyberspace: nations should not use cyberattacks to damage each other's critical infrastructure, should not target each other's computer emergency response teams, and should assist other nations investigating cyberattacks.[65] At the summit in September 2015, Presidents Xi and Obama "welcomed" the development of the first norm, declaring that neither country would be the first to use cyberweapons to cripple the other's critical infrastructure during peacetime. While such a declaration will face definitional issues—inasmuch as critical infrastructure could mean different things to the two sides—and will be difficult to verify because there are no means to inspect cyber operations or supervise the development of new malware, it may help generate shared norms on appropriate behavior. In an effort to identify common rules, the two leaders announced the formation of a senior experts group for continued discussion of these norms.

According to the consensus reached by the two presidents, the Senior Experts Group on International Norms in Cyberspace held its first meeting in May 2016 in Washington, D.C. Both sides discussed issues related to international cyberspace rules, including international norms of state behavior in cyberspace, confidence-building measures, and international law in cyberspace in a positive, in-depth, and constructive manner.[66] Prior to the meeting, Ambassador Wang Qun, who headed the Chinese delegation for the Senior Experts Group meeting, stated in a U.S. newspaper that infringements of individual privacy and cyber-enabled theft of intellectual property rights, cyber terrorism, and cyberattacks on national critical infrastructures are among the common challenges facing China and the United

States. Therefore, China and the United States must join hands to deal with these challenges together. It is the U.S. and China's "shared responsibility" to "work together for better global governance in cyberspace."[67]

The United Nations has authorized the continued meeting of the GGE and a new round of negotiations will start in August 2016. China and the United States remain far apart on the application of international law to cyberspace. The United States has argued that the laws of armed conflict should apply, and further discussions are needed to understand how states would concretely apply the principles of neutrality, distinction, and proportionality to cyberspace. Chinese officials have suggested that the difficulties of applying the principles are too great, that the current system should not just be copied to a new domain, and that countries should exclude the possibility of developing a new treaty for cyberspace. Due to a variety of unreconcilable differences, the GGE failed to produce any results. Nevertheless, the GGE remains the basis and direction for future discussions. Both Beijing and Washington have to think seriously about how to ensure that normal exchange mechanisms in the cyber domain not be interrupted by other non-cyber factors.

The 2015 report from the Group of Governmental Experts left many definitions and difficult issues for further clarification. For example, it notes that "states must not use proxies to commit internationally wrongful acts using ICTs, and should seek to ensure that their territory is not used by non-State actors to commit such acts."[68] It would be useful for U.S. and Chinese academics to discuss the definition of "proxy" and how it may relate to governments under existing international laws.

The two sides also have a shared interest in the stability and resilience of the Internet. This is an interest that extends beyond China and the United States to include the rest of the world. Stability has both a technical underpinning and a political component. In addition to discussing the rules of the road, the senior experts group should jointly identify facets of Internet functionality that are critical to the interests of both countries and develop a cooperative mechanism to ensure their security.

Developing new norms and building trust will require regular discussions. A U.S.-China cyber working group announced in April 2013 was suspended after the Department of Justice indicted five alleged PLA hackers for cyberespionage in May 2014. The two sides should work to ensure that the new high-level experts group does not become hostage to the ups and downs in the bilateral relationship. The need for the group to meet is bound to be most pressing when tensions between the two countries are highest.

Terrorist groups have so far shown greater dexterity in using the Internet for recruitment, fundraising, and propaganda than in launching destructive attacks, but that will change over time. The Islamic State of Iraq and Syria (ISIS), for example, has a stated desire to develop cyberweapons and has reportedly recruited hackers from Western Europe. Beijing and Washington share an interest in preventing extremist groups and other third parties from attacking critical infrastructure and should discuss joint measures to stop the proliferation of capabilities to nonstate actors. During early discussions, when trust remains low, this may just involve discussions of best practices for securing transportation, communications, and other critical infrastructure. In the first meeting of the cyber dialogue, the two sides agreed to work together to combat the posting on the Internet of instructions on how to build improvised explosive devices. As the discussions progress, the two sides could exchange intelligence on the capabilities of specific groups and share ideas on how to disrupt the development and distribution of cyberweapons.

Technology companies in both countries face competing demands from customers for greater security and privacy and from governments for surveillance and lawful access. The United States and China are among several countries considering policies that are designed to increase transparency and control over the products governments are procuring. These policies include local production requirements, access to source code, or methods for law or intelligence agencies to bypass encryption and other security measures. These policies, however, may decrease security and raise costs for technology firms. They may also be used to advantage local companies.

As Chinese firms enter new markets, they will also have an interest in the low-cost inputs, resiliency, proximity to suppliers, and economies of scale that are the outcomes of global supply chains. At the summit in September, China and Washington agreed that measures designed to ensure cybersecurity in commercial sectors "should be consistent with WTO agreements, be narrowly tailored, take into account international norms, be nondiscriminatory, and not impose nationality-based conditions or restrictions."[69] In order to build on this commitment and preserve the economic benefits, the two sides should establish a working group, drawn from the public and private sectors, to identify best practices on how to ensure the security of information and communications infrastructure and supply chain integrity.

The two sides also need to expand the conversation between Chinese and U.S. think tanks and universities. There are countless Sino-U.S. workshops, conferences, and joint research projects on conventional military, maritime, nuclear, and space issues. Many Chinese and U.S. experts in these areas have known each other for decades and participated in joint research projects. The Track 2 dialogue on cybersecurity cosponsored by the Center for Strategic and International Studies and the China Institute of Contemporary International Relations is a useful forum, but there is a need for more exchanges, collaborative research projects, and workshops on cyber issues. The dialogue, which began in 2009, has held 12 rounds of discussions and provided a valuable communications channel, especially before the official Cybersecurity Working Group was established in 2013. The dialogue has covered issues ranging from national cyber policy, norms of behavior, and the governance of cyberspace to the security of supply chains. The two think tanks jointly issued a memorandum in 2012 illustrating the convergence and divergence of views between China and the United States. Some recommendations from the February 2015 meeting held in Washington were echoed in the subsequent agreement between the two countries.

To facilitate such activities, U.S. think tanks and universities could share best practices with their Chinese counterparts. While U.S. think tanks have rapidly developed cyber programs, and the Hewlett Foundation has funded academic programs at Stanford University, the Massachusetts Institute of Technology, and the University of California–Berkeley, Chinese institutes have not moved as quickly. Moreover, the number of specialists that understand both Chinese and U.S. foreign policy and cyber challenges is small. U.S. and Chinese think tanks thus should work on identifying and mentoring the next generation of scholars and practitioners.

Areas of divergence and recommended mechanisms to reduce tension and manage crises

Although the summit statement on cyber-enabled intellectual property theft was an important first step, cyberespionage will continue to be an irritant in the U.S.-China relationship. Neither side agreed to reduce spying for political and military purposes; cyberespionage is too important to the national interests of both. The ideological battle over an open and free Internet will not end. Sovereignty in cyberspace will also continue to divide the two sides, as will the application of the law of armed conflict in cyberspace and the role of governments in the multi-stakeholder model of Internet governance.

Beijing and Washington want to prevent escalatory cyber operations—attacks that one side sees as legitimate surveillance but the other views as prepping the battlefield. Much like discussions about incidents at sea or in the air are meant to regularize interactions and prevent miscalculations, the senior experts group should work to clarify intentions in cyberspace. Formal discussions on acceptable norms of behavior and possible thresholds for use of force, as well as greater transparency on doctrine, can reduce the chance of misperception and thus diminish the likelihood that a conflict in cyberspace will become kinetic.

Attribution remains a point of contention, with Beijing calling the United States' claim that China was behind the attacks on the Office of Personnel Management "irresponsible and unscientific."[70] A shared understanding of what types of evidence can be used to attribute an attack and how that information is presented would be an important first step to defining norms of behavior. The 2015 UN Group of Governmental Experts report also calls on states to substantiate public accusations of state-sponsored cyberactivity and notes that "the indication that an ICT activity was launched or otherwise originates from a State's territory . . . may be insufficient in itself to attribute the activity to that state."[71] If this norm is truly accepted, it will mean that the United States, and other countries, will have to provide more public evidence of who is behind an attack.

At the June 2015 Strategic and Economic Dialogue, State Councilor Yang Jie-chi called for China to work with the United States to develop an "international code of conduct for cyber information sharing."[72] While the Chinese side did not offer any specifics, Washington and Beijing could establish a joint forensics team, made up of experts from the government, private sector, and academia, to investigate an attack on a third party and identify types of information to be shared.

Conclusion

Trust is currently a rare commodity in the Sino-U.S. bilateral relationship, and it is especially difficult to sustain in cyberspace. Much of what happens in this domain occurs in the shadows, out of the public sight. States do not take credit for cyberattacks, and there has been a widespread reluctance to talk publicly of the development of cyberweapons and offensive doctrines. In many cases, states outsource cyber operations to "patriotic hackers," criminals, and other proxies.

The 2015 agreement on cybersecurity was a significant symbolic step forward for China and the United States, but trust will be built and sustained through implementation. Both countries will test whether the high-level dialogue mechanism will successfully assist in cooperation and better incident response. While it is good that Washington and Beijing have agreed to further the discussion on the norms of cyberspace, the dialogue must be formalized, routinized, and insulated from political point scoring. Without practical progress, cybersecurity could quickly rise to the top of the bilateral agenda and threaten to undermine the U.S.-China relationship again.

In the last days of the Obama administration, cyber frictions that had bedeviled relations between China and the United States were largely mitigated peacefully on account of a multitude of cooperative mechanisms at the ministerial level. There are some uncertainties, however, regarding the Trump administration's cyber policy.

During his election campaign, Mr. Trump's position on cybersecurity was relatively limited and in fact, incoherent. Cybersecurity is not on the top of the agenda for the current administration. So far, it remains unclear whether or not the Trump administration may incline towards a more aggressive approach partly owing to the alleged cyber interference by the Russians during the 2016 presidential election. It is also unclear whether or not existing mechanisms can be maintained. During the first round of the U.S.-China Law Enforcement and Cybersecurity Dialogue, held in Washington, D.C., in October 2017, the two sides had reached consensus on a range of issues including counterterrorism, combating narcotics, and cybersecurity. The dialogue has since been effectively shelved, along with three other dialogue mechanisms, as the trade war as of the time of writing continues to be waged between the United States and China. It remains unclear whether the Trump administration intends to continue the U.S.-China dialogue within the context of existing frameworks, or whether it intends to find an alternative or suspend dialogue altogether.

Admittedly, cybersecurity has become one of the key issues of the U.S.-China bilateral relationship. In its first ever National Strategy of Cyberspace Security, the Chinese government has advocated for a peaceful, secure, open, cooperative, and orderly cyberspace. It therefore appears very worthwhile from a Chinese perspective at least, to continue dialogue as well as to re-clarify and reconfirm China's and well as the U.S.' vital interests in the cyber domain. Furthermore, the two sides should broaden the scope of the dialogue to include some potentially sensitive issues. For example, academic and industry efforts in both countries should be directed at initiating robust discussions on some tough but important topics such as the jurisdiction and flow of data, the rules and practices of the protection of private and sensitive data, the reciprocity of digital trade, and so on.

Notes

1 "President Xi Jinping's State Visit to the United States," White House, Office of the Press Secretary, Fact Sheet, September 25, 2015, www.whitehouse.gov/the-press-office/2015/09/25/fact-sheet-president-xi-jinpings-state-visit-united-states.

2 "Remarks by President Obama and President Xi of the People's Republic of China in Joint Press Conference," White House, Office of the Press Secretary, September 25, 2015, www.whitehouse.gov/the-press-office/2015/09/25/remarks-president-obama-and-president-xi-peoples-republic-china-joint.

3 Robert Abel, "G-20 Nations Agree: No Cyber-Theft of Intellectual Property," *SC Maga zine*, November 19, 2015, www.scmagazineuk.com/g-20-nations-agree-no-cyber-theft-of-intellectual-property/article/454845.

4 McAfee and the Center for Strategic and International Studies, "Net Losses: Estimating the Global Costs of Cybercrime," June 2014, www.mcafee.com/us/resources/reports/rp-economic-impact-cybercrime2.pdf.

5 Office of the President of the United States, *International Strategy on Cyberspace: Prosperity, Security, and Openness in a Networked World* (Washington, DC, May 2011), 3.

6 John D. Negroponte, Samuel J. Palmisano, and Adam Segal, *Defending an Open, Global, Secure, and Resilient Internet*, Independent Task Force Report 70 (New York: Council on Foreign Relations, 2013), 13, http://i.cfr.org/content/publications/attachments/TFR70_cyber_policy.pdf.pdf.

7 Tom Risen, "Study: The U.S. Internet Is Worth $966 Billion," *U.S. News*, December 11, 2015, www.usnews.com/news/blogs/data-mine/2015/12/11/the-internet-is-6-percent-of-the-us-economy-study-says.

8 Telecommunications Industry Association (TIA), "TIA's 2015–2018 ICT Market Review & Forecast," www.tiaonline.org/resources/market-forecast; and David Dean, Sebastian DiGrande, Dominic Field, Andreas Lundmark, James O'Day, John Pineda, and Paul Zwillenberg, "The Internet Economy in the G-20," Boston Consulting Group, March 19, 2012, www.bcgperspectives.com/content/articles/media_entertainment_strategic_planning_4_2_trillion_opportunity_internet_economy_g20.

9 "Top Sites in India," Alexa, www.alexa.com/topsites/countries/IN.

10 "Smartphone Market Share, 2015 Q2," International Data Corporation, www.idc.com/prodserv/smartphone-os-market-share.jsp.

11 Robert W. Holleyman II, "Digital Economy and Trade: A 21st Century Leadership Imperative" (remarks prepared for the New Democrat Network, Washington, DC, May 1, 2015), https://ustr.gov/about-us/policy-offices/press-office/speechestranscripts/2015/may/remarks-deputy-us-trade.

12 Hillary Rodham Clinton, "Remarks on Internet Freedom" (speech delivered at the Newseum, Washington, DC, January 21, 2010), www.state.gov/secretary/20092013clinton/rm/2010/01/135519.htm; Hillary Rodham Clinton, "Internet Rights and Wrongs: Choices & Challenges in a Networked World" (speech delivered at George Washington University, Washington, DC, February 15, 2011), www.state.gov/secretary/20092013clinton/rm/2011/02/156619.htm; and Hillary Rodham Clinton (speech delivered at the Conference on Internet Freedom, The Hague, Netherlands, December 8, 2011), http://thehague.usembassy.gov/news/events/events-2011/conference-on-internet-freedom.html.

13 Lorenzo Franceschi-Bicchierai, "Why the U.S. Government Is Investing Millions in Internet Freedom Technologies," Motherboard, September 29, 2015, http://motherboard.vice.com/read/why-the-us-government-is-investing-millions-in-internet-freedom-technologies.

14 James R. Clapper, "Worldwide Threat Assessment of the U.S. Intelligence Community," statement for the record to the U.S. Senate Armed Services Committee, Washington, DC,

February 26, 2015, www.dni.gov/files/documents/Unclassified_2015_ATA_SFR_-_SASC_FINAL.pdf.

15 U.S. Department of Defense, Defense Science Board, "Task Force Report: Resilient Military Systems and the Advanced Cyber Threat," January 2013, www.acq.osd.mil/dsb/reports/ResilientMilitarySystems.CyberThreat.pdf.

16 U.S. Department of Defense, *The Department of Defense Cyber Strategy* (Washington, DC, April 2015), www.defense.gov/Portals/1/features/2015/0415_cyber-strategy/Final_2015_DoD_CYBER_STRATEGY_for_web.pdf.

17 Henry Farrell, "The Political Science of Cybersecurity II: Why Cryptography Is So Important," *Washington Post*, February 12, 2014, www.washingtonpost.com/blogs/monkey-cage/wp/2014/02/12/the-political-science-of-cybersecurity-ii-why-cryptography-is-so-important; Nicole Perloth, Jeff Larson, and Scott Shane, "N.S.A. Able to Foil Basic Safeguards of Privacy on Web," *New York Times*, September 5, 2013; and Raul Zibechi, "South American Fiber Optic Ring," *Americas Program*, April 12, 2012, www.cipamericas.org/archives/6734.

18 Michael Hirsch, "How America's Top Tech Companies Created the Surveillance State," *National Journal*, July 25, 2013, www.nationaljournal.com/magazine/how-america-s-top-tech-companies-created-the-surveillance-state-20130725.

19 Ellen Nakashima, "Confidential Report Lists U.S. Weapons System Designs Compromised by Chinese Cyber spies," *Washington Post*, May 27, 2013, www.washingtonpost.com/world/national-security/confidential-report-lists-us-weapons-system-designs-compromised-by-chinese-cyberspies/2013/05/27/a42c3e1c-c2dd-11e2-8c3b-0b5e9247e8ca_story.html.

20 David Welna, "Top Intelligence Officials Warn against Growing Threat of Cyberattacks," *National Public Radio (NPR)*, September 10, 2015, www.npr.org/2015/09/10/439246971/top-intelligence-officials-warn-against-growing-threat-of-cyberattacks.

21 Barack Obama, "Remarks by the President to the Business Roundtable," White House, Office of the Press Secretary, September 16, 2015, www.whitehouse.gov/the-press-office/2015/09/16/remarks-president-business-roundtable.

22 Josh Rogin, "NSA Chief: Cybercrime Constitutes the 'Greatest Transfer of Wealth in History,'" *Foreign Policy*, July 9, 2012, http://foreignpolicy.com/2012/07/09/nsa-chief-cybercrime-constitutes-the-greatest-transfer-of-wealth-in-history; and Commission on the Theft of American Intellectual Property, "The Report of the Commission on the Theft of American Intellectual Property," National Bureau of Asian Research, May 2013, www.ipcommission.org/report/IP_Commission_Report_052213.pdf.

23 James R. Keith, "The Internet in China: A Tool for Freedom or Suppression?" testimony before the House Committee on International Relations, Washington, DC, February 15, 2006, http://chrissmith.house.gov/uploadedfiles/gofa_feb_15_2006_hearing.pdf.

24 Information Office of the State Council of the People's Republic of China (PRC), *The Internet in China* (Beijing, June 8, 2010), www.china.org.cn/government/whitepaper/node_7093508.htm.

25 Information Office of the State Council of the PRC, *The Internet in China.*

26 "China Internet Economy Exceeded $100B in 2014," *China Internet Watch*, April 9, 2015, www.chinainternetwatch.com/13097/china-internet-economy-2014/#ixzz3fawKZWsV.

27 Jonathan Woetzel et al., "China's Digital Transformation," *McKinsey Global Institute*, July 2014, www.mckinsey.com/insights/high_tech_telecoms_internet/chinas_digital_transformation.

28 Adam Segal, "Why China Hacks the World," *Christian Science Monitor*, February 1, 2016, www.csmonitor.com/World/Asia-Pacific/2016/0131/Why-China-hacks-the-world.

29 Paul Mozur, "China Tries to Extract Pledge of Compliance from U.S. Tech Firms," *New York Times*, September 16, 2015, www.nytimes.com/2015/09/17/technology/china-tries-to-extract-pledge-of-compliance-from-us-tech-firms.html.

30 Standing Committee of the 12th National People's Congress, "Counter-Terrorism Law of the People's Republic of China," trans. China Law Translate, December 27, 2015,

http://chinalawtranslate.com/%E5%8F%8D%E6%81%90%E6%80%96%E4%B8%B
B%E4%B9%89%E6%B3%95-%EF%BC%882015%EF%BC%89/?lang=en.

31 Office of the National Counterintelligence Executive, "Foreign Spies Stealing U.S. Economic Secrets in Cyberspace," *Report to Congress*, October 11, 2011, www.ncsc. gov/publications/reports/fecie_all/Foreign_Economic_Collection_2011.pdf.

32 Larry M. Wortzel, "Cyber Espionage and Theft of U.S. Intellectual Property," statement to the U.S. House Energy and Commerce Committee, Washington, DC, July 9, 2013, http://en ergycommerce.house.gov/hearing/cyber-espionage-and-theft-us-intellectual-property- and-technology.

33 Li Xiaokun, "China Is Victim of Hacking Attacks," *People's Daily*, June 5, 2013, http:// english.peopledaily.com.cn/90883/8271052.html.

34 Li Yan, "Cyber Deal Expected to Halt Disputes," *China News Service*, September 21, 2015, www.ecns.cn/2015/09-21/181825.shtml.

35 James R. Clapper, "Statement by Director of National Intelligence James R. Clapper on Allegations of Economic Espionage," Office of the Director of National Intelligence, IC on the Record, September 8, 2013, http://icontherecord.tumblr.com/ post/60712026846/statement-by-director-of-national-intelligence.

36 Obama, "Remarks by the President to the Business Roundtable."

37 U.S. Department of Defense, *Military and Security Developments Involving the People's Republic of China 2015* (Washington, DC, 2015), www.defense.gov/Portals/1/ Documents/pubs/2015_China_Military_Power_Report.pdf.

38 Adam Segal, "The Code Not Taken: China, the United States, and the Future of Cyber Espionage," *Bulletin of Atomic Scientists*, September 1, 2013.

39 "Xi Jinping: Ba woguo cong wangluo daguo jiancheng wangluo qiangguo" [Pushing China Transfer from a Big Power to a Great Power], *Xinhua*, February 27, 2014.

40 "Zhongguo huliangwang 20 nian fazhan baogao Wuzhen fabu tuxian 'wu ge shouci'" [Report of Twenty Years of Internet Development in China Released in Wuzhen, High- lighting Five First Times], *China Daily*, December 16, 2015, www.chinadaily.com.cn/ micro-reading/china/2015-12-16/content_14404589.html.

41 "Di shisan ge wunian guihua jianyi zhengshi fabu" [The Thirteenth Five-Year Plan Formally Published], *Xinhua*, November 3, 2015, http://finance.sina.com.cn/china/20 151103/160123664965.shtml.

42 "Wangluo anquan shi zhong da zhanlue wenti—fang guojia hulianwang xinxi ban- gongshi fuzhuren Wang Xiu Jun" [Cybersecurity Is an Important Strategic Issue— Interview with Deputy Director of National Internet Information Office Wang Xiu jun], *People's Daily*, May 18, 2014.

43 "Zhonghua renmin gongheguo guojia anquan fa" [National Security Law of the Peo- ple's Republic of China], *National People's Congress (PRC)*, art. 25, www.npc.gov.cn/ npc/xinwen/2015-07/07/content_1941161.htm.

44 "Qunian xinxi xiaofei guimo tongbi zengzhang 18%" [The Scale of Information Con- sumption Up by 18% Last Year], *Xinhua*, May 16, 2015.

45 "Zhongguo hulianwang fazhan baogao 2019: Zhongguo wangmin guimo da 8.54 yi" [China Internet Development Report 2019: The Number of China's Netizens Has Reached 854 Million], *The Beijing News*, October 20, 2019, www.bjnews.com.cn/feature/ 2019/10/20/639061.html.

46 Steve Morgan, "IBM's CEO on Hackers: 'Cyber Crime Is the Greatest Threat to Every Company in the World,'" *Forbes*, November 24, 2015.

47 Steve Morgan, "Cyber Crime Costs Projected to Reach $2 Trillion by 2019," *Forbes*, January 17, 2016.

48 "Xi Ji Ping jiu gongtong goujian wangluo kongjian mingyun gongtongti tichu wu dian zhuzhang" [President Xi Proposed Five Suggestions for Establishing a Community of Shared Future in Cyberspace], *Xinhua*, December 16, 2015, http://news.xinhuanet. com/world/2015-12/16/c_128536396.htm.

49 Xi Jinping's keynote speech at 2nd World Internet Conference, Wuzhen, December 16, 2015), www.wuzhenwic.org/2015-12/16/c_47521.htm.
50 "International Strategy for Cooperation on Cyberspace," March 1, 2017, www.xinhuanet.com/english/china/2017-03/01/c_136094371.htm.
51 Clinton, "Remarks on Internet Freedom"; and Clinton, "Internet Rights and Wrongs."
52 These kinds of articles and papers are not rare in Chinese media. For example, see "Baquanzhuyi wuchubuzai: Meiguo hulianwang guanli de shuangchongbiaozhun" [Hegemony Is Everywhere: Double Standards of U.S. Internet Management], *People's Daily*, October 24, 2014; "Meiguo you shenme zige zhize Zhongguo xianzhi hulianwang ziyou" [U.S. Is Not Qualified to Condemn China to Restrict Internet Freedom], *Xinhua*, October 24, 2010; and "Wangluo buying chengwei Meiguo ba quanxin gongju" [Cyber Should Not Be a New Tool of U.S. Hegemony], *QiuShi*, August 1, 2013.
53 "Xi Jin Ping zhuxi zai di er jie shijie hulianwang dahui de kaimu zhici" [President Xi Jinping's Opening Remarks at the 2nd World Internet Conference, Wuzhen], December 16, 2015.
54 Isaac Stone Fish, "If You Want Rule of Law, Respect Ours," *Foreign Policy*, November 2, 2014.
55 "Full Transcript: Interview with Chinese President Xi Jinping," *Wall Street Journal*, September 22, 2015, www.wsj.com/articles/full-transcript-interview-with-chinese-president-xi-jinping-1442894700.
56 Christopher Painter, "Cybersecurity: Setting the Rules for Responsible Global Behavior," testimony before the Senate Foreign Relations Committee Subcommittee on East Asia, the Pacific, and International Cybersecurity Policy, Washington, DC, May 14, 2015; and James Clapper, "Cybersecurity Policy," testimony before the Senate Armed Service Committee, Washington, DC, September 29, 2015.
57 Cory Bennett, "Chinese Malware Possibly Behind OPM Hack," *Hill*, July 2, 2015.
58 Mark Pomerleu, "White House Promotes Whole-of-Nation Cyber Deterrence Strategy," *Defense Systems*, December 23, 2015, https://defensesystems.com/articles/2015/12/23/obama-whole-of-nation-cyber-deterrence-strategy.aspx.
59 "Zue wangluo zhan, Meiguo yao fu shouyao zeren" [U.S. Should Take Primary Liability to Stop Cyberwarfare], *People's Daily*, February 7, 2013.
60 Yuli, "Cong hulianwang baquan kan xifang daguo de zhanlue shizhi yu mubiao" [Looking Inside the Strategic Nature and Goal of Western Big Power through Internet Hegemony], *Research on Marxism* 9 (2013).
61 James T. Areddy, "China Pushes to Rewrite Rules of Global Internet," *Wall Street Journal*, July 28, 2015.
62 Zhang Ling and Xu Weidi, "Zhongmei wangluo guanxi zhong de weixie, fengxian yu jiyu" [The Threat, Risk, and Opportunity in U.S. and China Cyber Relations], *Chinese Information Security* 9 (2015); and Xun Lei, "Qi zhi xianming changdao wangluo zhuquan" [Advocating Sovereignty in Cyberspace Unequivocally], *Guangming Daily*, January 9, 2016.
63 "Remarks by President Obama and President Xi of the People's Republic of China in Joint Press Conference."
64 "First U.S.-China High-Level Joint Dialogue on Cybercrime and Related Issues Summary of Outcomes," Department of Justice, Office of Public Affairs, December 2, 2015, www.justice.gov/opa/pr/first-us-china-high-level-joint-dialogue-cybercrime-and-related-issues-summary-outcomes-0.
65 Joseph Marks, "U.N. Body Agrees to U.S. Norms in Cyberspace," *Politico*, July 9, 2015, www.politico.com/story/2015/07/un-body-agrees-to-us-norms-in-cyberspace-119900.html.
66 "China and the U.S. Held First Senior Experts Group Meeting on International Norms in Cyberspace," March 13, 2016, *The People's Daily*, http://world.people.com.cn/n1/2016/0512/c1002-28345675.html.

67 Wang Qun, "Shared Interests and Responsibility: The US and China Must Join to Promote a Rule-based Cyberspace," *The Huffington Post*, May 11, 2016, www.huffpost.com/entry/shared-interests-and-resp_b_9873642.

68 "Group of Governmental Experts on Developments in the Field of Information and Telecommunications in the Context of International Security," UN General Assembly, no. A/70/174, July 22, 2015, 13, www.un.org/ga/search/view_doc.asp?symbol=A/70/174.

69 "U.S.-China Economic Relations," White House, Office of the Press Secretary, Fact Sheet, September 25, 2015, www.whitehouse.gov/the-press-office/2015/09/25/fact-sheet-us-china-economic-relations.

70 Eyder Peralta, "China Says U.S. Allegations That It Was Behind Cyberattack Are 'Irresponsible,'" *NPR*, June 5, 2015, www.npr.org/sections/thetwo-way/2015/06/05/412190405/china-says-u-s-allegations-that-it-was-behind-cyberattack-are-irresponsible.

71 "Group of Governmental Experts on Developments," 13.

72 Felicia Schwartz and Ian Talley, "U.S. Officials Warn Chinese Cyber Espionage Imperils Ties," *Wall Street Journal*, June 23, 2015, www.wsj.com/articles/biden-urges-honest-direct-talks-between-u-s-china-1435071461.

4 U.S.-China strategic relations in space

Brian Weeden and Xiao He

EXECUTIVE SUMMARY

This chapter examines the role of the space domain in the U.S.-China relationship, proposes cooperative initiatives to strengthen the relationship where U.S. and Chinese interests overlap, and recommends measures to mitigate tensions and crises where they diverge.

Main argument

The space domain will have a significant impact on the future of U.S.-China relations. Both countries see space as a domain that is critical to their national and economic security. The U.S. is focused on securing continued access to space and recapitalizing its space capabilities, while China is focused on developing its own capabilities in this domain. Although it is tempting to use the U.S.-Soviet competitive relationship in space as a model for the U.S.-China relationship, the analogy falls short due to the significant differences in context and the facts on the ground. At the very least, both the U.S. and China can take steps in the space domain to help stabilize their relationship and mitigate the worst-case scenario of armed conflict. But their efforts should not stop there: the ultimate goal should be to use space as a vehicle for positive engagement that helps shift the overall U.S.-China relationship toward cooperation and reduces the risk of conflict.

Policy implications

- Both the U.S. and China have strong national interests in contributing to multilateral efforts to bolster space governance and develop norms of responsible behavior in space. At the same time, they should look for ways to cooperate in civil and commercial space activities to create a positive element of their space relationship that offsets the military competition in this domain.
- If both countries develop operational offensive counter-space capabilities and a corresponding doctrine that relies on degrading the other's space capabilities during a conflict, the urge to strike first could be a significant source of instability and escalation in the event of a crisis scenario.

- Improving space situational awareness capabilities and enacting other transparency and confidence-building measures for the development and deployment of dual-use space technology could help manage tensions and mitigate escalatory risks during a crisis.

Innovations and activities in space will have a significant impact on the future of the U.S.-China relationship. Both countries have identified space as a strategic domain that is critical to their national interests and development.[1] Both are dedicating considerable resources to developing their civil, military, and commercial space sectors. Both countries also see their space accomplishments as critical to boosting national pride and international prestige, in addition to serving as a diplomatic tool to enhance soft power. Over time, space will increasingly play an important role in U.S.-China relations and could serve as either a source of instability or a means of strengthening the relationship.

The most significant historical example of how space affected a relationship between major powers was the Cold War relationship between the United States and the Soviet Union.[2] During that period, outer space emerged first as a domain for intense political and military competition and potential conflict. But in the 1960s and 1970s, agreements were made between the United States and the Soviet Union that reduced the most serious tensions, and over time the space domain became more of a stabilizing force in their relationship and eventually an avenue for cooperation after the fall of the Soviet Union. Both countries developed their own space-based technical capabilities to conduct intelligence and surveillance of each other. This allowed each side to develop a better understanding of the other's activities and enabled verification mechanisms to underpin arms control treaties and agreements, increase transparency, and reduce tensions.[3] The United States and the Soviet Union also developed collaborative exchanges between scientists, and even cooperated on human spaceflight with the Apollo-Soyuz program and eventually the International Space Station (ISS).[4] Along the way, they needed to overcome significant differences in perception of their relative power. The Soviet Union saw itself as an equal to the United States and pursued a parallel status in all the important domains, including space. But in the eyes of the United States, the two were not equals.[5] Partly as a result of this, much of the U.S.-Soviet relationship in space was not true cooperation but rather crisis management: attempting to prevent direct military collision and avoiding intervention in the other's sphere of influence.

While the U.S.-Soviet relationship in space is instructive, there are significant differences with the U.S.-China relationship today. The Cold War featured a hostile stand-off between two superpowers with opposing political and economic ideologies, and much of the rest of the world lined up behind one side or the other. The very real threat of mutual nuclear annihilation hung over every decision and crisis. Given that both sides were evenly matched in space capabilities, bilateral cooperation was an obvious choice.

The context today for U.S.-China relations in space is much different. China is much more integrated into the global economic and political system than the

Soviet Union was. Globalization has linked many of the world's economies and lowered barriers to technological diffusion.

Instead of two superpowers with allies and blocs lined up on one side or another, a much more complex set of relationships exists among countries, regions, and institutions. At least 60 other countries are involved in space activities in one form or another, with growing diversity of perspectives, interests, goals, and capabilities.[6] Although nuclear arsenals still exist, the likelihood of their use is greatly diminished, as is their link to conventional warfighting. There is also a significant difference in capabilities between the United States and China. China has been quickly developing its space capabilities, but the United States still has a decades-long lead in many areas. And while the U.S.-China relationship is important, space is only one of many domains that affects important issues. Moreover, the United States and China have differences in their goals and capabilities for space activities, making it more challenging to find projects in which they can collaborate as equals. Space capabilities are also now much more critical for each country's national security, increasing the chances and potential consequences of space being part of a potential conflict.

All these differences make it difficult to predict precisely what type of impact space will have on the U.S.-China relationship going forward. There is a chance for the space domain to have a positive impact and serve as a stable foundation on which to build a stronger overall relationship between the two countries. At the same time, it also has the potential to be a driver of mistrust and misperceptions that could lead to an overall worsening of relations between the United States and China, and perhaps even outright conflict. Whereas the Cold War relationship between the United States and Soviet Union focused on avoiding conflict, the United States and China should not be satisfied with just crisis control measures and negative cooperation for preventing confrontation. Instead, they need to find a way to realize more comprehensive and positive cooperation in space, which could have security and economic benefits for both. Failure to reconcile their differences in this domain could lead to a renewed arms race that would be to the detriment of both sides. Both countries have acknowledged the importance of developing a more stable, cooperative, and long-lasting bilateral relationship in space. The question is how to move beyond just rhetoric.

The remainder of this chapter provides an overview of the U.S.-China strategic relationship in the space domain and outlines concrete measures to improve cooperation. The first section discusses U.S. interests in space and U.S. perceptions of Chinese interests in this domain, while the second section examines Chinese interests in space and Chinese perceptions of U.S. interests. Based on both countries' relative interests and perceptions, the chapter next outlines where those interests overlap and proposes steps that can be taken to strengthen the U.S.-China strategic relationship. The fourth and final section analyzes where U.S. and Chinese interests diverge and proposes measures for managing tensions and minimizing instability in a potential crisis situation involving space.

U.S. views on Sino-U.S. relations in space

U.S. interests and priorities in space

The United States sees space as a critical domain to its security and prosperity. The current national space policy, issued by the Obama administration in 2010, states that "the United States considers the sustainability, stability, and free access to, and use of, space vital to its national interests."[7] This statement is a reflection of the fact that the United States currently spends the most on space activities (roughly $40 billion a year across national security and civil space programs)[8] and has the most satellites in orbit of any country. Out of more than 1,300 total active satellites, the United States has launched roughly 550, of which nearly 300 belong to the U.S. government.[9]

Space-based capabilities and services provide the foundation for U.S. national security. At the strategic level, they enable communications with U.S. nuclear and strategic forces. Space capabilities are also essential to the verification and monitoring of arms control treaties and form the cornerstone of the United States' intelligence, surveillance, and reconnaissance (ISR) capabilities. At the operational and tactical levels, space capabilities are the essential enablers for the United States' ability to defend its borders, project power to protect its allies and interests overseas, and defeat adversaries.

Space capabilities are also a critical piece of the U.S.—and the global—economy. Recent studies have estimated that the Global Positioning System (GPS) alone contributed more than $68 billion to the United States' economy just in 2013.[10] U.S. satellites also provide essential data to improve weather forecasting and modeling, the value of which is hard to measure but is likely in the billions. The global space economy is currently estimated to be more than $330 billion a year, with likely trillions more in indirect benefits to everything from crop management to international banking and trade, all of which benefits U.S. national and economic security.[11]

Civil space activities also continue to play a significant role in U.S. national prestige and soft power, but large-scale programs are increasingly hindered by political obstacles. Although human spaceflight and exploration are no longer the national priority they were during the race to the moon, there continues to be strong public interest in and support for U.S. civil space activities.[12] The ISS remains a vibrant symbol of international cooperation and collaboration on exploration and science, and robotic missions such as the Curiosity and Opportunity rovers on Mars and the New Horizons mission to Pluto continue to make global headlines. Much of the American public and many in Congress still feel a strong sense of pride in the United States' accomplishments in space, although this has not translated into a larger budget to achieve the goals that some space advocates would like NASA to achieve. There is still significant debate between the White House and Congress, and within Congress, over long-term strategy and goals for U.S. human spaceflight and exploration.[13]

In the midst of all this, the commercial space sector in the United States is currently undergoing a significant boom. Several companies continue to work on developing space tourism services, and three are competing for contracts from NASA to deliver personnel and cargo to the ISS.[14] Dozens of U.S. companies, largely funded by private capital, have also announced plans to utilize small satellites to provide a variety of services, including significantly increased remote sensing of the Earth, commercial weather data, tracking of ships at sea, and broadband Internet for the world.[15]

Although all these sectors factor into the U.S.-China strategic relationship in space, the national security sector weighs most heavily. There is growing concern within the U.S. national security community that the strategic situation in space is potentially unstable. The United States is much more reliant on space capabilities than any of its near-peer adversaries, and many of its space capabilities that are most critical for national security are vulnerable to attack, particularly kinetic attacks. This vulnerability has heightened U.S. concern that a potential adversary will develop counter-space capabilities to threaten U.S. space capabilities, thereby undermining the ability of the United States to win a major engagement with a near-peer adversary.[16]

The 2011 National Security Space Strategy (NSSS) provided an initial plan for addressing such instability.[17] The NSSS laid out high-level concepts for dealing with what it described as an "increasingly congested, contested, and competitive" environment in space.[18] The strategy proposed the following set of interrelated strategic approaches for meeting U.S. national security objectives in space:

- Promote responsible, peaceful, and safe use of space;
- Provide improved U.S. space capabilities;
- Partner with responsible nations, international organizations, and commercial firms;
- Prevent and deter aggression against space infrastructure that supports U.S. national security;
- Prepare to defeat attacks and to operate in a degraded environment.[19]

In October 2012 the U.S. Department of Defense published an updated directive on space policy that expanded on the NSSS and provided direction on its implementation.[20] The new policy emphasized the importance of strengthening the safety, sustainability, stability, and security of the space environment. It also outlined four elements that the United States will use to deter attacks on its own or allied space systems:

- Support the development of international norms of responsible behavior that promote the safety, stability, and security of the space domain.
- Build coalitions to enhance collective security capabilities.
- Mitigate the benefits to an adversary of attacking U.S. space systems by enhancing the resilience of our space enterprise and by ensuring that U.S.

forces can operate effectively even when our space-derived capabilities have been degraded.
- Possess capabilities, not limited to space, to respond to an attack on U.S. or allied space systems in an asymmetric manner by using any or all elements of national power.[21]

Since these strategies were released, Chinese anti-satellite (ASAT) testing and development has progressed. A growing body of evidence suggests that China has been actively developing at least two hit-to-kill ASAT weapon systems over the past decade. The development process has included at least seven tests of these systems, including one test that created thousands of pieces of space debris in one of the most congested regions of the Earth's orbit.[22] In particular, China's apparent test in May 2013 of a kinetic-kill capability to reach geostationary Earth orbit has created a very high level of concern in U.S. national security circles.[23] This high-altitude region (approximately 22,000 miles above the equator) is where many critical U.S. intelligence, strategic communications, and missile early warning satellites reside. These satellites had long been considered safe from attack, partly because of the understanding that an attack on them could quickly escalate toward nuclear war.[24] However, some U.S. observers have concluded that China's emerging military space doctrine may not include the same reluctance to attack strategic U.S. satellites and that the ASAT testing is intended to develop capabilities to hold at risk U.S. satellites in every orbital region.[25]

The resulting concern has led to a significant shift in the U.S. military's planning and attitude toward a greater focus on space protection and warfighting. In the summer of 2014, the U.S. Department of Defense completed a Space Strategic Portfolio Review (SPR) of the entire space enterprise pertaining to national security. The SPR concluded that it is critical for the United States to be able to identify threats in space, ensure that its space capabilities can withstand aggressive counter-space programs, and counter the space capabilities of adversaries that target U.S. forces.[26] As a result of the review, the Department of Defense reprogrammed a reported $5 billion to $8 billion in the budget request for fiscal year (FY) 2016 toward space protection over the next five years.[27] Senior officials are openly discussing the need to "prepare for a war in space" and are developing programs and capabilities to detect, deter, and defeat attacks on U.S. space capabilities.[28] The Department of Defense and intelligence community also created both the Joint Space Doctrine and Tactics Forum to establish a warfighting culture within the national security space community and the Joint Interagency Combined Space Operations Center to experiment with future scenarios and develop tactics, techniques, and procedures to respond to attacks on space capabilities.[29]

The U.S. Congress has also signaled a shift toward a more aggressive posture toward space. The National Defense Authorization Act (NDAA) for FY16, the primary piece of legislation that authorizes and directs the activities of the U.S. military, calls on the U.S. national security space community to report to Congress on how it plans to "protect and preserve the rights, access, capabilities, use, and freedom of action of the United States in space and the right of the United

States to respond to an attack in space and, if necessary, deny adversaries the use of space capabilities hostile to the national interests of the United States."[30] The FY15 NDAA also required the secretary of defense and the director of national intelligence to produce a study on the role of offensive space operations and specified that the majority of the $32.3 million allocated to the Space Security and Defense Program for FY15 must be used for "the development of offensive space control and active defensive strategies and capabilities."[31]

U.S. perceptions of Chinese interests and activities in space

U.S. perceptions of China's development of space capabilities can best be described as wary. The United States understands the need to develop such capabilities to support national security and defense but is concerned that some Chinese space capabilities appear to be offensive in nature and aimed at undermining U.S. space power, particularly in light of a new Chinese doctrinal focus on "active defense."[32] The recent major realignment of China's military forces and command structure is seen by some in the United States as reinforcing the perception that China is preparing to fight a war in space. At the same time, there seems to be little appreciation that many of the Chinese doctrinal positions are exactly the same as what the U.S. military has proposed in decades past or is considering again now. In the civil space sector, the United States is less concerned with China's achievements in human spaceflight and exploration but is beginning to be troubled about China's use of those achievements for soft power.

As part of this wariness, the United States has voiced strong objections to China's major proposal on space security, the Treaty on the Prevention of the Placement of Weapons in Outer Space (PPWT).[33] The objections are partly due to a disagreement over the salience of the issue. For the United States and a number of its allies, the most pressing issues are assured access to space and protecting existing space capabilities from threats (intentional and unintentional).[34] But the United States also sees the PPWT as fundamentally flawed because it is not verifiable and would only apply to weapons "placed in orbit." Under that definition, the treaty would ban potential U.S. space-based missile defenses or orbital counterspace systems but not the ground- or air-based ASAT capabilities that China is developing.[35]

Some U.S. observers are also suspicious of recent Chinese co-orbital rendezvous and proximity operations (RPO) as being tests of potential co-orbital ASAT capabilities. In 2010 a Chinese satellite (SJ-12) conducted a series of maneuvers to rendezvous with another Chinese satellite (SJ-06F) in low Earth orbit and likely bumped into it.[36] A similar scenario (without the bumping) occurred again in 2013.[37] These activities are very similar in nature to the United States' recent demonstrations of its own RPO technology, such as the Defense Advanced Research Projects Agency's Experimental Satellite System–11 (XSS-11) and NASA's Demonstration for Autonomous Rendezvous Technology (DART) satellite.[38] However, there is still strong suspicion in the U.S. national security community that the Chinese RPO activities are proof that the PPWT is no more than a political ploy, or at the very least part of a hedging strategy that signals China may not be as interested in peace in space as it professes publicly.

However, this skepticism does not mean that the United States sees China as an outright enemy. While Washington is concerned about China's rise, it also encourages Beijing to become a partner for greater international security.[39] Defense planners in the United States see the world entering into a much more complex and uncertain era, and the overall strategy is one of hedging against the most dangerous threats. The stated goal of the increased U.S. emphasis on protection and preparedness for warfighting is to deter attacks and prevent conflict in space. In that sense, the U.S. military sees itself as taking steps to mitigate a threat from China. Whether that strategy will be counterproductive and will actually end up increasing the risk of conflict remains to be seen.

In a similar fashion, the United States is wary, and even borderline distrustful, of commercial and civil cooperation with China in space. The two biggest concerns are technology theft via espionage and the significant role the People's Liberation Army (PLA) plays in all aspects of Chinese space activities. There is also a debate in the United States over whether space cooperation should be used as an incentive to encourage China to change its behavior or as a reward for actual change, particularly on human rights and religious freedom. The latter sentiment was behind the passage of the Wolf Amendment as part of the FY12 NASA appropriations bill, which prohibited NASA and the Office of Science and Technology Policy from spending any money on bilateral space activities with China without explicit congressional approval.[40] The Wolf Amendment continues to hinder any significant efforts at bilateral civil space cooperation between the United States and China.

The United States has cautiously encouraged China's participation in enhancing the space governance regime. China was one of the 15 countries with direct participation in the UN Group of Governmental Experts on transparency and confidence-building measures (TCBM) for outer space activities.[41] To date, China has played a mostly positive role in the discussions of best-practice guidelines for the long-term sustainability of space activities in the UN Committee on the Peaceful Uses of Outer Space.[42] And while Beijing voiced some concerns during the negotiations of the International Code of Conduct for Space Activities that was proposed by the European Union, it was meaningfully engaged in the process. As long as China continues to participate constructively in these and similar efforts and advance its interests in a positive way, the United States is likely to welcome Chinese involvement in future discussions of space governance.

Finally, it is important to note other developments that may affect the U.S.-China relationship and complicate the management of space-related issues. Notably, U.S. concerns over a more uncertain and risky future are driven as much by recent Russian activities in Eastern Europe as they are by any of China's activities. Russia's annexation of Crimea, involvement in Ukraine, and more bellicose attitude toward Europe and NATO greatly concern U.S. military planners, as these developments may signal a weakening of international rule of law and norms of behavior.[43] Some reports also suggest that Russia may be testing its own ASAT weapons again.[44] The combination of recent Russian aggression and China's growing military capabilities is what is causing the shift in U.S. national security circles away from diplomatic and cooperative approaches toward more militaristic solutions to dealing with the perceived threat.

While this analysis does lend a pessimistic tone to the future of U.S.-China relations in space, it does not necessarily mean that the relationship is fatalistic and destined to end in conflict. Both the United States and China have acknowledged the dangers of outright conflict and pledged their interest in avoiding such an outcome. It is critical for that pledge to move beyond just rhetoric to include specific proposals.

Chinese views on Sino-U.S. relations in space

China's interests and priorities in space

Outer space is the new global commons with great strategic importance, and China will increasingly depend on space-based assets for both economic and military aims that may be partly incompatible and even in competition with other key players, especially the United States. Therefore, it sees outer space as a domain full of both opportunities and risks. China has as large a stake in the space area as the other major powers, and the importance of developing a comprehensive and sound space policy cannot be overestimated.

China has four broad national interests in outer space: national security, soft power in international regimes, scientific and economic benefits, and bridges for cooperation with other states. First, China sees space as critical to maintaining strategic stability and defending national security. Space capabilities are the most effective force multipliers. The PLA must develop its space assets to collect information, detect threats, and guide operations.

From China's perspective, the most urgent problem is that the space capability gap between the United States and China is growing. U.S. space technology is more advanced and still moving forward rapidly. If China cannot narrow the gap, it will face more and more security risks and challenges. Through its new space-based assets and related missile defense technology, the United States may even acquire the ability to neutralize China's limited nuclear deterrence.[45] Without developing its space capabilities, China thus might be unable to maintain bilateral strategic stability or defend its core interests, such as in Taiwan.

In recent years, the U.S. Department of Defense has focused on developing more space-reliant capabilities, including the controversial Terminal High Altitude Area Defense (THAAD) theater missile defense system and other proposed weapon systems as part of its air-sea battle strategy.[46] China is concerned that these systems, and in particular the THAAD radars, could be used to gather intelligence or degrade its nuclear deterrent. One option for China may be to engage in negotiations with the United States to limit the placement of such assets. But Beijing cannot merely count on the goodwill of Washington to make concessions. If the United States possesses capabilities to neutralize China's nuclear deterrent,

U.S. policies and actions in the Asia-Pacific may be more unilateral and proactive. Thus, China believes that it must possess considerable space capabilities to protect its national security and maintain strategic stability in East Asia.

China's second major interest in space is to have a voice in the creation of international rules and institutions. There are many transnational governance problems in the space domain, including physical and electromagnetic congestion and the weaponization of outer space. China is a newcomer in many other domains where the United States has already created the institutions and set the rules, such as in the governance of global monetary issues through the World Bank and the International Monetary Fund and of nuclear issues through the international non-proliferation regime. China does not have a strong voice in these organizations, and joining them largely means that it must accept rules that have been decided mainly by the United States. Thus, proactive participation in international governance of outer space could enhance China's stance and help make future international regimes more beneficial to China's interests.

In recent years, China has devoted great financial, diplomatic, and intelligence resources to acquiring more institutional power on the international stage. It is therefore not surprising for China to assume a positive attitude toward the formation of international rules in space. Examples are the UN Group of Governmental Experts on TCBMs in outer space, the EU-led negotiations on an International Code of Conduct for Space Activities, and the Russian- and Chinese-proposed PPWT. China believes that engaging constructively in these treaties and other efforts may improve its international reputation, national prestige, and soft power. However, China has met considerable difficulties in achieving these goals. Despite strong support from the international community for the PPWT, the United States has refused to support the proposal on the grounds that it lacks effective verification mechanisms and is not equitable.[47] This kind of "supervision stalemate" is not a new problem. China sees the further development of its space or counter-space systems as a way to gain more bargaining power and perhaps break the deadlock.

The third major focus of Chinese space activities is to increase scientific knowledge and expand commercial activities. Advancement of space capabilities can benefit many industries, facilitate scientific research, boost innovation in relevant areas, and increase commercial profits, such as by launching satellites for foreign customers.[48] In the long run, resources invested in space technology could see significant returns. However, many Chinese state-owned enterprises (SOE) in the space sector are restricted in the world market or sanctioned by the United States. Chinese astronauts and scientists are also excluded from the U.S.-led international joint program. These restrictions have significantly impaired China's research and industrial development in the space domain, and the country continues to attempt to persuade the United States to relax, and ultimately abolish, these restrictions.[49]

Increased technology transfers or trade could help China accelerate its space program and other related research. But even if barriers to technology transfer remain, relaxing restrictions to allow China to participate in joint activities would still have benefits. Chinese participation in joint programs such as human space exploration, the ISS, or other cooperative projects could increase China's operational know-how in the space domain. And even if there is no bilateral cooperation between the United States and China, a change in U.S. export control policy could allow Chinese companies to dramatically expand their presence in the international commercial space market.

The fourth and final focus of China's space activities is to strengthen cooperation and improve bilateral relationships with other major powers, of which the most prominent is the United States. China has stated that the development of its space capabilities should not be achieved at the cost of bilateral relations or mutual confidence with other states.[50] A space arms race may seriously deteriorate China's external environment and divert precious and limited resources away from urgent domestic areas. In addition, it could shift China's broader foreign policy and grand strategy from competitive cooperation to total confrontation. The costs of a hostile space arms race and direct conflict with the United States would thus far outweigh the benefits provided by new space capabilities.

Therefore, China has a clear interest in using its development of space capabilities to promote bilateral cooperation and the formation of international regimes. At the very least, such development should not harm these important diplomatic goals. Effective cooperation in the space domain may help China and the United States show goodwill to each other and set a model for bilateral cooperation to handle security and governance problems. No matter whether this is called a "new type of great-power relationship" or a "new-model major-country relationship," a desirable Sino-U.S. bilateral relationship in space should not only encourage mutual respect and avoid confrontation but also contribute to solving global challenges such as climate change.

China's perceptions of U.S. interests and activities in space

China perceives the goal of the United States' space policy as to maintain U.S. dominance in outer space and enlarge the power disparity between the United States and other states.[51] The United States desires as much "freedom of action in space" as possible so that it can use space for military aims such as maintaining and developing space-based assets to support strategic planning and military operations. Improving national security is a natural and inevitable goal, but China does not acknowledge that the militarization and weaponization of outer space is a legitimate part of that freedom. China fully supports the principle of the peaceful use of space.

Lack of agreement over what is included under the principle of the peaceful use of space could increase tensions in the U.S.-China relationship. In general, Beijing advocates that all states should follow the principle of peaceful use in space activities, but it also believes that U.S. advancements surpass the requirements for national security. Given that the United States already possesses far more military capabilities than China, the upgrading and further developing of U.S. space assets is easily interpreted as a potential threat. In particular, the U.S. national security community's recent emphasis on greater "space protection" appears to China to be ultimately offensive in nature, as it would enlarge the power gap and ensure U.S. hegemony in space.[52] China sees the United States' pursuit of space protection in a similar light as the development of missile defense. Although the United States and its East Asian allies say that the purpose of such systems is merely to protect themselves from a possible North Korean missile attack, China is concerned that they will inevitably undermine the credibility of its nuclear and conventional deterrent.

More specifically, China does not perceive any benefits to its own security from increased U.S. space capabilities but only potential threats. Although the United States often claims that its efforts in advancing space-based capabilities are not directed against China, the latter only feels more insecure. The growing U.S. space capabilities provide no public goods that benefit China's national security or other strategic goals but only serve to undermine China's strategic posture. By comparison, although the strong U.S. military presence in East Asia does have some negative influence on China's national security and external environment, China nevertheless does benefit from a relatively stable East Asia and the reduced incentive for Japan to bolster its own military capabilities.

Moreover, the United States and China do not share a common threat in space. China's main concern is a potential U.S. attack on its important satellites, and while there is some interest in the management of space debris, weather research, and distribution of orbits, these and other common interests are too marginal to be the basis for mutual understanding and confidence.[53] In China's view, the governance problems are not as sensitive and important as the security ones, not in the center stage of international politics. China welcomes cooperation on these environmental issues but will not give as high priority to their achievement as it would to security issues. It will be a very difficult task for the United States to dispel China's suspicion about its intentions and demonstrate that increased U.S. space capabilities will have some benefits for China.

The end result of the grave concerns by strategic analysts on both sides is likely to be a mixed blessing. It is unlikely that China will directly challenge U.S. national interests in space in the near future because its own space capabilities are still in their infancy. China also realizes that the United States will never limit itself through an arms control treaty in space or other bilateral agreements as long as it still maintains a significant advantage in power and capability. Thus, China's most likely course of action is not to try to persuade the United States to join a multilateral space regime but rather to develop its own space power rapidly.[54]

The continued power gap in space will also lead China to link space to other diplomatic and national security issues. Since Beijing has no effective negotiating tools in the space domain, this strategy is seen as one potential way to influence U.S. policy. One example is the debate surrounding the deployment of THAAD in South Korea. If the United States insists on deploying this system on the Korean Peninsula, China may become much tougher on issues such as nuclear transparency and the reduction in nuclear material stockpiles.[55] Further deterioration in the U.S.-China relationship due to the THAAD system or any other space-related technology may also negatively affect military-to-military communications and other bilateral mechanisms. Of course, this strategy will likely have a negative impact on the overall relationship through hindering cooperation in other issue areas and undermining mutual trust. But for China, linking space to other issues is one of the few negotiating levers at its disposal.

Ultimately, improving U.S.-China relations in space may depend on resolving the great-power gap between the two countries in this domain. At the moment, they do not have much common language, and there is little cooperation and even direct rivalry. With Washington's continued refusal to engage in Chinese proposals to limit what Beijing perceives as the U.S. militarization and weaponization of space, China has likely concluded that only by bolstering its own national security space capabilities can it bring the United States back to the negotiating table. Yet this strategy has many risks, the most worrisome of which is that it will likely heighten tensions and could lead to conflict. Thus, it would appear to be in the best interests of both countries to put in place mechanisms to increase positive engagement and potentially even enable cooperation before the situation gets dire.

Comparison of U.S. and Chinese interests in space and policy recommendations

The previous two sections on U.S. and Chinese perceptions of their own and each other's interests in space revealed several areas of overlapping interests. These areas present opportunities for cooperation and bilateral engagement that could help strengthen the bilateral relationship. At the same time, it is clear that stark differences and disagreements also exist between the two countries in the space domain. These areas of divergence are the result of major structural, cultural, and political differences that are unlikely to be resolved in the near to medium term. Thus, mechanisms are needed to help manage tensions and crises that may occur over time. The following discussion identifies these areas of convergence and divergence and proposes steps that can be taken to strengthen the U.S.-China relationship in space while also reducing tensions and the risk of conflict.

Areas of convergence and recommended cooperative initiatives

The long-term sustainability of space

The biggest area of overlap is both countries' desire to maintain the long-term sustainability of the space domain. The United States, as well as increasingly China, has invested significant resources in developing space capabilities to support national security, economic, and political goals. Thus, both have a keen interest in mitigating the negative impacts that environmental concerns such as space debris, space weather, and radio-frequency interference have on day-to-day space operations and the long-term ability of all countries to use space. While these dangers often get less attention than intentional threats such as ASAT weapons, they are more probable and could have just as devastating an impact on space capabilities.

Both the United States and China should thus continue to engage in both bilateral and multilateral initiatives that enhance the long-term sustainability of space.

Over the last several years, space sustainability has become an increasingly important issue and the focus of a number of initiatives. Working together, and with other stakeholders, to help ensure the success of these initiatives would go a long way toward reinforcing the desire of both the United States and China to be seen as playing a leadership role in space governance and being responsible space powers.

Multilaterally, both countries should work to ensure that the UN Committee on the Peaceful Uses of Outer Space's effort to develop long-term sustainability guidelines reaches a consensus. This initiative began in 2007 as an attempt to solidify existing best practices on the use of space to support sustainable development on Earth, safe space operations, strategies for dealing with space weather, and national regulations.[56] After making good progress for several years, the process has lost momentum recently as a result of concerns over security-related aspects of the guidelines and increased tensions between Russia and the United States and Europe. The outright failure of the initiative, or its implicit demise through stagnation, would jeopardize real progress that would benefit the United States and China, along with all spacefaring countries.

In a bilateral context, both countries should consider putting in place mechanisms that enhance the transparency of day-to-day nonmilitary activities in space. Recent efforts to enhance the sharing of space situational awareness (SSA) data between the U.S. military and Chinese satellite operators and to organize technical exchanges on space surveillance are good first steps.[57] They should be followed by additional measures, such as technical exchanges and dialogue on conjunction assessment and collision avoidance procedures, as well as the creation of more robust communications channels between SSA data providers and Chinese satellite operators.

The peaceful use of space as a geopolitical tool for engagement and cooperation

The second major area of overlap between the United States and China is their desire for the peaceful use of space as a geopolitical tool for engagement and cooperation. Both countries have invested significant resources in developing civil space programs for science and exploration that are seen as key areas for building prestige and soft power. The United States and China should develop more bilateral and international cooperation on civil space projects. Continuing to exclude China from such cooperation will not prevent it from developing its own capabilities, as some in the United States had hoped, but only ensure that China cooperates with other countries in space in a way that advances its own national interests and goals. The exclusion of civil space cooperation also leaves military-to-military engagement as the only venue for cooperation. Such engagement is more useful for mitigating tensions and crisis instability than for building a positive relationship.

However, there are significant challenges to work through in this area. On the U.S. side, Congress will continue to have significant concerns over technology transfer and the potential spillover benefits that civil cooperation could have for the PLA. Both countries also currently have different goals and objectives for their human spaceflight programs. The United States is focused on extending the ISS through 2024 and plans to send humans to an asteroid and Mars by the 2030s.[58] Although China also has long-term interests in the moon and Mars, its primary focus for the next two decades is building and operating its own space station in Earth orbit, Tiangong 3.

Rather than proposing a specific destination or goal for civil space cooperation, the United States and China should instead focus on developing a clear strategy for engagement that mixes both top-down and bottom-up joint initiatives.[59] The objectives and potential benefits and risks of the strategy should be well-defined and clearly explained to national interest groups. Top-down initiatives involving high-profile activities such as human spaceflight will require significant involvement and political capital from national leaders to overcome bureaucratic inertia and resistance to cooperation. Bottom-up approaches involving low-profile areas of cooperation such as collaborative scientific research and missions will require organizational champions on both sides.

Commercial and private sector cooperation

A final potential, albeit more difficult, area of cooperation is the commercial and private sector. The United States, as well as China to a much lesser extent, is currently experiencing a massive increase in commercial companies engaged in space activities. Lowering the barriers to commercial cooperation and competition and allowing Chinese companies to gradually re-enter the global market could yield significant benefits. Increased competition and supply, particularly in space launch, could lead to lower costs and greater innovation. In addition, SOEs, which conduct the vast majority of China's commercial space activities, wield important influence in Chinese policymaking. SOEs have pushed for meaningful changes in Chinese policy in other domains and could do so in space if they have the incentive of freer markets to compete in as a result.

That said, there are significant hurdles to overcome in increasing commercial space cooperation. Both the United States and China have different definitions of "commercial," largely driven by differences in ideology. The United States generally believes that commercial implies separate and distinct from the government, whereas China is still transitioning from a centrally managed economy to a market economy. As a result, many in the United States will be concerned that commercial cooperation will lead to direct benefits for the Chinese government, and particularly for the PLA's military capabilities. In addition, the U.S. government and private sector alike will have strong concerns that commercial engagement in space could enable Chinese economic espionage and intellectual property theft.

Areas of divergence and recommended mechanisms to manage tensions and crises

THE DEVELOPMENT, TESTING, AND EMPLOYMENT OF DUAL-USE CAPABILITIES

One of the most significant areas of tension will be the development, testing, and employment of dual-use capabilities that have both military and nonmilitary uses.

Many space technologies are dual-use in nature: rockets are used to loft humans and peaceful satellites into orbit as well as to hurl conventional and nuclear warheads at targets on Earth. Many satellite applications such as remote sensing, communications, and navigation have both commercial and military applications and end users. The commoditization of space technology and the expansion of commercial activity in space are increasingly breaking down traditional silos between military, civil, and commercial uses of space, thereby blurring the lines even further.

The development of robotic RPO, which involves the close approach and potential docking of two or more unmanned space objects, currently poses a significant challenge to a stable relationship. Such operations form the foundation of capabilities essential to the next generation of space activities, including on-orbit satellite servicing, refueling, repairs, formation flying, and the ability to actively remove large space debris. However, they are also vital to on-orbit inspection of satellites and intelligence gathering as well as co-orbital ASAT weapons.[60]

A second area of tension over dual-use capabilities is the development, testing, and employment of direct ascent kinetic-kill weapons. Such systems utilize rockets to place a kill vehicle on a ballistic trajectory to intercept and destroy a space object by colliding with it. The United States has been developing direct ascent kinetic-kill technology for decades. Although it has used the technology for ASAT capabilities in the past,[61] it currently does not have any acknowledged kinetic-kill ASAT programs and states that current programs are for missile defense only.[62] China's activity in this area has been more recent and has focused on developing and testing direct ascent kinetic-kill technology for ASAT capabilities, although it has recently justified the testing as related to missile defense.[63]

In the case of a conflict, the presence of operational ASAT capabilities on both sides could be a strong driver for crisis instability. Chinese military authors writing about space doctrine are increasingly focused on the importance of first strikes against U.S. space assets in order to seize the initiative and deter a U.S. attack.[64] At the same time, the United States is increasingly worried about Chinese conventional ballistic missile attacks on carrier battle groups and land bases in the Asia-Pacific, which utilize ISR satellites for targeting. In response, the United States is considering "left of launch" capabilities that could include using ASAT systems against Chinese satellites to disrupt the ballistic missile kill chain.[65] Thus, a crisis scenario between the United States and China could include a race condition where both sides move to strike first against the other's space assets, which could cause the situation to escalate out of control.

Transparency and confidence-building mechanisms for managing tensions and crises

The prospects of banning or prohibiting the development of direct ascent kinetic-kill and RPO technologies are slim. RPO technology has many legitimate peaceful uses and potentially significant commercial applications. Both the United States and China are likewise developing their direct ascent kinetic-kill technologies as a result of strong, but different, national interests that are unlikely to disappear in the foreseeable future. Moreover, verification challenges associated with the space domain will continue to impede any arms control initiative that is built on bans or limits on deployment of technology or capabilities.

A more promising approach is to focus on transparency and confidence-building measures for both direct ascent and RPO. TCBMs are a means by which governments can share information to help create mutual understanding and trust and reduce misperceptions and miscalculations. Although not new, TCBMs represent a shift for the space world, which has long focused its efforts on pushing for legally binding arms control agreements and treaties. The recent report from the UN Group of Governmental Experts, in which the United States and China both participated, highlights several areas for space TCBMs: information exchange on space policies, information exchange and notifications related to outer space activities, risk reduction notifications, and contact and visits to space launch sites and facilities.[66]

Improving information on activities in space likely holds the most promise for mitigating tensions in the U.S.-China relationship in this domain. While determining a satellite's exact capabilities and function is still difficult, SSA capabilities have developed to the point where it is becoming possible to verify actions and activities in space. The U.S. military already maintains a catalog of more than 22,000 human-generated space objects in Earth's orbit, much of which is available publicly and also shared with all satellite operators.[67] China is currently developing its own SSA capabilities and, presumably, its own catalog of space objects. Russia, several European countries, India, and many other spacefaring nations are also increasing their own SSA capabilities, and most recently actors in the private sector have started to develop such capabilities as well.[68]

As SSA capabilities continue to improve and proliferate to other countries, it becomes increasingly possible that they may be able to serve as a new type of national technical means to underpin bilateral and multilateral political agreements on responsible and irresponsible behavior in space.[69] Such agreements should be aimed at limiting dangerous or provocative actions, such as close approaches of national security satellites,[70] signaling restraint for kinetic testing and deployment of new capabilities, and making political pledges to refrain from first use of destructive counter-space weapons.[71]

A key challenge in developing these agreements will be overcoming cultural and bureaucratic incentives for opacity on both sides. In the United States, the national security community has a deeply rooted culture of secrecy and unilateralism in the space domain that results from policy decisions made during the Kennedy administration as well as the consideration that space remains the last domain where the United States has a decisive advantage. For China, which sees itself as significantly inferior to the United States, opacity in space activities and programs is seen as one of the few tools to offset overwhelming U.S. capabilities and resources. Both countries also have the usual organizational silos and impediments to sharing information internally that are inherent to all large bureaucracies and undermine bilateral sharing.

Both countries need to come to the realization that enhancing SSA capabilities and increasing transparency on activities in space are in their national interests. While some more exquisite national SSA capabilities should be reserved for security uses, there is a much broader set of basic SSA capabilities that are relatively common among all spacefaring nations and essential to safe space activities, including those of commercial satellite operators. Increased sharing of data from these capabilities and collaboration on enhancing and improving them will result in positive externalities that will benefit all countries.

Conclusion

Given that both the United States and China have considerable national security, civil, and commercial interests in space, this domain will have a significant impact on the future of bilateral relations. Although it is tempting to view the U.S.-China relationship in space through a similar lens as the U.S.-Soviet relationship, the differences between the two relationships and their contexts may ultimately matter more than the similarities. The key question is whether space will be a source of tension that creates instability and risk or an area of positive engagement that can strengthen the relationship.

Both the United States and China should look at where their interests in space overlap to find potential areas to strengthen their relationship. Both have interests in working with the rest of the international community to strengthen the space governance regime in a manner that enhances the long-term sustainability of space, including by addressing both environmental threats and security challenges. Both countries should also find a way to engage in bilateral and multilateral civil space projects, including science and exploration. Doing so would create an element to their relationship that has a different dynamic from military-to-military interactions.

At the same time, both the United States and China should be cognizant of where their interests in space differ and look to enact confidence-building measures to reduce tensions and the risk of a crisis escalating into outright conflict. While the prospects for legally binding arms control measures are slim at this stage, they could put in place unilateral and bilateral measures to reduce tensions created by the testing and development of direct ascent kinetic-kill and RPO capabilities. Finally, both countries would benefit significantly from improving their national SSA capabilities and increasing data sharing with each other.

In recent years, there have been both positive developments as well as potential obstacles in the U.S.-China relationship as it pertains to outer space. On the positive side, the United States and China agreed to begin two-part bilateral dialogue on space, one focused on civilian aspects of outer space and the other on security-related matters. The first Civil Space Dialogue was held in Beijing in September 2015, and the second took place in Washington in October 2016, while on the other hand the first Space Security Exchange was held in Washington in May 2016. One of the potential challenges that confronts effective U.S.-China cooperation in outer space has been none other than the changing nature of U.S. domestic politics, particularly the U.S. presidential election of November 2016 which resulted in the election of Donald Trump as the 45th president of the United States and which saw the Republican Party take control of both houses of Congress. It will be recalled that in November 2017, the third Civil Space Dialogue was held in Beijing, with the two sides exchanging plans for human and robotics space exploration and discussing engagement through multilateral mechanisms. However, as the Trump administration identified China as a "strategic competitor" and initiated a trade war against it, this dialogue was effectively suspended along with other dialogue mechanisms. With super-hawks in the United States now advocating a "New Cold War" with China, it is unclear whether the space domain will remain a sphere of cooperation between Beijing and Washington or whether it will be turned into a theater of conflict and confrontation.

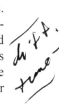

Notes

1 For the U.S. perspective, see Executive Office of the President of the United States, *National Space Policy of the United States of America* (Washington, DC, June 28, 2010), www.whitehouse.gov/sites/default/files/national_space_policy_6-28-10.pdf. For the Chinese perspective, see Information Office of the State Council of the People's Republic of China (PRC), *China's Space Activities in 2011* (Beijing, 2011), www.china. org.cn/government/whitepaper/2011-12/29/content_24280462.htm; and Ministry of National Defense (PRC), *China's Military Strategy* (Beijing, May 2015), http://eng.mod. gov.cn/Database/WhitePapers/2015-05/26/content_4586688.htm.

2 For two excellent books that provide a historical overview of this relationship, see William E. Burrows, *This New Ocean: The Story of the First Space Age* (New York: Random House, 1998); and Walter McDougall, *The Heavens and the Earth: A Political History of the Space Age* (Baltimore: Johns Hopkins University Press, 1997).

3 Pat Norris, *Spies in the Sky: Surveillance Satellites in War and Peace* (Berlin: Springer Praxis Books, 2008).

4 For an overview of U.S.-Soviet cooperation in space, see Roald Sagdeev and Susan Eisenhower, "United States—Soviet Space Cooperation during the Cold War," *NASA*, www.nasa.gov/50th/50th_magazine/coldWarCoOp.html.

5 George Kennan clearly argued that the Soviet Union's power was much weaker than the United States' in the early Cold War. See George F. Kennan, *Memoirs, 1925–1950* (Boston: Little, Brown and Company, 1967).

6 For a listing of all the countries that have had one or more satellites in space, see Secure World Foundation, "Space Sustainability: A Practical Guide," 2014, http://swfound. org/media/121399/swf_space_sustainability-a_practical_guide_20141_.pdf.

7 Executive Office of the President of the United States, *National Space Policy of the United States of America.*

8 "Space Foundation Report Reveals Global Space Economy Climb to $330 Billion," *Space Foundation*, July 7, 2015, www.spacefoundation.org/media/press-releases/ space-foundation-report-reveals-global-space-economy-climb-330-billion.

9 "UCS Satellite Database," Union of Concerned Scientists, September 1, 2015, www. ucsusa.org/nuclear_weapons_and_global_security/solutions/space-weapons/ucs-satellite-database.html.

10 Dee Ann Divis, "Study: GPS Contributed More Than $68 Billion to the U.S. Economy," *Inside GNSS*, June 16, 2015, www.insidegnss. com/node/4535.

11 "Space Foundation Report Reveals Global Space Economy Climb to $330 Billion."

12 Benjamin Wormald, "Americans Keen on Space Exploration, Less So on Paying for It," Pew Research Center, Fact Tank, April 23, 2014, www.pewresearch.org/fact-tank/2014/04/23/americans-keen-on-space-exploration-less-so-on-paying-for-it.

13 Jeff Foust, "Impatience for Mars," *Space Review*, May 18, 2015, www.thespacereview.com/article/2755/1.

14 Tariq Malik, "Competition Heats Up for NASA's Space Cargo Contract," *Space.com*, May 31, 2006, www.space.com/2444-competition-heats-nasa-space-cargo-contract.html.

15 For an overview of recent developments in the commercial space sector, see Tauri Group, "2015 State of the Satellite Industry Report," September 2015, http://space.taurigroup.com/reports/SIA_SSIR_2015.pdf.

16 U.S. Air Force Space Command, *Resiliency and Disaggregated Space Architectures* (Peterson Air Force Base, 2013), www.afspc.af.mil/shared/media/document/AFD-130821-034.pdf.

17 U.S. Department of Defense, *National Security Space Strategy Unclassified Summary* (Washington, DC, January 2011), www.defense.gov/Portals/1/features/2011/0111_nsss/docs/NationalSecuritySpaceStrategyUnclassifiedSummary_Jan2011.pdf.

18 Ibid., i.

19 Ibid., 5.

20 U.S. Department of Defense, "Space Policy," Directive, no. 3100.10, October 12, 2012, www.dtic.mil/whs/directives/corres/pdf/310010p.pdf.

21 U.S. Department of Defense, "Space Policy," 2.

22 Brian Weeden, "Anti-Satellite Tests in Space—The Case of China," Secure World Foundation, May 18, 2005, http://swfound.org/media/115643/china_asat_fact_sheet_may2015.pdf.

23 Brian Weeden, "Through a Glass Darkly: Chinese, American, and Russian Anti-Satellite Testing in Space," Secure World Foundation, Space Review, March 17, 2014, www.thespacereview.com/article/2473/1.

24 Laura Grego, "Preventing Space War," Union of Concerned Scientists, All Things Nuclear, July 7, 2015, http://allthingsnuclear.org/preventing-space-war.

25 Dean Cheng, "The PLA's Interest in Space Dominance," testimony before the U.S.-China Economic and Security Review Commission, Washington, DC, February 18, 2015, www.uscc.gov/sites/default/files/Cheng_Testimony.pdf.

26 Mike Gruss, "Disaggregation Giving Way to Broader Space Protection Strategy," *Space News*, April 26, 2015, http://spacenews.com/disaggregation-giving-way-to-broader-space-protection-strategy.

27 Mike Gruss, "U.S. Spending on Space Protection Could Hit $8 Billion Through 2020," *SpaceNews*, July 2, 2015, http://spacenews.com/u-s-spending-on-space-protection-could-hit-8-billion-through-2020.

28 Andrea Shalal, "U.S. Eyes New Ways to Prepare and Win Future War in Space," Reuters, April 17, 2015, www.reuters.com/article/2015/04/17/us-usa-military-space-future-idUSKBN0N82E820150417.

29 Sydney Freedberg Jr., "STRATCOM Must Be Warfighters, Not FAA in Space: Lt. Gen. Kowalski," *Breaking Defense*, June 16, 2015, http://breakingdefense.com/2015/06/stratcom-must-be-warfighters-not-faa-in-space-lt-gen-kowalski; and "New Joint Interagency Combined Space Operations Center to Be Established," U.S. Department of Defense, September 11, 2015, www.defense.gov/News/News-Releases/News-Release-View/Article/616969/new-joint-interagency-combined-space-operations-center-to-be-established.

30 U.S. House of Representatives, *An Act to Authorize Appropriations for Fiscal Year 2016 for Military Activities of the Department of Defense, for Military Construction, and for Defense Activities of the Department of Energy, to Prescribe Military Personnel Strengths for Such Fiscal Year, and for Other Purposes*, 114th Cong., Amendment H.R. 1735 (Washington, DC, June 18, 2015), www.gpo.gov/fdsys/pkg/BILLS-114hr1735pap/pdf/BILLS-114hr1735pap.pdf.

31 U.S. House of Representatives, *Carl Levin and Howard P. "Buck" McKeon National Defense Authorization Act for Fiscal Year 2015*, 113th Cong., H.R. 3979 (Washington, DC, December 19, 2014), www.congress.gov/bill/113th-congress/house-bill/3979/text# toc-H107A2 990469548E49DDB5A7A69A2EBEC.

32 Cheng, "The PLA's Interest in Space Dominance."

33 "Press Conference: Deputy Assistant Secretary Frank A. Rose—U.S. National Space Policy 2010," U.S. Mission to Geneva, July 13, 2010, https://geneva.usmission. gov/2010/07/13/rose-press-briefing.

34 Frank A. Rose, "Ensuring the Long-Term Sustainability and Security of the Space Environment," U.S. Department of State, August 13, 2014, www.state.gov/t/avc/ rls/2014/230611.htm.

35 Michael Listner and Rajeswari Pillai Rajagopalan, "The 2014 PPWT: A New Drat But with the Same and Different Problems," *Space Review*, August 11, 2014, www.thespace review.com/article/2575/1.

36 Brian Weeden, "Dancing in the Dark: The Orbital Rendezvous of SJ-12 and SJ-06F," *Space Review*, August 30, 2010, www.thespacereview.com/article/1689/1.

37 Marcia S. Smith, "Surprise Chinese Satellite Maneuvers Mystify Western Experts," *Space Policy Online*, August 19, 2013, www.spacepolicyonline.com/news/surprise-chinese-satelllite-maneuvers-mystify-western-experts.

38 Leonard David, "Military Micro-Sat Explores Space Inspection, Servicing Technologies," *Space.com*, July 22, 2005, www.space.com/1336-military-micro-sat-explores-space-inspection-servicing-technologies.html; and NASA, "Demonstration of Autonomous Rendezvous Technology Mishap Review Board," NASA Engineering and Safety Center Report, no. RP-06–119, December 2006, www.nasa.gov/pdf/167813main_RP-06-119_05-020-E_DART_Report_Final_Dec_27.pdf.

39 U.S. Joint Chiefs of Staff, *The National Military Strategy of the United States of America 2015* (Washington, DC, June 2015), www.jcs.mil/Portals/36/Documents/Publications/ 2015_National_Military_Strategy.pdf.

40 Marcia S. Smith, "Rep. Wolf Tells Bolden No to China on ISS," *Space Policy Online*, March 6, 2012, www.spacepolicyonline.com/news/rep-wolf-tells-bolden-no-to-china-on-iss.

41 Christopher Johnson, "The UN Group of Governmental Experts on Space TCBMs," Secure World Foundation, Fact Sheet, April 2014, http://swfound.org/media/109311/ swf_gge_on_space_tcbms_fact_sheet_april_2014.pdf.

42 Christopher Johnson, "The UN COPUOS Guidelines on the Long-Term Sustainability of Outer Space Activities," Secure World Foundation, Fact Sheet, December 2014, http://swfound.org/media/189048/SWF_UN_COPUOS_LTS_Guidelines_Fact_ Sheet_December_2014.pdf.

43 Deb Riechmann, "Russia Is the Biggest Threat to U.S. National Security, Joint Chiefs Nominee Tells Congress," *Associated Press*, July 9, 2015, www.usnews.com/news/politics/ articles/2015/07/09/joint-chiefs-nominee-says-he-will-assess-strategy-against-is.

44 Bill Gertz, "Russia Flight Tests Anti-Satellite Missile," *Washington Free Beacon*, December 2, 2015, http://freebeacon.com/national-security/russia-conducts-successful-flight-test-of-anti-satellite-missile.

45 Zhang Hui, "Action/Reaction: U.S. Space Weaponization and China," *Arms Control Today*, December 2005, www.armscontrol.org/print/1943.

46 John K. Warden and Brad Glosserman, "China's THAAD Gamble Is Unlikely to Pay Off," *Diplomat*, April 15, 2015, http://thediplomat.com/2015/04/chinas-thaad-gamble-is-unlikely-to-pay-off; and Elbridge Colby, "Don't Sweat AirSea Battle," *National Interest*, July 31, 2013, http://nationalinterest.org/commentary/dont-sweat-airsea-battle-8804.

47 Listner and Rajagopalan, "The 2014 PPWT."

48 Zhao Weibin, "Sino-U.S. Competition and Cooperation in Outer Space," *China U.S. Focus Digest*, July 2014, www.chinausfocus.com/foreign-policy/sino-us-competition-and-cooperation-in-outer-space.

49 "U.S. Needs to Reexamine NASA's China Exclusion Policy," *China Daily*, June 5, 2014, www.chinadaily.com.cn/world/2014-06/05/content_17563848.htm.

50 Marcia S. Smith, "China Issues New Five Year Space Plan," *Space Policy Online*, 2011, www.spacepolicyonline.com/news/china-issues-new-five-year-space-plan.

51 Bao Shixiu, "Deterrence Revisited: Outer Space," *China Security*, no. 5, 2007, 5.

52 Greater protection of U.S. space capabilities from counter-space attacks could reduce the deterrent effect of Chinese counter-space capabilities and thus increase the likelihood that the United States might use military force against China. In addition, some of the "protection" measures being considered by the United States are offensive in nature, and some U.S. commentators are even calling for preemptive attacks on space objects that may pose a future threat to U.S. satellites. See Brian Chow, "Fund Pre-Emptive Self-Defense in Space," *Defense News*, October 20, 2015, www.defensenews.com/story/defense/commentary/2015/10/20/fund-pre-emptive-self-defense-space/74263522.

53 Xu Nengwu, "Taikong anquan waijiao nuli de kunjing ji qi sikao" [Some Thoughts on the Space Security Plight], *Foreign Affairs Reviews*, June 2007, 59.

54 Ling Shengli, "Taikong zhili yu Zhongguo de conyu zhanlue" [Space Governance and China's Participation Strategy], *International Studies* (China) 3 (2015): 121–22.

55 He Qisong, "Taikong anquan wenti ji qi duobian zhuyi boyi" [Space Security Issue and Its Multilateral Gambling], *Contemporary International Relations* 5 (2015).

56 Johnson, "The UN COPUOS Guidelines."

57 Mike Gruss, "U.S. to Expedite Orbital Collision Avoidance Warnings to China," *SpaceNews*, December 5, 2014, http://spacenews.com/42869us-to-expedite-orbital-collision-avoidance-warnings-to-china.

58 John P. Holdren and Charles Bolden, "Obama Administration Extends International Space Station Until at Least 2024," *White House*, January 8, 2014, www.whitehouse.gov/blog/2014/01/08/obama-administration-extends-international-space-station-until-least-2024.

59 Brian Weeden, "U.S.-China Cooperation in Space: Constraints, Possibilities, and Options," in *Anti-Satellite Weapons, Deterrence, and Sino-American Relations*, ed. Michael Krepon and Julia Thompson (Washington, DC: Stimson Center, 2013), www.stimson.org/images/uploads/Anti-satellite_Weapons.pdf.

60 For a discussion of Chinese RPO and a comparison with U.S. and European RPO activities, see Weeden, "Dancing in the Dark."

61 Laura Grego, "A History of Anti-Satellite Programs," Union of Concerned Scientists, 2011, www.ucsusa.org/sites/default/files/legacy/assets/documents/nwgs/a-history-of-ASAT-programs_lo-res.pdf.

62 Many are skeptical of this claim, particularly after a U.S. missile defense system was used to destroy an ailing U.S. satellite in 2008. For a discussion of the latent ASAT capability of U.S. missile defense programs, see Laura Grego, "The Anti-Satellite Capability of the Phased Adaptive Approach Missile Defense System," Federation of American Scientists, Public Interest Report, Winter 2011, https://fas.org/pubs/pir/2011winter/2011Winter-Anti-Satellite.pdf.

63 Weeden, "Through a Glass Darkly."

64 Kevin Pollpeter, "Chinese Military Writings about Counterspace" (presentation at the Mitchell Institute for Space Studies, Arlington, VA, November 3, 2015).

65 Sydney Freedberg, "Joint Staff Studies New Options for Missile Defense," *Breaking Defense*, September 16, 2015, http://breakingdefense.com/2015/09/joint-staff-studies-new-options-for-missile-defense.

66 UN General Assembly, "Group of Governmental Experts on Transparency and Confidence-Building Measures in Outer Space Activities," July 29, 2013, www.un.org/ga/search/view_doc.asp?symbol=A/68/189.

67 For background and details on this program, see Tiffany Chow, "Space Situational Awareness Sharing Program: An SWF Issue Brief," *Secure World Foundation*, September 22, 2011, http://swfound.org/media/3584/ssa_sharing_program_issue_brief_nov2011.pdf.

68 An overview of current SSA capabilities can be found in Brian Weeden, "Space Situational Awareness," Secure World Foundation, Fact Sheet, September 2014, http://swfound.org/media/1800/swf_ssa_fact_sheet_sept2014.pdf.

69 "National Technical Means" was the euphemism for reconnaissance satellites and other verification mechanisms used as the foundation for arms control agreements between the United States and the Soviet Union.

70 For an example, see Brian Chow, "Avoiding Space War Needs a New Approach," *Defense News*, September 16, 2015, www.defensenews.com/story/defense/commentary/2015/09/16/avoiding-space-war-needs-new-approach/32523905.

71 David C. Gompert and Phillip C. Saunders, *Paradox of Power: Sino-American Strategic Restraint in an Age of Vulnerability* (Washington, DC: National Defense University, 2011), www.dtic.mil/cgi-bin/GetTRDoc?AD=ADA582221.

5 Stepping up investments in U.S.-China relations*

Making people-to-people exchange a strategic priority

Travis Tanner and Zhao Minghao

EXECUTIVE SUMMARY

This chapter examines people-to-people (P2P) exchange between the U.S. and China and argues that this mechanism can serve as a vehicle to increase collaboration and reduce tension between the two countries on issues related to national security concerns.

Main argument

The U.S.-China relationship faces a critical juncture. Today the relationship is marked by progress in certain areas, while simultaneously experiencing a continued stalemate and simmering tensions in others. The stakes are high given the global implications of the two nations' interactions with each other across a wide range of issues. One important mechanism to facilitate positive engagement and collaboration, as well as successfully manage tension and areas of disagreement, is P2P exchange. Though the impact of such exchanges is not always immediate, the long-term benefits of building common understanding, an ecosystem of experts on challenging security issues in both countries, clear communication channels, ground rules and mutually agreed-upon vocabulary for dialogue, and intellectual support for government officials are well worth the investment of time and resources.

Policy implications

- As the U.S.-China relationship matures, the type of P2P exchange should also evolve to include more dialogues oriented toward national security. Specifically, the two countries should consider creating a high-level channel to orchestrate P2P activities (both Track 1.5 and Track 2) focused specifically on building collaboration on global strategic issues.
- P2P activities that focus on areas where the U.S. and China can collaborate will intrinsically build mutual understanding and trust, allowing for the two nations to engage in productive discussions on more sensitive issues. Washington and Beijing should develop a methodology to evaluate the effectiveness and impact of specific P2P exchanges.

- It is critical that the profile of individuals who participate in P2P exchange related to national security concerns expand beyond government officials and think tank scholars to include experts in the business, scientific, NGO, academic, and other expert communities.
- Given that the key for the future of the bilateral relationship rests in the hands of the next generation of leaders, the U.S. and China should invest in providing more opportunities for student exchanges to train this future generation of relationship managers.

The U.S.-China relationship has changed significantly over the past three decades and continues to evolve. As ties between the two countries appear to be entering a new and important phase—marked by high international stakes, increased tensions over strategic and economic issues, and a growing number of overlapping interests—the senior leaders in both nations must counter the buildup of strategic mistrust and rivalry. As the world's two largest military powers, two largest economies, and arguably the two most influential actors on the global stage, the United States and China must determine how to manage strategic tensions, avoid conflict, and collaborate to solve global challenges. One key mechanism to achieve these goals is to seek new and innovative ways to cultivate and leverage people-to-people (P2P) ties—a long-standing bright spot in the relationship—in order to address challenges in strategic domains. The United States and China have a long history of regular P2P exchange in the fields of education, culture, tourism, commerce, leadership, and sports, which has already made a significant impact on bilateral ties. Some of these activities occur as part of government-sponsored programs, while others take place in a more ad hoc and organic fashion. This chapter, however, does not provide a comprehensive overview or analysis of these many forms of exchange and interaction but instead focuses on how, if at all, P2P activity could be applied to enhance cooperation in areas of converging interests in the security domain. For the purposes of this project, P2P exchange in the security domain is defined as engagement at the Track 1.5 and Track 2 levels. Track 1.5 dialogue refers to situations where official and nonofficial actors engage, while Track 2 dialogue refers to nongovernmental, informal, and unofficial contacts and activities between private citizens or groups of individuals or nonstate actors.[1]

Although P2P activities have historically played a valuable role in strengthening the U.S.-China relationship, they do not always result in immediate and measurable outcomes. Often results appear gradually and incrementally over time. P2P exchange is conducted to provide long-term results, which are critical for ensuring that the bilateral relationship remains on a positive trajectory long into the future. In order for both countries to manage differences and capitalize on common interests in the coming years, decades, and centuries, they must engage in the kind of discussions and constructive dealings that are most effectively facilitated through P2P exchange.

From a national security perspective, P2P activities have traditionally been considered an issue of secondary importance and viewed more as a tool of cultural and public diplomacy, beneficial only for achieving "soft" diplomatic objectives. Altering this view and utilizing P2P as a mechanism to tackle strategic issues could help reduce tensions over cybersecurity, outer space activities, nuclear weapons, maritime disputes in the East and South China Seas, and other sensitive security-related topics, as well as address the general trust deficit in the bilateral relationship. By elevating the status of P2P exchange beyond a "nice thing to do," senior leaders in both countries will open doors to new and innovative ways to manage several of the most sensitive issues plaguing the U.S.-China relationship. As the relationship becomes more sophisticated, interests increasingly overlap, and China moves into larger and more significant global roles, robust P2P activities are needed to provide a stable foundation on which the relationship can grow and mature. The greater the web of P2P ties and the more levels of cooperation that can be cultivated between the two nations, the higher the cost of a potential conflict and the greater the incentives to maintain stability.

Furthermore, the chapter assesses whether P2P can serve as an effective mechanism to manage areas of tension where interests diverge—for example, in the cyber, nuclear, space, and maritime domains. The chapter argues that as the U.S.-China relationship continues to expand, P2P exchange should be broadened beyond its traditional realm. Specifically, the environment is ripe to improve bilateral relations by increasing and expanding the number of P2P engagements at both the Track 1.5 and Track 2 levels between officials, scholars, scientists, private sector representatives, NGO leaders, and other specialists in a range of strategic domains.

The chapter begins by outlining the positive impact P2P exchange has had on the U.S.-China relationship across many dimensions. Against this backdrop, it then contrasts the different systems and organizational styles through which P2P exchange is coordinated in and between the two countries and highlights specific obstacles for expanding P2P to more strategic domains. Finally, the chapter concludes by laying out a series of recommendations to overcome these obstacles and developing innovative ways in which P2P exchange can address several challenging emerging strategic areas where risks for increased tension are highest. In sum, the chapter aims to highlight the valuable role P2P could play in strengthening U.S.-China relations by serving as a catalyst to facilitate more dialogue, engagement, and interaction between nonofficial interlocutors on topics related to national security.

Role of P2P exchange in U.S.-China relations

The value of P2P ties

P2P relations have long played a critical role in the development of the U.S.-China relationship. More than 200 years ago, the U.S. commercial vessel *Empress of China* visited the Guangzhou port, marking the beginning of P2P ties. Over 40 years ago, ping-pong players broke the diplomatic ice between the United States and China, heralding the normalization of the bilateral relationship several years later. Since then, P2P efforts have contributed to the deepening of understanding between the people of both countries, thereby expanding communication channels, addressing challenges, generating economic activity, and improving relationship management. While many difficult and sensitive issues continue to plague bilateral relations in the strategic and economic areas, the P2P aspect of the U.S.-China relationship has reached an unprecedented level. More than 10,000 American and Chinese citizens cross the Pacific each day,[2] and in 2014 alone there were 4.3 million trips made between the two countries.[3] Countless Chinese and American citizens also interact daily via the Internet and social media.

Since the first student exchange took place in 1978, the number of Chinese students studying in the United States at the tertiary level has grown to 304,040 students in 2014.[4] Between 2010 and 2014, more than 100,000 American students studied in China—achieving the goal of President Barack Obama's 100,000 Strong Initiative to increase the number and diversity of young Americans who learn Chinese and study abroad in China.[5] Likewise, the U.S. Department of Commerce estimates that in the 2013–14 academic year, Chinese students contributed $8.04 billion to the U.S. economy.[6]

The number of exchanges occurring between students, scientists, artists, tourists, leaders at the subnational level, and athletes is growing. There are sports competitions, online conversations, technical workshops, social leadership exchanges, tourism, cultural and media interactions, and academic exchanges occurring across a broad range of cities in both countries. There are now more than 1,100 cooperating institutions and programs between the United States and China, one-third of which were established during the Obama years.[7] Over 80 U.S. universities are involved in partnerships to offer undergraduate degrees in China, and over 30 are involved in partnerships to offer graduate degrees.[8] These universities represent more than 36 U.S. states.[9] Over 240 pairs of sister provinces, states, and cities also exist between the United States and China.[10] Finally, the number of American tourists visiting China has increased 10%, from 1.9 million in 2007 to 2.09 million in 2014.[11] Over the same time period the number of Chinese tourists in the United States increased from 397,000 to 2.19 million, representing a 451% increase.[12]

P2P activities have produced a wide range of short- and long-term benefits for the bilateral relationship, some profound and others intangible. However, as the relationship matures, dedicated and targeted P2P exchange is needed to address the strategic challenges that the U.S.-China relationship faces. Tensions are rising over cybersecurity, maritime disputes in the East and South China Seas, interactions in space, and obstacles impeding trade and financial flows between the two countries. These frustrations, along with other friction points, have heightened the level of strategic rivalry between the world's two largest military powers.

While there does not appear to be a direct transition mechanism between the number or depth of P2P exchange and the general health of the overall U.S.-China relationship, historically P2P exchange has served as a ballast, allowing the U.S.-China relationship to weather difficult storms. When tensions have been high, relationship managers have relied on human relationships, unofficial communication channels, and a deep and personal understanding of the other country's interests to steady the boat and move the relationship out of troubled waters.

Strong relationships between citizens in both nations can also mitigate the potential policy excesses that either side might otherwise be tempted to pursue—the "don't go there" concept. Public participation and public opinion can weigh heavily on the making of domestic and foreign policy. When government officials know that private citizens are invested in policy outcomes and the general management of the bilateral relationship, accountability is higher, providing an important variable for consideration in the policymaking process. The public can also encourage public officials to overcome short-term obstacles in order to achieve long-term objectives—the "hang in there" concept.

Furthermore, educational exchange and other P2P activities lead to increased mutual understanding. The more the future leaders and relationship managers understand the perspectives, interests, considerations, and policy environments that their counterparts face, the more successful they will be in steering the relationship in a positive direction. Increased understanding helps build shared norms and obviate misunderstandings and miscalculations.

Graham Allison, a professor at Harvard University, has argued that if leaders in China and the United States perform no better than their predecessors in classical Greece or Europe at the beginning of the 20th century, historians of the 21st century will cite Thucydides in explaining the catastrophe that follows.[13] The rise of power alone does not necessarily lead to violent clashes. The key lies in what strategy a rising country chooses and how an established power responds to the associated challenges. Therefore, in order to effectively address the fear and mistrust that exist between the United States and China, a strategy to create a more vibrant and substantively deep series of P2P exchanges is required.

Official vs. nonofficial P2P channels

P2P exchange has played an important role in the positive development of the bilateral relationship. The need to mitigate heightening tensions calls for both the U.S. and Chinese governments to elevate the successful P2P platform and further utilize it as a strategic tool.

The United States and China currently discuss bilateral issues in more than 90 different intergovernmental bodies.[14] A few examples include the U.S.-China Strategic Security Dialogue, U.S.-China Cybersecurity Working Group Dialogue, U.S.-China Labor Dialogue, U.S.-China Workplace Safety and Health Dialogue, U.S.-China Legal Experts Dialogue, U.S.-China Human Rights Dialogue, U.S.-China Joint Commission on Commerce and Trade, U.S.-China Joint Committee on Environmental Cooperation, U.S.-China Climate Change Working Group, U.S.-China Ten-Year Framework for Energy and Environment Cooperation, U.S.-China Consultation on People-to-People Exchange (CPE), and U.S.-China Strategic and Economic Dialogue (S&ED).[15] These exchanges are incredibly valuable.

The largest and most visible of these dialogues is the S&ED, which was established by President Obama and former Chinese president Hu Jintao in April 2009 and which represents the highest-level bilateral forum to discuss a broad range of issues between the two nations.[16] The S&ED is held on an annual, rotating basis and addresses shared opportunities and challenges in the 21st century. At the seventh session, held in Washington, D.C., in June 2015, U.S. secretary of state John Kerry and Chinese state councilor Yang Jiechi co-chaired the strategic track, while U.S. secretary of treasury Jacob Lew and Chinese vice premier Wang Yang co-chaired the economic track. Leaders from 19 U.S. government agencies and senior officials representing key Chinese ministries and agencies joined them.

From 2010–16, the U.S. and Chinese governments had held an annual companion dialogue focused on enhancing P2P—the U.S.-China Consultation on People-to-People Exchange. Launched in 2010, this dialogue has served as an incredibly valuable tool for promoting enhanced engagement and was the first of its kind to be held at the cabinet level. The CPE has been led by Vice Premier Liu Yandong on the Chinese side and Secretary of State Hillary Clinton (2010–12) followed by Secretary of State John Kerry (2012–16) on the U.S. side.[17] It has convened a broad range of stakeholders from both countries to advance initiatives and projects that range across six pillars—education, science and technology, culture, health, sports, and women's issues—resulting in over 400 bilateral deliverables, each of which represents a significant interaction between individuals in both nations.[18] Universities, foundations, advocacy groups, sports organizations, and many other institutions have collaborated with both governments in carrying out these initiatives. After Trump came into power, the U.S. and Chinese governments instituted a new dialogue mechanism—the U.S.-China Social and Cultural Dialogue (SCD) for promoting P2P between the two countries. The SCD was launched by U.S. president Donald Trump and Chinese president Xi Jinping in April 2017 at Mar-a-Lago. The first SCD was co-chaired by U.S. secretary of state Rex Tillerson and Chinese vice premier Liu Yandong on September 28, 2017, in Washington, D.C. The stated goal of the SCD is to advance U.S.-China social and cultural relations "consistent with result-oriented approach of the new Comprehensive Dialogue Mechanism."[19]

The need to elevate P2P exchange

Although it is clear that P2P exchange addresses a broad range of issues and creates positive outcomes for the bilateral relationship, is this enough? P2P activity today looks significantly different than it did 30 years ago. It is important to ensure that P2P exchange continues to evolve to encompass more topics related to national security, which are the source of many of the tensions in the bilateral relationship. It is imperative to increase mutual understanding and provide opportunities for collaboration between people across a full range of professions—such as scientists, engineers, soldiers, technicians, diplomats, scholars, and journalists—with a focus on those involved in the strategic domains of cyber, nuclear, maritime, and space.

As discussed earlier, the two governments convene regular discussions through official dialogue mechanisms such as the S&ED (during the Obama administration) and the CDM (during the Trump administration) to address topics related to national security, including nuclear weapons proliferation, space, and cybersecurity. Many of these dialogues originated as Track 2 scholarly discussions that over time became critically important communication channels between academics and government officials on both sides. Track 2 interactions allow the United States and China to engage in a safe environment that is conducive to more free and open dialogue about sensitive topics. Specifically, Track 2 discussions between experts from both countries provide a platform to educate a larger number of interlocutors, identify areas of concern, define norms and vocabulary, identify negotiating positions, explore red lines, and provide sustained intellectual support to government officials involved in Track 1 discussions. Furthermore, Track 2 talks provide a less risky venue for airing controversial proposals and allow for negotiations outside the domestic bureaucracies. In some cases, participants serve as de facto staff or advisers who vet recommendations before passing them to officials.[20] One expert on conflict resolution identified seven specific benefits of Track 2 dialogue:[21]

- *Exploratory function.* Help both sides learn more about each other and understand the interests that inform official positions.
- *Innovation function.* Create a forum to empower elites with additional credibility when proposing policy to officials by granting them an opportunity to vet new ideas with the other side.
- *Legitimization effect.* Help break taboos against negotiations, especially when nonrecognition or a long period of hostility is the backdrop for talks.
- *Accumulation effect.* Build a critical mass of elites on each side who have participated in informal negotiations and can bolster the pro-negotiation camp within their national political arena.
- *Clarification effect.* Help identify and discuss difficult details and sticking points.
- *Preparatory effect.* Allow Track 1 officials to develop mutual familiarity before official talks begin.
- *Latency effect.* Create equitable ideas that, while perhaps not immediately actionable because of conditions on the ground, can be preserved in case a better opportunity arises in the future.

Commenting on the importance of dialogue in managing the U.S.-China relationship, then vice premier Wang Yang stated the following:

> There are different ways of resolving difference and frictions, and dialogue is certainly the most cost-effective means for doing so. The establishment of the high-level, comprehensive dialogue serves the need for peace, development and cooperation of our times and is a sign of the growing maturity of China-U.S. relations. Any time or energy the two countries put into the dialogue is more than worthwhile considering the enormous progress that results there . . . for both sides. . . . The convergence of interests between our two countries has gone beyond many people's imaginations. It is now such that neither of us could afford non-cooperation or even all-out confrontation.[22]

P2P exchange between countries has benefited many nations and improved even some of the most contested bilateral relationships. For example, "cricket diplomacy" between India and Pakistan helped contribute to a better bilateral relationship in 2011–12.[23] Israel and Palestine have likewise conducted a range of P2P activities, including Track 2 dialogues, educational exchanges, visits by scholars to research centers, and civil society exchanges.[24] Though difficult to ascertain the precise impact of these activities, they potentially helped calm tensions and increased mutual understanding—developments that may have deterred violence and conflict. In both cases, P2P, though not a panacea for the discord and tension between the nations involved, contributed to creating a more conducive environment for managing the relationship in a positive way. Both cases are of course quite different from the U.S.-China relationship. Although P2P exchange will not likely dissolve all mutual suspicion that exists between the United States and China, it holds the potential to diminish mistrust, enhance mutual understanding, and ultimately contribute to a more healthy and robust bilateral relationship.

Opportunities for increasing the role of P2P exchange

The following discussion highlights several ways in which P2P exchange could produce greater value for the U.S.-China relationship.

Sustained intellectual support

P2P exchange could play a constructive role in reducing tensions surrounding the range of strategic issues facing the U.S.-China relationship. Coordinated Track 1.5 and 2 dialogues around emerging cyber, space, maritime, and nuclear issues would provide sustained intellectual support for government officials and opportunities to educate and expand the number of qualified interlocutors capable of discussing key issues in both countries. In certain strategic domains, only a limited number of individuals can effectively engage with counterparts in the other country. In order to ensure that a wide range of views, policy options, and considerations are explored, a new and larger cohort of experts must be cultivated and trained to manage critically important aspects of the relationship.

For example, when China joined the World Trade Organization (WTO), its ongoing participation in the Asia-Pacific Economic Cooperation (APEC) had equipped a cadre of Chinese economists and diplomats with the requisite knowledge and skills to facilitate the country's entry into the WTO. This included familiarity with international norms for negotiation, language skills, knowledge of international law, and comprehension of obligations. Without acquiring this expertise, China would have been at a severe disadvantage during the negotiation process. Moreover, without a sufficient number of well-informed and competent trade professionals, it would have been impossible for China to conduct the necessary enforcement to ensure that the nation met its WTO obligations.

Norms, ground rules, and a shared vocabulary

Increased opportunities for dialogue at the Track 1.5 and 2 levels would provide occasions to discuss and establish norms, basic ground rules, and mutually consistent vocabulary that will allow both sides to engage more effectively at the official level on newly emerging areas of strategic concern, such as cybersecurity and space. In both areas, there is little mutual understanding of how the other side views even some of the most fundamental issues, let alone more complex dimensions. Because China and the United States maintain their own doctrines and perspectives within these strategic domains, they must establish basic ground rules and terms for discussing particular topics. Doing so would also help develop an environment in which miscommunications and misunderstandings could be avoided.

For example, during President Xi's state visit to the United States in September 2015, the two presidents announced a new agreement on cyber issues. This outcome represents a step in a positive direction, although possibly only a small one, depending on implementation. The agreement includes measures for China and the United States to avoid engaging in commercial cyberespionage, cooperate in conducting investigations and collecting evidence, identify and endorse norms of behavior in cyberspace, and establish two high-level working groups and a hotline between the two sides.[25] It is interesting to note that one of the main obstacles to reaching this agreement was the fundamental difference in how the countries define and discuss cybertheft. Whereas the United States draws a line between traditional state espionage and corporate theft of intellectual property, Chinese experts and officials see a close link between economic and security-related cyberactivity and allege that Chinese companies, including the telecommunications company Huawei, are the victims of hacking by U.S. state actors like the National Security Agency.[26] This difference in the definition of cybertheft has been a major stumbling block, and the September 2015 agreement signals that progress has been made to align the two perspectives. The agreement followed a series of Track 1.5 and 2 dialogues focused on cybersecurity that had been held over the past several years. P2P exchange and dialogue thus helped lay the groundwork for future negotiations by establishing a mutually consistent vocabulary and set of norms related to the cyber domain.

New networks

More robust P2P engagement on emerging strategic issues would allow for the development of professional working networks between decision-makers, advisers, technicians, and future policymakers involved in these critical domains. Furthermore, dialogue between a broader range of individuals would open up new communication channels and help both sides more effectively navigate complicated security-related issues.

Climate change provides one example of the value of cultivating professional relationships to ensure optimal communication. At one time, Beijing and Washington were in a bitter disagreement over this issue. Today, however, cooperation on climate change has become a highlight in the bilateral relationship and helped advance global efforts to address this challenge. In November 2014, when President Obama visited China, the two countries announced a pathbreaking joint statement on climate change. The consensus and deals made during President Xi's state visit to the United States in September 2015 further injected momentum into global climate negotiations and contributed to the adoption of a new pact at the UN Climate Change Conference in Paris in December.

To a large extent, this progress resulted from increased and more substantive P2P activities. Through the U.S.-China Ten-Year Framework for Cooperation on Energy and Environment, launched in 2008, not only did government officials meet annually to exchange views, but U.S. and Chinese businesses, NGOs, universities, and local government officials also participated via the EcoPartnerships initiative.[27] At the U.S.-China Clean Energy Research Center, established in 2009, experts from the two countries worked together to create new energy technologies to help both societies counter climate change challenges.

As discussed earlier, cybersecurity is one critical area that has benefited and could continue to benefit from coordinated P2P dialogue. Given the lack of relevant knowledge, ability, and experience within both governments, addressing cybersecurity challenges will require input and intellectual support from nongovernmental actors. These private sector actors could provide valuable insights, information, and recommendations that will enable both governments to achieve more productive outcomes. Through this process of inviting private sector agents to contribute to Track 1.5 and 2 dialogues, ground rules and norms that all actors agree on could be established. Finally, there needs to be a more active and broad-based policymaking network created that involves cyber experts and enterprises outside the government. During his September 2015 visit to the United States, President Xi met with business leaders from the information technology sector who were participants in the eighth U.S.-China Internet Industry Forum, including the heads of Microsoft, Apple, and Facebook. Xi called for a constructive dialogue between China and the United States on cyber issues. Arguably, in the area of cybersecurity, P2P can play a key role in creating an ecosystem of experts in both countries, establishing ground rules and a shared vocabulary, and generating the intellectual support that government officials need to be effective in their negotiations.

In early rounds of interaction and discussion, the forums should aim to deal with areas where common ground can most easily be found—for example, maintaining an open, reliable Internet that fosters international trade and individual privacy. After mutual understanding and trust have been built in those areas, discussions could then expand to more sensitive issues of espionage and cyberattacks on critical infrastructure targets.

Obstacles to improving P2P exchange

Both China and the United States recognize the importance of P2P exchange and support a broad range of activities. Therefore, elevating P2P as a tool for addressing the emerging strategic issues that challenge the relationship should be a rather straightforward adjustment. Nonetheless, significant challenges exist that impede, or at least will complicate, efforts to elevate P2P exchange to address more strategic issues.

Societal ties between the United States and China have grown rapidly and are expected to continue to do so in the years to come. For example, between 2009 and 2015, the direct investment from Chinese enterprises into the United States has grown fivefold and created more than 80,000 jobs across the country.[28] It is estimated that Chinese investment in the United States will rise to between $100 billion and $200 billion by 2020, creating 200,000 to 400,000 jobs.[29] This kind of economic activity will require a variety of innovative P2P interactions to reduce cultural misunderstandings and friction. Chinese entrepreneurs may experience conflicts with their American employees over labor rights, management styles, and gender identity, among other issues. Some U.S. politicians continue to cite China as an enemy or at the very least a fierce competitor that must be carefully managed and in some cases thwarted. When ordinary Chinese people hear these types of statements from U.S. business leaders or politicians, it does not help advance bilateral ties. Therefore, P2P exchange should also aim to deepen mutual understanding between ordinary people in both countries and shatter mistaken attitudes about the U.S.-China relationship.

Since normalization in 1978, P2P relations between the United States and China have improved at almost all levels. However, the following obstacles threaten to hinder the further deepening of ties.

Definition of P2P

One challenge is the fact there is no universally accepted definition of what constitutes P2P exchange. As a result, evaluating the impact of activities is difficult. The diplomatic conceptualization of P2P has generally been framed in the context of a broad range of bilateral and multilateral interactions. It can be short term or long term and may range from grassroots outreach programs to widely publicized broadcast efforts to elite-level negotiations that take place alongside traditional diplomacy tracks.

Nicholas Cull, an expert on public diplomacy, divides nontraditional diplomatic activities into five categories: listening, advocacy, cultural diplomacy, exchange diplomacy, and international broadcasting.[30] This suggests a more holistic vision of P2P diplomacy, one that encompasses high-level dialogue, national media, online interaction, NGO outreach programs, and real-world exchanges between countries. While this definition is certainly comprehensive enough to cover the many ways in which P2P is understood, it may be too broad to have any substantive use. Other scholars focus on the semiofficial Track 2 potential of P2P exchanges instead of attempting to qualify the more intangible effects of soft power. Harold Saunders, a former assistant secretary for Near East affairs and the director of international affairs at the Kettering Foundation, carefully differentiates the potential power of Track 2 dialogues to enact policy change from "people-to-people diplomacy where the objective is solely 'getting to know the other side' and deepening personal experiences with one's adversaries (such as [through] student exchanges) rather than finding solutions to problems."[31] In China, P2P has also been defined very broadly, and the term is often used to describe human exchange activities to help promote foreign relations. For many Chinese officials and scholars, P2P could refer to exerting the function of public diplomacy, which is usually conducted by the government to cultivate public opinion in other countries. Previously, in China the phrase "people-to-people diplomacy" was often used to describe public diplomacy activities.

The issue of what precisely P2P consists of is further complicated in the U.S.-China bilateral context because concepts such as soft power, public diplomacy, and P2P diplomacy are understood differently by both nations. On the U.S. side, policymakers are quick to laud the benefits of P2P in "warming" interpersonal relations but tend, as Saunders does, to dismiss its impact in high-level politics. Consequently, P2P tends to be driven by nongovernmental actors. While it may have a large influence on society-to-society interactions, P2P is often disorganized, short term, and restricted to the social rather than the political sphere.

In China, high-level officials have explicitly tied the promotion of P2P activities to the country's foreign policy strategy. Some Chinese scholars assert that P2P should be understood to be one of the "three pillars" of China's foreign policy, alongside mutual political trust and economic and trade cooperation. Both Xi and Liu have quoted the scholar Han Feizi to suggest that P2P diplomacy is important because "state-to-state relations are dependent on the closeness between peoples, while P2P relations are dependent on mutual understanding" (*guozhi jiao zaiyu min xiangqin, min xiangqin zaiyu xin xiangtong*).[32] However, because of the close alliance between P2P and national interests, Chinese P2P efforts have often been viewed critically, if not outright suspiciously, by some U.S. actors as an insidious effort to increase Chinese influence abroad. Similar problems plague U.S. activities in China. Many Chinese are still suspicious of some P2P efforts originated by the U.S. side because they think invisible connections between U.S. NGOs and government agencies exist or that P2P activities might be veiled attempts orchestrated by the U.S. government to foment instability in China.

While P2P programs can warm interstate relations, when their intentions are miscommunicated or misunderstood, they can also contribute to increased antagonism. Differing views of what constitutes P2P, and the resulting difficulty in how to evaluate its success, make it challenging to build consensus between the two countries around how to organize and increase the efficacy of P2P.

Bureaucratic differences

A second obstacle for P2P exchange is that the bureaucratic systems and mechanisms for organizing these activities vary significantly between the two countries. In China, most P2P activities are originally promoted or organized by government agencies, though more and more universities, foundations, and other nonprofit organizations are beginning to play important coordinating roles. In the United States, P2P activities are arranged in a more ad hoc environment, with civil society taking the lead. The fragmented nature of P2P in the United States has its benefits but also produces real problems, such as program repetition, missed opportunities, and an inability to comprehensively evaluate program outcomes. (Similar challenges exist in China but to a lesser degree.) In addition, because institutions operate very differently in both countries, there is a risk that increased engagement may fall short of expectations if Chinese and Americans fail to examine closely their differing assumptions, motives, objectives, professional and educational standards, laws, and regulations—which underscores the need for dialogue and exchanges.[33]

As a result of the different bureaucratic processes, the types of funding streams for P2P activities also differ. With respect to the CPE, on the Chinese side many of the related P2P activities have received government support. On the U.S. side, though the government does financially support a number of high-quality scholarship and fellowship programs, relatively few CPE-originated P2P activities have received direct financial support from the government. Instead, nonprofit organizations, universities, and other nongovernmental entities have sought funding from the private sector and foundations to underwrite the activities.[34]

Value systems

The third potential obstacle, and a simultaneous rationale for more P2P exchange, is profound and consequential disagreements between value systems. A joint study on U.S.-China strategic distrust by Wang Jisi and Kenneth Lieberthal notes that because many Chinese elites "believe that the ultimate goal of the U.S. . . . is to maintain its global hegemony, they conclude that America will seek to constrain or even upset China's rise." The study observes that "America's democracy promotion agenda is understood in China as designed to sabotage the Communist Party's leadership. The leadership therefore actively promotes efforts to guard against the influence of American ideology and U.S. thinking about democracy, human rights, and related issues."[35]

Recently, many American observers criticized the Chinese government's campaign to guard against the influence of Western thought. According to U.S. media reports, in 2013 some of China's leaders categorized Western values as one of several nontraditional threats that must be vigilantly guarded against.[36] In June 2015, the House Committee on Foreign Affairs held a hearing to assess China's influence on academic freedom at U.S. universities. Susan Lawrence, among other American experts, asserted that the Chinese government identifies subjects that are not to be openly discussed in the media or university classrooms, including Western constitutional democracy, neoliberal economics, Western ideas about journalism, and universal values.[37] In early 2015, Chinese universities reportedly were instructed to reduce the number of textbooks that disseminate "misleading" (*cuowude*) Western values in their classrooms.[38] Many Americans who participate in P2P activities worry that if the Chinese government categorizes Western textbooks as a risk to young Chinese minds and a threat to the country, then Western faculty and universities must be seen as even more dangerous. This suspicion of American education is captured in China's draft law on the regulation of foreign NGOs.[39]

Despite long-standing policies to encourage cooperation with international organizations and individuals, some Chinese officials are skeptical of P2P exchange in security-related fields. These leaders would prefer to limit activities to the cultural and other "soft" domains and avoid expanding and organizing engagements to address more substantive issues in the security domain.[40] Another example is the U.S. government's desire to establish and operate more American Cultural Centers in China, which are small institutions commonly given seed funding by a U.S. embassy and operated jointly by U.S. and Chinese universities or by a U.S. embassy or consulate. They provide programing to introduce local populations to a wide range of American culture—similar to the function played by Confucius Institutes that operate across the United States. The U.S. government would like to open and operate more cultural centers but has encountered challenges receiving permission from Chinese authorities. To date, the United States has funded 25 cultural centers on university campuses throughout China. However, currently only 14 are open, with various levels of activity, although more are scheduled to open in the future.

From the Chinese perspective, value-oriented activities conducted by government agencies and some NGOs have been critical instruments of U.S. foreign policy, and American senior officials and members of Congress often openly express criticism of China's value system.[41] "The war of ideas" advanced by a number of high-level U.S. policymakers and NGO practitioners sounds aggressive and threatening to Chinese ears. For example, in 2011, then secretary of state Clinton claimed that the "Chinese system is doomed" during an interview with the *Atlantic*.[42] In the Chinese opinion, the American value system is not universally applicable, while the United States' value-related foreign policy, such as "transforming" the greater Middle East,[43] is costly and could be considered self-defeating. Some Americans tend to view the ideological differences between China and the United States through the "we win and you lose" perspective, which leads to constant Chinese vigilance against American value–based P2P activities.

Moreover, the Chinese side believes that the United States also attempts to restrain certain P2P activities based on concerns over differences in values. In most cases, Confucius Institutes are established jointly through partnerships between U.S. and Chinese universities. Most are autonomously run programs and operate on university campuses. In 2012 a dozen Chinese teachers at Confucius Institutes in the United States were forced to leave due to a U.S. State Department directive on visa regulations. Taylor Reveley, president of the College of William and Mary in Virginia, wrote to the State Department that the policy directive may "inadvertently interfere with the very positive contributions made by Confucius Institutes to higher education in the U.S., as well as to U.S.-China relations more broadly."[44] In May 2015 a Chinese professor from Tianjin University, Zhang Hao, was arrested by the United States on charges of economic espionage. Many Chinese observers believe that Zhang's case might be at most a dispute over intellectual property and that this incident demonstrates the U.S. government's hostility and unfair treatment toward some Chinese studying and working in the United States. In addition, a number of legal obstacles still exist in the United States that impede U.S.-China engagement in sensitive security-related fields, similar to the restrictions that exist in China.

Evaluation metrics

Another major obstacle is the lack of quantifiable data to demonstrate the impact of P2P exchange on the bilateral relationship. The nature of P2P activities—medium-to long-term and geared toward building trust, strengthening relationships, and enhancing mutual understanding—makes it difficult to measure their impact. Evaluating the benefits of P2P exchange is also difficult because outcomes are gradual and incremental. The difficulty of measuring and quantifying the results of P2P exchange presents a key obstacle to convincing policymakers and other leaders in both countries that P2P should be elevated and utilized as a strategic tool, despite the fact that P2P engagement in other areas is at an all-time high.

Lack of resources

A related challenge is the lack of resources dedicated for P2P activities. Coordinating productive P2P activities requires considerable resources. Track 1.5 and 2 dialogues, for example, necessitate that individuals travel and spend time face to face with one another. Because it is difficult to quantify and measure immediate results of P2P interactions, it can be difficult to demonstrate their value to potential funders and secure financial support. As previously mentioned, the U.S. government financially supports a number of high-quality scholarships and public diplomacy programs but does not contribute funding to many of the P2P activities it currently supports in word and action. Most Track 1.5 and 2 dialogues are sponsored by universities, think tanks, and NGOs. Securing additional resources from Congress in order to expand and execute new P2P exchange geared toward strategic issues would be difficult. Securing funding for P2P activities is also a challenge in China. Although the government provides financial support for initiating P2P programs, ensuring their long-term sustainability requires the private sector's involvement.

Political apathy

General apathy in the policymaking community toward the value of P2P is another hurdle that must be overcome in order to shift gears and elevate how P2P is utilized in the bilateral relationship. Many believe that P2P exchange does not serve a strategic purpose and are unwilling to allocate the time and financial investment necessary to sustain regular Track 1.5 and 2 dialogues. Countering this apathy and convincing those in decision-making positions of the strategic role that P2P activity can and should fulfill is an important step toward developing more P2P exchange focused on security-related themes.

Negative perceptions of the other country are also a challenge. Robust P2P activity does not necessarily equate to harmonious bilateral relations and positive mutual perceptions. A 2014 survey by the Pew Research Center found that only 35% of Americans view China favorably, down from over 50% in 2011.[45] In a 2013 survey on U.S.-China security perceptions published jointly by the Carnegie

Endowment for International Peace and the China Strategic Culture Promotion Association, 27% of Chinese government elites regarded the United States as an enemy, and 45% of the general Chinese public viewed the United States as a competitor.[46] Yet while negative attitudes about the other country can serve as an obstacle to P2P activities and reduce their effectiveness, the solution, as the next section will argue, is to conduct more engagement between the people of both nations to enhance mutual understanding—in particular, on issues related to national security.

Recommendations

The previous section considered how definitional differences, government policies, different value systems, lack of resources, the absence of robust metrics, and political apathy threaten to slow or derail gains from P2P exchange and limit opportunities to utilize this mechanism to counter strategic mistrust. In order to move beyond the status quo, both governments must put aside their suspicions and be open to dialogues, workshops, seminars, and travel groups with the broadest array of participants from business, academic, NGO, scientific, media, and other communities that are focused on more strategic issues.

Although U.S. and Chinese leaders often express a desire to cooperate more on key strategic issues and major global challenges, a gap exists between this stated willingness and actual practice. This chapter proposes that an important way to bridge this gap is for senior leadership in both countries to agree to expand P2P exchange and support more Track 1.5 and 2 dialogues on sensitive strategic issues facing the relationship. This is not an easy task, as the preceding discussion makes clear. Orchestrating P2P exchange to build trust around the most sensitive issues will require long-term strategic vision by leaders in both nations. Though this is no doubt a tall order, the risk of continuing along the current path of high-level strategic mistrust is far too great. Actions must be taken today to ensure the future stability of the U.S.-China relationship. Thus, we recommend the following steps to expand P2P exchange to strategic domains.

Educate and increase P2P participants' understanding of the broad context of the U.S.-China relationship and how their specific engagement fits into the big picture

When it comes to many of the most challenging emerging policy issues, such as cybersecurity, space, climate change, energy security, and public health, there exists a lack of knowledge, ability, experience, and personnel in both governments. Many officials are still unfamiliar with the nature, scope, and consequences of these challenges. They also encounter difficulty explaining the complexity of these issues to the public and often default to oversimplified explanations. Meanwhile, some expert participants in P2P exchange do not understand the broad policy implications of their narrow area of expertise. In this proposed new wave of P2P activities focused on addressing security-related issues, it is key to involve a variety of experts, including scientists, educators, soldiers, retired military officers, NGO leaders, public policy experts, politicians, and journalists. Therefore, methods must be developed to educate these interlocutors on the broad political, economic, and security aspects of the issues they deal with in their Track 1.5 and 2 dialogues. By so doing, these individuals will be better equipped to take into consideration how their work contributes to the bilateral relationship. In addition, ensuring that professionals who help shape public opinion are well informed can result in productive second-, third-, and fourth-order effects on the bilateral relationship.

The participation of an increased number of interlocutors on both sides in Track 1.5 and 2 dialogues will help develop a new generation of informed professionals capable of providing advice and intellectual support to both governments and serving as communication channels on important topics. In the future, addressing complex challenges will require more input from nonstate actors. Therefore, a more effective and broader-based policymaking network is needed that involves experts on key emerging issues such as cybersecurity, space, and climate change. A larger, better-informed cohort of P2P participants will help foster new, innovative ideas and recommendations for how to constructively deal with the most pressing issues facing the bilateral relationship. To this end, the U.S. government should allocate more resources to support student exchange and other P2P activities, while the Chinese government should encourage more involvement from the nongovernmental sector in executing P2P activities.

Develop a methodology to evaluate the effectiveness and impact of P2P exchange

The first step in this process is conducting an evaluation to assess the effectiveness of the P2P deliverables and programs created through the CPE and S&ED. The survey could be administered to P2P exchange participants in both forums to evaluate how they view the achievements, obstacles, and potential future opportunities that have been created over the past six years. A series of best practices and lessons learned would be derived from the survey results and adopted to ensure that future P2P activities in strategic domains are executed as effectively as possible. These survey results could then be utilized to develop a sound methodology for evaluating the general effectiveness and impact of P2P exchange across cultural, educational, economic, and other domains. Such an evaluation tool would help shape future activities to be as effective and productive as possible.

Leverage the largely positive but uncoordinated P2P activities occurring at the subnational level to benefit state-to-state relations

As a first step, surveys should be conducted at the U.S. state and Chinese provincial levels to assess the depth and breadth of these exchanges—something akin to the joint National Committee on U.S.-China Relations and Rhodium Group China

Investment Monitor project that assesses Chinese investment on a state-by-state basis.[47] Aggregating this information, which is available but not effectively collated, would produce new perspectives on lessons learned and other insights helpful to improving the role of P2P in the bilateral relationship. In addition, collecting and making available this information would help institutionalize subnational exchanges that often result in positive outcomes in commercial, educational, and cultural spheres.

Invest in more opportunities for student exchange

The key for the future of the bilateral relationship rests in the hands of the next generation of leaders. Therefore, ensuring that future leaders are equipped with the skills to collaborate with each other will keep the most important bilateral relationship in the world on an even keel, and thus should be a key priority for both Washington and Beijing. Both governments should directly invest in and encourage private-sector support for increased and improved student exchange opportunities. In addition, Chinese institutions should learn from the U.S. Foreign Policy Colloquium, run annually by the National Committee on U.S.-China Relations, and seek to help American students studying in China to better understand Chinese policies and policymaking mechanisms.

Conclusion

Early 2017 saw the inauguration of Donald J. Trump as the new president of the United States. On the campaign trail, Mr. Trump took a hardline approach towards China, citing plans to designate the country as a currency manipulator as well as to impose steep tariffs, and to call on China to cease any provocative activity in the South China Sea. In December 2017, the White House published the National Security Strategy Report, labeling China as its main "strategic competitor." The Trump administration quickly declared the decades-long U.S. strategy of engagement with China a failure and began to emphasize "strategic competition" with Beijing. In the domain of P2P exchanges, the Trump administration, citing national security concerns, took measures to curtail Confucius Institutes in the United States, created hurdles for Chinese students aiming to study in the U.S. in the fields of STEM (Science, Technology, Engineering, and Mathematics), and even barred many Chinese scholars from entering the United States.

Given this reality, will the current nature of people-to-people activity be sufficient to further strengthen the U.S.-China bilateral relationship? For example, will Washington and Beijing continue to hold the annual Comprehensive Dialogue Mechanism including the Social and Cultural Dialogue that promotes discussion of key issues facing the bilateral relations and that promotes people-to-people relations? Will U.S. immigration laws hinder the number of Chinese students studying in the United States? Will strategic and economic dialogue take place only among a few top leaders in both governments instead of through a broader approach that also encompasses Track 1.5/2 dialogues? The answers to these questions and others will determine to a large extent the strength of the foundation of the bilateral relationship and its ability to promote new cooperation and to withstand any possible future storms.

Notes

* The views presented in this chapter are entirely the authors' and do not reflect the views of U.S.-China Strong Foundation or Fudan University. The authors would like to thank Elizabeth Chen, Kyle Churchman, Lei Yingdi, Li Zhaoying, Liang Xiaodon, and Justine Ty for their insightful research assistance.

1 William D. Davidson and Joseph V. Montville, "Foreign Policy According to Freud," *Foreign Policy*, no. 45 (1981–82): 145–57.

2 "The U.S.-China Strategic & Economic Dialogue/Consultation on People-to-People Exchange" (remarks at the Joint Opening Session with Vice President Joe Biden, Chinese vice premier Liu Yandong, Chinese vice premier Wang Yang, Secretary of Treasury Jack Lew, and Chinese state councilor Yang Jiechi, Washington, DC, June 23, 2015), www.state.gov/secretary/remarks/2015/06/244120.htm.

3 Liu Yandong, "Cultural Ties That Bind: Liu Yandong," *USA Today*, June 22, 2015, www.usatoday.com/story/opinion/2015/06/22/liu-yandong-vice-premier-china-united-states-people-to-people/29110417.

4 "Top 25 Places of Origin of International Students, 2013/14–2014/15," Institute of International Education, Open Doors Data, www.iie.org/Research-and-Publications/Open-Doors/Data/International-Students/Leading-Places-of-Origin/2013-15.

5 "U.S. Reaches Major Milestone: 100,000 American Students Study in China," 100,000 Strong Foundation, July 10, 2014, http://100kstrong.org/2014/07/11/us-reaches-major-milestone-100000-american-students-study-in-china.

6 "Open Doors Fact Sheet: China," Institute of International Education, 2014.

7 Liu Yandong (speech at the second U.S.-China University Presidents Roundtable Forum, Houston, June 21–22, 2015).

8 The website of the Ministry of Education of the People's Republic of China (PRC) carries lists of approved Chinese educational partnerships with foreign countries. For more on this issue, see Susan V. Lawrence, "Is Academic Freedom Threatened by China's Influence on U.S. Universities?" testimony before the House Committee on Foreign Affairs Subcommittee on Africa, Global Health, Global Human Rights and International Organizations, Washington, DC, June 25, 2015, http://docs.house.gov/meetings/FA/FA16/20150625/103688/HHRG-114-FA16-Wstate-LawrenceS-20150625.pdf.

9 Lawrence, "Is Academic Freedom Threatened?"

10 Liu, "Cultural Ties That Bind."

11 China National Tourism Administration, "Annually Inbound Tourists Report," 2007, www.travelchinaguide.com/tourism/2006statistics/inbound; and China National Tourism Administration, "Annually Inbound Tourists Report," 2014, www.travelchinaguide.com/tourism/2014statistics/inbound.htm.

12 "2014 Market Profile: China," National Travel and Tourism Office, U.S. Department of Commerce, http://travel.trade.gov/outreachpages/download_data_table/2014_China_Market_Profile.pdf.

13 Graham Allison, "Thucydides's Trap Has Been Sprung in the Pacific," *Financial Times*, August 21, 2012, www.t.com/cms/s/0/5d695b5a-ead3-11e1-984b-00144feab49a.html#axzz3rOqvTH4x. Athens and Sparta fought a war due to complicated reasons that extended beyond the rise of Athens. The arrogance of the Athenians intensified the fear of the Spartans, and to some degree the Spartans were overly fearful.

14 "Yang Jiechi's Remarks on the Results of the Presidential Meeting between Xi Jinping and Obama at the Annenberg Estate," Embassy of the PRC in the United States of America, June 9, 2013, www.china-embassy.org/eng/zmgxss/t1049301.htm.

15 Susan V. Lawrence, "U.S.-China Relations: An Overview of Policy Issues," Congressional Research Service, CRS Report for Congress, R41108, August 1, 2013, 10–11, www.fas.org/sgp/crs/row/R41108.pdf; and Congressional-Executive Commission on China, *Annual Report 2014* (Washington, DC, October 9, 2014), www.gpo.gov/fdsys/pkg/CHRG-113hhrg89906/html/CHRG-113hhrg89906.htm.

16 The U.S.-China Strategic and Economic Dialogue upgraded and replaced the Senior Dialogue and Strategic Economic Dialogue started under the George W. Bush administration.

17 "U.S.-China Consultation on People-to-People Exchange (CPE)," U.S. Department of State, Fact Sheet, June 24, 2015, www.state. gov/r/pa/prs/ps/2015/06/244183.htm.

18 "People-to-People Exchange Helps Deepen China-U.S. Relations: Chinese Vice Premier," *Xinhua*, June 25, 2015, http://news.xinhuanet.com/english/2015-06/25/c_134355253.htm; and "The U.S.-China Strategic & Economic Dialogue/Consultation."

19 "U.S.-China Social and Cultural Exchange," Office of the Spokesperson, U.S. Department of State, Washington, DC, September 29, 2017, www.state.gov/r/pa/prs/ps/2017/09/274520.htm; "Joint Statement of China-U.S. Social and Cultural Dialogue," *People.cn*, September 29, 2017, http://world.people.com.cn/n1/2017/0929/c1002-29567251.html.

20 Susan L. Shirk, "The Northeast Asia Cooperation Dialogue: An Experiment in Track II Multilateral Diplomacy," in *Security Cooperation in Northeast Asia: Architecture and Beyond*, ed. T.J. Pempel and Chung-min Lee (New York: Routledge, 2012), 193–211.

21 Nadim N. Rouhana, "Interactive Conflict Resolution: Issues in Theory, Methodology, and Evaluation," in *International Conflict Resolution after the Cold War*, ed. Paul C. Stern and Daniel Druckman (Washington, DC: National Academies Press, 2000), 301, 303, 313–18.

22 Wang Yang, "U.S.-China Dialogue Pays Dividends?" *Wall Street Journal*, June 21, 2015, www.wsj.com/articles/u-s-china-dialogue-pays-dividends-1434922739.

23 Nayeem Showkat, "Cricket Diplomacy between India and Pakistan: A Case Study of Leading National Dailies of Both the Countries (The Hindu & Dawn)," *Journal of Mass Communication and Journalism* 3, no. 1 (2013).

24 Lee Yaniv, "People-to-People Peace Making: The Role of Citizen Diplomacy in the Israeli-Palestinian Conflict," USC Center on Public Diplomacy, May 9, 2013.

25 "President Xi Jinping's State Visit to the United States," White House, Office of the Press Secretary, Fact Sheet, September 25, 2015, www.whitehouse.gov/the-press-office/2015/09/25/fact-sheet-president-xi-jinpings-state-visit-united-states.

26 "China on Frontlines of Cyber Security Threat," *Xinhua*, April 19, 2014, www.chinadaily.com.cn/china/2014-04/19/content_17447912.htm.

27 For more information on this initiative, see the EcoPartnerships program website at https://ecopartnerships.lbl.gov.

28 National Committee on U.S.-China Relations and the Rhodium Group, "New Neighbors: Chinese Investment in the United States by Congressional District," May 2015, 5.

29 Ibid.

30 Nicholas J. Cull, *Public Diplomacy: Lessons from the Past* (Los Angeles: Figueroa Press, 2009).

31 Harold Saunders, "Officials and Citizens in International Relationships: The Dartmouth Conference," in *The Psychodynamics of International Relationships, Volume II: Unofficial Diplomacy at Work*, ed. Vamik D. Volkan, Joseph V. Montville, and Demetrios A. Julius (Lexington: Lexington Books, 1991), 49–50.

32 Xi Jinping, "Zai zhongguo guoji youhao dahui ji zhongguo renmin duiwai youhao xiehui chengli 60 zhounian jinian huodong shang de jianghua" [Speech by H.E. Xi Jinping President of the People's Republic of China at China International Friendship Conference in Commemoration of the 60th Anniversary of the CPAFFC], *Xinhua*, May 15, 2014, http://news.xinhuanet.com/politics/2014-05/15/c_1110712488.htm.

33 Terry Lautz, "The Cultural Relationship," in *Tangled Titans: The United States and China*, ed. David Shambaugh (Plymouth: Rowman & Littlefield Publishers, 2013), 211–34.

34 This is a general description of the situation, but the reverse conditions apply in both countries on a smaller scale as well. For example, the project from which this chapter derived did not receive government funding but received support from the China-U.S. Exchange Foundation based in Hong Kong and the Carnegie Corporation of New York.

35 Kenneth Lieberthal and Wang Jisi, "Addressing U.S.-China Strategic Distrust," Brookings Institution, John L. Thornton China Center Monograph Series, no. 4, March 2012, viii, www.brookings.edu/~/media/research/files/papers/2012/3/30-us-china-lieberthal/0330_ china_lieberthal.pdf.

36 Chris Buckley, "China Takes Aim at Western Ideas," *New York Times*, August 19, 2013, www.nytimes.com/2013/08/20/world/asia/chinas-new-leadership-takes-hard-line-in-secret-memo.html.

37 Lawrence, "Is Academic Freedom Threatened?"

38 "China Vows No Western Values in University Textbooks," *Straits Times*, January 30, 2015, www.straitstimes.com/asia/east-asia/china-vows-no-western-values-in-university-textbooks.

39 National People's Congress of the PRC, "Jingwai fei zhengfu zuzhi guanli fa (zhang an er ci shenyi gao)" [Overseas NGO Management Law (Second Drat)], April 2015, www.npc.gov.cn/npc/xinwen/lfgz/flca/2015-05/05/content_1935666.htm. A translation is available from the China Development Brief, http://chinadevelopmentbrief.cn/articles/cdb-english-translation-of-the-overseas-ngo-management-law-second-drat.

40 Yiwei Wang, "Public Diplomacy and the Rise of Chinese Soft Power," *Annals of the American Academy of Science* 616 (2008): 261.

41 Patrick Sookhdeo and Katharine C. Gorka, *Fighting the Ideological War: Winning Strategies from Communism to Islamism* (McLean: Isaac Publishing, 2012).

42 Jeffrey Goldberg, "Hillary Clinton: Chinese System Is Doomed, Leaders on a 'Fool's Errand,'" *Atlantic*, May 10, 2011, www.theatlantic.com/international/archive/2011/05/hillary-clinton-chinese-system-is-doomed-leaders-on-a-fools-errand/238591.

43 John Lewis Gaddis, "A Grand Strategy of Transformation," *Foreign Policy*, November 10, 2009, http://foreignpolicy.com/2009/11/10/a-grand-strategy-of-transformation.

44 Cheng Yingqi, Luo Wangshu, and Tan Yingzi, "U.S. Targets Confucius Institutes Over Visas," *China Daily* (U.S. edition), May 25, 2012, http://usa.chinadaily.com.cn/china/2012-05/25/content_15382551.htm.

45 Pew Research Center, "Global Opposition to U.S. Surveillance and Drones, But Limited Harm to America's Image: Many in Asia Worry about Conflict with China," July 14, 2014, 26–31, www.pewglobal.org/files/2014/07/2014-07-14-Balance-of-Power.pdf.

46 Carnegie Endowment for International Peace and China Strategic Culture Promotion Association, "U.S.-China Security Perceptions Survey: Findings and Implications," December 12, 2013, 10–11, http://carnegieendowment.org/files/us_china_security_perceptions_report.pdf.

47 For more information, see "China Investment Monitor," Rhodium Group, http://rhg.com/interactive/china-investment-monitor.

6 Sino-U.S. military-to-military relations*

Roy D. Kamphausen with Jessica Drun

EXECUTIVE SUMMARY

This chapter examines U.S.-China military-to-military (mil-mil) relations, providing recommendations on strengthening cooperation in areas of shared interests and presenting mechanisms for managing tensions in areas of conflicting interests.

Main argument

The mil-mil relationship between the United States and China has seen periods of both cooperation and conflict since its inception during the Cold War. While the state of mil-mil relations hinges largely on the overall state of the bilateral relationship, three decades of exchanges have revealed not only the inadvertent risks and shortcomings associated with these exchanges but also their utility and importance in maintaining stability in the Asia-Pacific and safeguarding U.S. interests. At the same time, these interactions have led to a deeper understanding of Chinese interests—and highlighted areas of convergence and divergence with U.S. interests. Acknowledgement of the limitations and differences has paved the way for a more sophisticated mil-mil relationship. Future steps—ones that are modest, incorporate shared goals, and avoid constraints—can contribute to a more effective mil-mil relationship that is optimal for both parties, bringing forth a new paradigm of U.S.-China engagement.

Policy implications

- The Sino-U.S. mil-mil relationship has matured over the years, bringing a heightened awareness of the importance of maintaining the relationship (and more restraint in suspending it) as well as an adaptability to change amid fluctuations in the strategic environment. This emerging adaptability suggests that a window of opportunity exists to foster a more robust mil-mil relationship—one that enhances regional stability and international security.

- Enhancing communication mechanisms between the two sides—for example, in mutually determining the correct mix of mil-mil activities or in clarifying interests to the other party—serves to reduce miscalculations and assuage differences.
- The nature of each country's position vis-à-vis the other, both in the region and in the international system, results in inherently conflicting interests. A realistic approach to the relationship thus must be modest in its expectations.

The dimension of military-to-military (mil-mil) relations is one of the long-standing components of the Sino-U.S. bilateral relationship. In recent years, the relationship between Washington and Beijing has been marked by not only growing cooperation but also increasing competition. Mitigating the effects of spillover from the latter into the former is a key factor in advancing the overall U.S.-China relationship. Consequently, the National Bureau of Asian Research (NBR), in partnership with the Institute for Global Cooperation and Understanding (iGCU) at Peking University, has undertaken a two-year project that seeks to identify challenges within key strategic domains and put forth pragmatic policy recommendations on how to best manage tensions and enhance bilateral relations.

The mil-mil domain is growing ever more consequential in light of recent developments in the Asia-Pacific. Increasing militarization in the region and China's assertion of its claims in the South China Sea through island-building and patrols by military and paramilitary vessels heighten the need for mil-mil contacts as a means of defusing tensions, ensuring stability, and communicating each side's respective objectives and interests to avoid miscalculations. As China's military expands its breadth and reach in the region, and increasingly beyond, addressing the disconnects between the two militaries will become all the more critical in the years to come.

This chapter contributes to the debate over the optimal formulation for a bilateral U.S.-China mil-mil relationship. The topic has been addressed from a variety of perspectives to date. An examination of the existing literature on mil-mil relations finds that there is agreement on the utility of this dimension of the bilateral relationship for risk reduction and conflict management, but that barriers exist and certain limitations are necessary in order to safeguard U.S. capabilities and interests. For instance, Kurt Campbell and Richard Weitz stress—reflecting a general consensus among experts—that conditions for mil-mil exchanges lie largely in the state of the overall bilateral relationship, and thus any expected progress on the mil-mil front must be preceded by improvements in the broader U.S.-China relationship. James Nolan finds that personnel exchanges neither have much operational value nor contribute to trust-building, but nonetheless have benefits for diplomacy and deterrence. Kevin Pollpeter argues for a security management approach to mil-mil relations over a security cooperation one, which would mitigate risks associated with imbalances in transparency and reciprocity in the relationship.[1]

Scholars also note that there are inherent structural and cultural constraints—particularly divergent worldviews and institutional barriers—that must be recognized in order to manage expectations of the relationship and focus on areas with the most room for cooperation. Scott Harold suggests a dual-directional approach to engagement, both top-down and bottom-up, in order to address challenges and raise the cost for China of severing mil-mil ties—as Beijing is wont to do when expressing its discontent with elements of the bilateral relationship. Finally, Christopher Yung calls for increased cooperation on nontraditional security threats as a way of expanding the relationship even further.[2]

Existing studies have framed differences in the U.S.-China mil-mil relationship as fundamentally inconsistent, seeking instead to find lower-common-denominator areas of cooperation, without adequate consideration of Chinese views. This chapter attempts to break new ground in several ways and complements the coauthored chapters in this joint study of strategic domains in U.S.-China relations. While representing U.S. views, the chapter incorporates decades of interactions and discussions with Chinese government and military officials. These perspectives are interwoven into the text of the study—following a similar structure as the coauthored pieces—and are instructive in that they relay both long-held and adaptive views, demonstrating how the mil-mil relationship has evolved.

The chapter first provides an overview of the Sino-U.S. mil-mil relationship since 1989. It then assesses the significance of the mil-mil relationship to overall U.S.-China relations and considers both U.S. interests and U.S. perspectives on Chinese interests. The next section examines the areas of convergence between the two sides' interests and proposes recommendations for increased cooperation. Finally, the chapter identifies areas of divergence and proposes options for mitigating risk and reducing tension.

The evolution of the mil-mil relationship

Historical backdrop

Borne of a plan to take strategic advantage of China's tilt away from the Soviet Union during the Cold War, the early Sino-U.S. mil-mil relationship had essential aspects that served each side's strategic interests: throughout the 1980s, the United States provided cooperative defense programs that supported China's nascent military modernization program, and China's nonsupport of its former Communist ally further isolated the Soviet Union at the end of the Cold War.[3] All in all, the bilateral mil-mil relationship was so successful that this dimension became an important component of the overall relationship in this period.

This phase of the relationship ended in Tiananmen Square in June 1989. Immediately after the crisis, the administration of President George H.W. Bush canceled existing arms sales programs, sent equipment and personnel back to China, and curtailed ongoing training. The relationship lay dormant until 1993, when Assistant Secretary of Defense Charles Freeman's visit to Beijing began the slow movement toward normalization.

Following the restart of mil-mil activities in 1993, the Sino-U.S. relationship hit a snag in 1995–96 when Taiwanese leader Lee Teng-hui's visit to the United States triggered strong reactions from the mainland. In response to what Beijing perceived as pro-independence provocations, the People's Liberation Army (PLA) carried out missile exercises off the northern and southern coasts of Taiwan and large-scale amphibious exercises in the Chinese mainland's coastal areas across from Taiwan. Beijing's moves were interpreted as coercive measures intended to shape the 1996 presidential election in Taipei. The U.S. response, which included the deployment of two U.S. Navy aircraft carriers near the Taiwan Strait, elicited a strong reaction from the PLA.[4]

Tensions declined in the aftermath of the mini-crisis, but two important trends were now evident, and these have informed the development of bilateral mil-mil relations ever since. First, military planners in both China and the United States began to consider that a military crisis over Taiwan might involve direct conflict between the United States and China. In 1995–96 the United States was surprised at the apparent use of kinetic force to achieve political effects. For its part, China was surprised at the level of the U.S. response but encouraged that the United States now understood how seriously it regards moves toward independence in Taiwan.[5] Intelligence activities increased to support operational military planning, and much of the activity and research of the nongovernmental PLA-watching community focused on understanding PLA modernization efforts so as to better inform U.S. policy and operational responses.[6]

However, at a policy level, the approach was much different. Following a return to normalcy in early 1997, the United States began to pursue an approach that can best be characterized as "deter by engagement." The logic of this approach was centered on the idea that if senior PLA leaders fully understood the capabilities of the U.S. military, they would avoid conflict at all costs. It was determined that the best means to convey the power and capabilities of the U.S. Armed Forces would be to demonstrate these capabilities directly during official mil-mil visits by senior PLA visitors to the United States. Thus, between 1997 and 2000, six of seven members of China's top military body—the Central Military Commission—were hosted in the United States for precisely this purpose.[7] The United States sought to engage at a high level so as to deter the possibility of conflict, and thus deter by engagement.[8]

These twin motivations—preparing for conflict while engaging at very high levels so as to avoid this outcome—while not unique to the U.S.-China relationship, form the essential components of the contemporary relationship's mil-mil domain. A third aspect, the role of the U.S. Congress, derives directly from the tension between these two ideas. In the late 1990s, culminating in the National Defense Authorization Act of 2000, Congress showed that it did not agree with the policy of deterring by engagement if the engagement could result in direct or inadvertent assistance to the PLA's own military modernization efforts and in the process threaten Taiwan.

By the late 1990s—with these three factors playing interacting roles in the development of mil-mil relations, at least from a U.S. perspective—other bilateral mil-mil activities, including functional visits and educational exchanges, also saw a sharp increase. By the time President Bill Clinton conducted his historically long nine-day visit to China in June 1998, the mil-mil dimension had developed to the point that it was seen as one of the leading elements of the overall bilateral relationship. However, a mere 11 months later, mil-mil activities once again came to a halt as China responded to the inadvertent, yet inexplicable, NATO bombing of the Chinese embassy in Belgrade, Yugoslavia, on May 8, 1999, by canceling planned activities and putting other ongoing programs on hold.[9] The mil-mil deep freeze continued until late November 1999, when the bans were lifted and activities resumed.[10] By mid-2000 the level of mil-mil activity had nearly returned to pre–Belgrade bombing levels, and by year's end the U.S. chairman of the Joint Chiefs of Staff, General Henry Shelton, had conducted an official visit to China.[11]

After months of close, even dangerous, intercepts of U.S. reconnaissance flights in international airspace above the East and South China Seas in late 2000 and early 2001, a Chinese F-8II jet fighter collided with a propeller-driven U.S. EP-3 surveillance aircraft on April 1, 2001.[12] The Chinese pilot, Lieutenant Commander Wang Wei, was lost and the 24 member crew of the EP-3 conducted an emergency landing on Hainan Island, where they were detained for 11 days. At that point, the new leadership in the U.S. Department of Defense, led by Secretary of Defense Donald Rumsfeld, had come to believe that mil-mil relations were not yielding the expected results in terms of assisting in crisis management, and the United States canceled all exchanges until they could be reviewed and approved. Activities were thereafter conducted in an atmosphere of high scrutiny and tight supervision on the U.S. side. Relations had improved enough by October 2003, however, that Rumsfeld hosted his counterpart General Cao Gangchuan, the first PLA minister of national defense to visit the Pentagon in seven years.[13] Rumsfeld himself visited China as secretary of defense in 2005. During the early period of Robert Gates's tenure as secretary of defense, mil-mil activities increased in quantity and substance, including Gates's own visit to Beijing in late 2007.

Reflecting China's displeasure with the U.S. announcement of a large arms sale to Taiwan in October 2008, the PLA put mil-mil relations on hold again, not restarting them until several months after the Obama administration was in office.[14] Mil-mil relations were also suspended in January 2010 after an announcement of a further arms sale to Taiwan.

Recent developments

Since mil-mil relations were restarted several months after their suspension in January 2010,[15] the type and sophistication of ties have markedly increased. New types of cooperation include Chinese participation in the Rim of the Pacific (RIMPAC) 2014 naval exercise, as well as RIMPAC 2016; a first-ever naval exercise involving cross-deck helicopter landings (2013); and army-army collective training for disaster management in Hawaii (2014), with follow-on reciprocal humanitarian assistance and disaster relief exercises in Haikou and Seattle in 2015. Significantly, the mechanism for notification of major military activities was strengthened in 2015, and an air annex for the rules of behavior for the safety of maritime and air encounters was completed.[16] Moreover, the institution of bilateral army staff talks in June 2015 offers promise of a new mechanism for high-level and strategic dialogue, perhaps taking on more importance with the establishment of a new ground force service in the PLA in January 2016.[17] The number of high-level exchanges in both directions are also at or near an all-time high, perhaps epitomized by the fact that before his retirement in September 2015, U.S. chief of naval operations Jonathan Greenert had met with his counterpart, PLA admiral Wu Shengli, five times in the previous three years.[18] And perhaps portending well for future relations, the two sides have found ways to continue their bilateral relationship, despite existing tensions. For instance, the commander of U.S. Pacific Command (PACOM), Admiral Harry Harris, visited Beijing in November 2015, just days after the USS *Lassen* conducted a freedom of navigation operation in the South China Sea and held high-level meetings with PLA leadership, including the Central Military Commission vice chairman, General Fan Changlong.[19] In previous years, such a visit would have been "postponed" at such a point of tension, which suggests a level of maturity or a new learned ability to manage the tensions in bilateral mil-mil relations.

However, the specter of unpredicted interruptions in the bilateral mil-mil relationship still looms, and a concern about this "go-stop-go" history reflects a number of factors. First, mil-mil engagement has always been closely linked to the overall quality of the bilateral relationship, which has included varying amounts of cooperation and confrontation. Mil-mil relations have not been immune from these broader trends, and indeed in some cases military interactions have themselves been the source of broader bilateral tension. Second, as noted earlier, the institutions in each country that are asked to carry out meaningful mil-mil activities are also the institutions that must, at some level, prepare to conduct military operations against the other if so ordered by national command authorities. This too is not an entirely new phenomenon; certainly in the latter days of the Cold War, U.S. and Soviet forces faced a similar conundrum. But it is worth remembering that both militaries know this problem, and this awareness inevitably affects their interactions. Finally, despite the uncertainties in the political dimensions of the relationship, both sides have shown the ability to adjust. For instance, they eventually adapted to a new environment after Tiananmen in 1989. In addition, the tensions arising from the cross-strait crisis in 1995–96, the bombing of the Chinese embassy in Belgrade in 1999, and the EP-3 crisis of 2001 were mitigated over time, and mil-mil relations moved forward after arms sales announcements without fundamental adjustments to policy in either capital. This suggests a level of durability in the relationship and the promise that current obstacles have at least some possibility of being managed. That a similar go-stop-go pattern can be observed in the U.S. mil-mil relationship with other countries as well (for example, the Philippines and Indonesia), which halt and then later return to productive and consistent relations, further supports the notion that this pattern in the U.S.-China mil-mil relationship can transition to a more consistent approach.

The significance of the mil-mil dimension of U.S.-China relations

Conflict avoidance

Both Washington and Beijing have acknowledged the importance of the U.S.-China relationship for maintaining stability in the Asia-Pacific. Indeed, some have argued that it is the most important bilateral relationship for the 21st century.[20] To that end, stability in the mil-mil dimension is critical for providing crisis stability between the two militaries—clearly both sides want to avoid military tensions or armed conflict because they recognize that conflict would be disastrous for both countries and catastrophic for the region. In order to achieve this end, the United States and China need to mitigate the likelihood of any strategic miscalculations and establish means of de-escalation if a conflict were to arise. Simply put, an effective mil-mil program could contribute to conflict avoidance.

As such, Presidents Barack Obama and Xi Jinping have jointly advocated for a more mature and robust mil-mil relationship between the United States and China. Indeed, at the state visit of President Obama to China in November 2014, the two sides agreed to an agenda of increasing mil-mil confidence-building mechanisms (CBM), including notification of major military activities (with annexes on notification of policy and strategy developments and observation of military exercises) and rules of behavior for the safety of air and maritime encounters (with annexes on terms of reference and rules of behavior for encounters between naval surface vessels).[21] When President Xi visited Washington ten months later in September 2015, the CBM agreements were further enhanced, with new annexes on air-to-air safety and crisis communications, and new work was done on the major military activities agreement. Moreover, Presidents Obama and Xi made friendly statements about each side's contribution to international peacekeeping, suggesting new areas for cooperation.[22]

Risk reduction

Mil-mil engagement can also contribute to risk reduction in the overall bilateral relationship, especially in areas of shared threat and vulnerability. Improved mil-mil relations support and facilitate broader collaborative efforts in counterterrorism, antipiracy, disaster response and relief, and, more recently, climate change mitigation. Collaboration between the United States and China can help ensure stability and prosperity in the Asia-Pacific and offers the promise of the provision of public goods for the shared benefit of all in the region.

Management of tensions

An effective mil-mil relationship can manage tensions over issues on which the two sides do not agree and cannot make concessions, but which they need the other side to at least understand. For example, the United States has critically important alliance relationships in the Asia-Pacific that cannot be sacrificed for improved U.S.-China relations. An example of managing tensions in this regard was the suggestion by a senior adviser to this project that China was willing to engage in trilateral dialogues on a variety of security topics in a "United States + Asian ally + China" formulation. On the Chinese side, Beijing affirms its sovereign right to "rise" and pursue national security goals—such as defense of sovereignty and territorial integrity—that contribute to modernization and development within the current window of opportunity. Beijing often views U.S. actions in the region that appear to endanger these goals as part of a concerted containment policy to prevent China from attaining its development efforts. Thus, U.S. actions and statements that reassure Beijing on this point serve broader purposes of managing tension.

This reality of conflicting national interests is compounded by misperceptions and unilateral moves that have largely exacerbated existing distrust in U.S.-China relations. The Obama administration's Rebalance to Asia is a high priority to Washington. The rebalance, however, is viewed by Beijing as primarily military focused, not least due to perceptions of increased U.S. military activities in the Chinese periphery. Conversely, the United States is wary of China's deployment of its military, coast guard, and other security services in the South China Sea and elsewhere—apparently to pursue changes in the status quo to favor Chinese interests—which both threatens U.S. leadership in the region and affects perceptions of U.S. commitment among regional allies. In the absence of real conflict, the usefulness of the United States' unmatched military power in East Asia is potentially limited. It is worth noting, however, that Washington's commitment to allies and security partners remains firm, and if called on, the U.S. Armed Forces would execute contingency plans in defense of those relationships.

Enhanced mil-mil contacts can reduce the risk of miscalculation through the confidence building that declining security tensions might bring. Neither side wants to engage in a war, given fiscal constraints and high personnel and recapitulation costs, as well as the untold impact on each country and the region as a whole. A U.S.-China conflict would impose unimaginably high costs and prove disastrous for not only the two countries involved but the entire Asia-Pacific.

Interests and challenges in mil-mil relations

The U.S.-China relationship faces numerous challenges that are grounded in the very nature of the dynamic between the two countries. The United States is the established power, and China is the rising power. Their military relationship reflects the challenges posed by a power transition. Although the two militaries are not actively engaged in competition, planners on both sides are considering such possibilities. To be sure, the two militaries cannot change this core dynamic, but when they interact this reality makes their engagement fraught with more consequence than might be fair or realistic.

Managing security challenges

The United States' principal interests in effective U.S.-China mil-mil relations are to avoid conflict, reduce risk, and manage existing and emerging security challenges in ways that avoid security dilemma outcomes and do not undermine the United States' prerogatives or military posture, nor limit potential future opportunities in the Asia-Pacific.[23] Achieving these goals would be a substantive contribution to the broader bilateral relationship. Moreover, it is imperative that the United States engage in mil-mil activities with China because of how consequential both countries' militaries are; for Washington to do otherwise would be destabilizing in the region and strongly opposed by friends and adversaries alike.

The United States perceives that China has similar interests in conflict avoidance, risk reduction, and tension management but expresses these goals in somewhat different terms. For instance, Chinese counterparts in this project have emphasized that the proper framework for managing bilateral issues would be under the rubric of "building a new type of major-power relations" (*xinxing daguo guanxi*). In the process, they emphasize the framework for addressing the issues as much as, or even more than, the outcomes themselves.

Moreover, the United States fully understands that China firmly opposes U.S. military operations in the air and sea off China's coast but outside its territorial waters. The United States hears Chinese assertions that these acts are constituent elements of a strategy to contain China, but it strongly believes that this Chinese perception is belied by more than 40 years—and six presidential administrations—of policy and practice. Finally, U.S. leaders wonder whether China's historically defensive national security orientation—and the doctrine, disposition, and development that support such an orientation—might be changing as new activities (e.g., land reclamation) are observed and new weapons systems (e.g., anti-ship ballistic missiles) come online.

Improving the overall bilateral relationship

A second U.S. interest is to see positive improvement in the bilateral mil-mil relationship in ways that do not diminish or weaken U.S. alliance relationships. To be sure, the principal purpose of mil-mil engagement is as a means of addressing bilateral issues in ways that avoid conflict, reduce risk, or manage tensions. However, closely related is whether and how those means contribute to the strengthening of U.S. alliances—or conversely, avoid the diminution of these important relationships. For example, intensified Chinese claims and actions in the East and South China Seas might conflict both with U.S. interests in ensuring freedom of navigation and protecting sea lines of communication and with U.S. efforts to assure allies and reduce regional tensions.

The United States' perceptions of Chinese views of U.S. alliances are informed by the overtly negative statements offered by the Chinese side. Chinese interlocutors in this project frequently asserted that the United States overemphasizes and is overly committed to its allies, that its nonsupport for a particular side's claims in disputed areas is de facto support for the U.S. ally's claims, and that a strong United States emboldens weaker allies in their relationships with China. To be sure, the ways in which alliances have historically been diverted from their intent, such as through entanglement and abandonment, can be found at times in U.S. alliances in Asia. But alliance management is art, not science, and the U.S. side perceives that Chinese judgments about how the United States interacts with its allies overestimate the degree to which these exchanges are China focused, underestimate the costs to maintaining the relationships, and seriously undervalue the contributions of the alliance relationships to regional stability more generally.

Reducing mistrust

A third U.S. interest is in reducing the high levels of mistrust between the two militaries, but this is an enabling interest that serves to support the achievement of the larger interests. The goal of reducing mistrust stems from the complicated bilateral history of military interactions, which has experienced numerous low points. As described earlier, the abrupt termination of cooperative defense programs following the June 4 incident in 1989, the United States' accidental bombing of the Chinese embassy in Belgrade in May 1999, and the EP-3 collision in April 2001 have weighed heavily on the Sino-U.S. military relationship, as have more recent events, such as the ongoing U.S. military presence in China's exclusive economic zone. These incidents have increased Chinese wariness of military engagement with the United States, not least because they raise questions of U.S. intent toward China.

The United States also harbors mistrust, but the origins of this mistrust are different. The United States sees its own World War II and postwar security commitments as creating the security environment in which unprecedented economic prosperity in Asia—including in China—occurred. This view is deeply embedded within the consciousness of the "broad middle" of U.S. foreign policy toward Asia. Thus, challenges to the benign hegemonic role that the United States has played, or claims to have played, create mistrust on the U.S. side because they suggest that fundamental change is in order that could put at risk enduring U.S. policy and commitment in the region. Moreover, U.S. leaders perceive that China is pursuing changes to the status quo in incremental, below-the-radar ways—so-called salami-slicing tactics—that preclude direct military responses. The United States worries that such moves serve to undermine its credibility in the region, particularly to vested allies and partners.

It should be noted, however, that mistrust is not *ipso facto* an impediment to an enhanced mil-mil relationship. In fact, both sides acknowledge that trust is not a necessary precondition and can be established as the relationship progresses. One of China's leading security experts, Yan Xuetong, has argued that "it is not even clear what mutual trust between nations means. There are countless examples throughout history of cooperation between major powers that lacked any of this so-called mutual trust. In fact, the lack of trust has been the norm in successful international relationships."[24] Indeed, as Nolan has noted, by a wide margin, U.S. military leaders do not trust their counterparts.[25]

Advancing cooperation on the global stage

A fourth, more limited interest lies in advancing cooperation on shared global security issues, with the Gulf of Aden patrols serving as a notable example. Such an interest does not suggest that the United States regards a "G-2" arrangement as either optimal or desirable. What it does suggest is that the two great powers have militaries with highly complementary capabilities, which, if organized effectively, might make useful contributions to the global good of international security. The challenge, of course, is that each side tends to regard security engagement with the other primarily through the prism of its impact on bilateral relations, and this nips in the bud many potential collaborative endeavors with broader potential benefits.

Even so, the United States perceives that such shared global security interests are of growing importance to China but are not necessarily of greatest consequence. In part, this is related to the fact that the global dimensions of China's military modernization are still only nascent. Additionally, China has endured much criticism for its unilateral military activities outside Asia—for example, the development of bases at ports in the western Indian Ocean and its activities in Africa—and hardly wants to invite more criticism. The United States also perceives that Chinese concerns about nonintervention still play a strong role in arguing against out-of-region deployments of the PLA to deal with security issues.[26]

Managing domestic constraints

Finally, the United States must manage domestic constraints in conducting mil-mil relations, particularly those imposed by the U.S. Congress. The National Defense Authorization Act of 2000 (as amended in 2010) limits the types of operational engagements that the United State can pursue between the U.S. military and the PLA, unless the secretary of defense judges the risk of exposure to be manageable. Congress maintains keen oversight of Sino-U.S. military contacts in order to ensure adherence to the act, and for a variety of reasons the Department of Defense must be responsive to congressional concerns.

The U.S. side perceives that China regards congressional involvement as a large impediment to bilateral mil-mil relations moving forward. This judgment has changed over time, evolving from a point in which the PLA viewed congressional engagement as something to be avoided or circumvented to a more subtle contemporary position. This trend suggests that any U.S. administration should strive to more effectively manage Congress rather than resort to blaming congressional oversight for failure to move ahead in the mil-mil relationship.

Areas of convergence in the mil-mil dimension

Setting realistic expectations

A common thread that has emerged from experiences in carrying out mil-mil programs, as well as numerous interviews conducted with senior officers and policymakers on both sides, is that the optimal mil-mil program must recognize the aforementioned challenges and thereby avoid some of the more dramatic swings in the relationship. This necessitates—and both sides have argued for—modest steps, despite the fact that the mil-mil relationship is already more than 30 years old. The first area of convergence is this shared interest in moving mil-mil engagement forward while keeping expectations modest.

Demonstrating the value of an enduring mil-mil relationship

A second area of convergence is the judgment that cancelation of mil-mil activities to demonstrate displeasure with policy decisions or military developments by the other side is an approach that has outlived its utility. As noted earlier, both parties have engaged in this practice in the past. It is precisely because both sides perceived the costs of canceling mil-mil to be low that such an approach was so often employed. Mercifully, both sides are realizing that setting a low bar for suspending engagement serves neither country's interests, nor for that matter the interests of the region, and a higher standard—no cancelations—is now more generally accepted. Indeed, after the most recent U.S. decision to sell a package of weapons to Taiwan, China chose not to cancel mil-mil activities, which is a sign of progress.[27]

Establishing parameters for the U.S.-China relationship

A third area of convergence is that both countries share an interest in defining and delimiting what the new great-power relationship between the United States and China will become in terms of mil-mil engagement. This includes several dimensions. The first is declaratory and centers on the objectives for what the relationship might become, whether it results in a fourth Sino-U.S. communiqué on the emerging relationship or is defined progressively by presidents after bilateral visits. A second dimension of such an effort is to clarify the intentions each state has for the Asia-Pacific. China desires that the United States continue to avow that it does not seek to contain China's rise and that it will respect China's sovereignty, integrity, and system. The United States, for its part, among other things, desires to hear that China does not seek the end of U.S. military presence in the region, that U.S. relationships with allies and strong partners (including Taiwan) will not be threatened, and that freedom of operations in international air and sea are guaranteed. A final aspect of this area of convergence is to discuss what the two militaries might usefully accomplish together that will strengthen the existing international order.

Determining an appropriate set of mil-mil activities

A fourth area of convergence is both sides' efforts to find a mix of mil-mil activities that will help define an appropriate new great-power relationship. Whether through raising the level of participants from the military side in the annual Strategic and Economic Dialogue, building on the newly established army-army staff talks, enhancing existing strategic dialogues, increasing personnel exchanges, or other measures, there are many opportunities.

In some respects, the agreements on mil-mil CBMs reached during the last two presidential visits are a template for the way ahead in finding the right set of mil-mil activities. These CBMs address major concerns on each side, including

China's concerns about the U.S. military's close proximity to the Chinese coast and the United States' concerns about the safe operations of its aircraft and ships anywhere, but especially when they are close to those of the PLA. They also address both countries' desire to know more about the policy and operations of the other.

However, these are really just very basic first steps. Indeed, the CBM agreements indicate that each country still judges success by the limited ways in which it "gets what it wants"—the epitome of a self-referential relationship—and not by whether some greater good is accomplished. Ultimately, effective mil-mil relations may have only a limited effect on resolving the core political and security concerns that the United States and China have with one another—and this might be the wrong metric by which to judge the relationship anyway. The structural challenge embedded in the engagement of a rising and an established power simply cannot be solved through mil-mil activities alone. The quality and improvements in the trading relationship, the development of even more enhanced diplomatic collaboration on global foreign policy challenges, and the deepening of people-to-people ties also play important roles in managing this process of power transition.

Future steps

Looking ahead, the development of a collaborative agenda that delivers security benefits on a range of issues could both increase security and strengthen the relationship in important ways. That said, these types of activities almost certainly should begin outside Asia. The antipiracy exercise in the Gulf of Aden provides an interesting template for consideration: a common threat in a geographic area that is unchallenged between the two countries, poses relatively low lethal risk, and involves no core interests. But whether other such areas for collaboration exist—or whether the Gulf of Aden antipiracy exercise was a one-off opportunity—remains to be seen. The two sides' commitment to enhancing peacekeeping efforts certainly suggests a new area of exploration. There thus seems to be scope for the United States and China to develop a framework of mil-mil engagement through activities that avoid each other's important constraints and deal with existing challenges, while emphasizing those actions that increase regional and global security.

Areas of divergence and mechanisms for managing tensions

The Chinese side believes that U.S. congressional oversight, the U.S. military's reconnaissance operations in the international airspace off China's east coast, the United States' alliances in Asia, and U.S. arms sales to Taiwan pose obstacles to the smooth development of the mil-mil relationship. The U.S. side assesses that China's support for the North Korean regime, pressure on Taiwan, and unclear territorial intentions in the maritime space of the Asian littoral are areas of divergence. Several suggestions follow for managing and reducing tensions in these areas.

Involve Congress

The United States ought to continue emphasizing Congress's relevant role; this branch of government cannot be dismissed simply because its inputs are not desired. But more importantly, active engagement with Capitol Hill during mil-mil exchanges ought to increase. Key members of Congress and their staff ought to be brought into the process more than is currently desired, despite the complications that such efforts might bring. While congressional staff have ample opportunities to visit China, consideration should be given to encouraging their active involvement in regular mil-mil activities. Potential options include congressional representation at the Defense Consultative Talks, staff participation in major mil-mil exercises, more regular Armed Services Committee engagement with the process, and even participation by counterparts in the National People's Congress. When rejecting a mil-mil activity, the Department of Defense ought to give a merit-based reason rather than using Congress as an excuse.

Consider changes in surveillance patterns

The long-standing nature of Chinese objections to U.S. reconnaissance and surveillance to date has only considered the Chinese perspective. In short, the operations are categorized as "unfriendly" because they occur near China and are assumed to "target" Chinese capabilities and intentions. In this regard, the Chinese side has often asked the United States how it would feel if Chinese ships and planes operated 13 nautical miles off California's coast, just outside U.S. territorial waters.[28] This line of questioning implies that the United States only engages in such activities because it can. The typical response by senior U.S. leaders—that while the United States would not like such a development, it would not object as long as China adhered to customary international law—has not proved persuasive to Chinese counterparts. To be sure, a change in surveillance patterns by the United States merits consideration because of ongoing Chinese concerns, although there are inherent risks with giving up a right according to customary international law. But for the U.S. side to even brook such considerations, acknowledgment from China of the stabilizing effects of good information on the effective functioning of a regional security system would be constructive.

Pursue trilateral security dialogues

U.S. alliance relationships in the Asia-Pacific are an integral element of the security fabric of the region. Though costing considerable resources and commitment and requiring extraordinary levels of policy attention by U.S. leaders, these alliances serve important security goals and pave the way for enhanced economic and trading partnerships. China has no comparable set of relationships. The Chinese perception that U.S. alliances are primarily about achieving containment of China is unnecessarily limited in perspective, and China's actions to weaken these alliances are almost making themselves a self-fulfilling prophecy. Indeed, they only reinforce the notion that the alliances are intended to limit China. A suggestion that emerged from project discussions about engaging in a variety of trilateral security dialogues with the United States and its allies merits serious consideration. The potential benefits from dispelling misperceptions about intent—perhaps by sharing information about the costs of alliance management and suggesting real ways in which the network of alliances contributes to regional stability—are huge.[29]

Address common challenges

Over the longer term, the Sino-U.S. mil-mil relationship will become more durable and effective when it serves to strengthen regional and global security, even as it addresses common challenges that both countries face or emerging international security challenges. An example of a common challenge with implications for regional and global security involves crisis scenarios in North Korea. Each side has common policy interests in the denuclearization of the Korean Peninsula, even if timelines vary. But there has been little discussion or de-confliction regarding crisis scenarios involving regime viability—and ultimately the security of strategic sites in the North. It is not hard to imagine a situation in which special operations forces from both the United States and China are operating in North Korea during a crisis in uncoordinated ways that put at risk the safety and security of each force and the achievement of their broader security goals. Project advisers from both countries suggested caution in making a recommendation for mil-mil engagement on this front. They noted high levels of political and strategic uncertainty surrounding such an approach within China, in the bilateral China–North Korea relationship, and potentially among U.S. allies as well. These are worthy concerns that argue for caution and constraint. Yet it is noteworthy that the early period of Sino-U.S. mil-mil engagement was fraught with strategic uncertainty as well, and the U.S. military and the PLA were able to find sufficient common ground to enable the development of a mil-mil relationship.

An example of emerging security challenges includes a consideration of either space or cyberspace and possible interactions with nuclear strategic security.[30] While such an approach involves issues that are broader than the mil-mil dimension, there are essential military components that make mil-mil engagement on these issues both appropriate and potentially productive. A further example of cooperation on emerging security challenges would be enhanced collaboration on humanitarian assistance and disaster relief. To be sure, natural disasters are not new, and the Asia-Pacific has long suffered the effects of such disasters to a much greater degree than other regions.[31] What is somewhat new is the prospect for collaboration. The U.S. and Chinese militaries have complementary capabilities. For example, U.S. Air Force lift capabilities could be used to deploy Chinese heavy equipment to disaster-stricken locations.

Conclusion

Elements of cooperation and competition have been inherent in the Sino-U.S. relationship since its inception in the early 1980s. Moreover, the history of the relationship reveals that political dimensions have all along interacted with military operational dimensions in ways that complicate the effective implementation of a mil-mil program. In part, this reflects the natural dynamic of two great powers that do not always have common interests but are not committed adversaries. And to be sure, suggesting that "all would be well" if only the political constraints were to be removed is wishful thinking; rather, the complexities of the Sino-U.S. mil-mil relationship are what make it challenging, but what also introduce opportunities.

This chapter argues that there are indeed areas of convergence in the relationship, including having modest expectations and giving mutual assurances that neither side will arbitrarily cancel mil-mil activities or freeze out this dimension more generally. The sides also converge in assessing that, in an era in which China's rise has achieved certain impressive effects, continued work—at the most senior policy levels all the way down to tactical military engagements—must be undertaken to better understand the dynamics of this evolving relationship in a new period. The two sides also agree that continuing effort must be made to find the optimal mix of mil-mil activities to better define the great-power relationship in the new era. This chapter proposes options for developing decision-making processes that would help in this process. All in all, these areas of convergence present opportunities for strengthening the overall bilateral relationship.

This chapter also identifies areas of divergence, which are often sources of tension. Of note, the Chinese side highlights how the degree to which international media emphasize the metanarrative of tension between a rising and an established power serves to color all interactions. The facts, however, suggest that the two militaries are less constrained by this metanarrative, and several data points in the chapter indicate that an adjustment is underway. For instance, U.S. PACOM commander Admiral Harry Harris and U.S. Pacific Fleet commander Admiral Scott Swift proceeded with their visits to China in November 2015, even after the USS *Lassen* conducted a freedom-of-navigation action in the South China Sea in late October. Their decision to execute preplanned activities reflects a level of maturity that might not have existed in previous years. The latter part of 2016 saw the continuation and expansion of mil-mil activities, including visits to China by Chief of Naval Operations Admiral John Richardson and Army Chief of Staff General Mark Milley, as well as China's participation in RIMPAC 2016.

Notwithstanding, the election of U.S. president Donald Trump in November 2016 further complicates an already complex U.S.-China relationship. The Trump administration has now declared the decade-long, bipartisan engagement strategy towards China a "failure," and yet it remains uncertain what a kind of new framework Washington will adopt. And it remains likewise unclear if necessary attention will be paid to ensuring positive momentum on the mil-mil front.

A central finding of this chapter is that mil-mil has reached a new level of maturity, enabling it to weather temporal challenges and avoid disruptions. An announcement of a decision by the Trump administration to make large arms sales to Taiwan, for example, would be an early test of this finding.

It can be argued that continuing and advancing the U.S.-China mil-mil relationship is conducive to both the administration's broader policy objectives and U.S.

interests in the Asia-Pacific. The Trump administration has touted the importance of revitalizing the U.S. economy. Stability in the Asia-Pacific region supports this end, given the amount of global trade passing through vital waterways and the growing economic clout of Asian countries. Sustained mil-mil engagements can contribute greatly to this end through the creation and use of mechanisms to manage tensions and prevent conflict escalation, while also reassuring allies about enduring U.S. commitment to the region.

Ultimately, this chapter finds that the key to developing a more effective mil-mil relationship will be to move beyond the type of relationship defined by the satisfaction of each party with direct exchanges to a new paradigm in which Sino-U.S. mil-mil engagement makes real contributions to regional and global security. In many respects, such a development will help define how the two great powers interact in the mil-mil domain going forward.

Notes

* This chapter presents the personal views of the authors.

1 Kurt Campbell and Richard Weitz, "The Limits of U.S.-China Military Cooperation: Lessons from 1995–1999," *Washington Quarterly* 29, no. 1 (2005–6): 169–86; James P. Nolan, "Why Can't We Be Friends? Assessing the Operational Value of Engaging PLA Leadership," *Asia Policy*, no. 20 (2015): 45–79; and Kevin Pollpeter, *U.S.-China Security Management: Assessing the Military-to-Military Relationship* (Santa Monica: RAND Corporation, 2004).

2 Scott W. Harold, "Expanding Contacts to Enhance Durability: A Strategy for Improving U.S.-China Military-to-Military Relations," *Asia Policy*, no. 16, (2013): 103–37; and Christopher D. Yung, "Continuity and Change in Sino-U.S. Military-to-Military Relations," in *Conflict and Cooperation in Sino-U.S. Relations: Change and Continuity, Causes and Cures*, ed. Jean-Marc F. Blanchard and Simon Shen (New York: Routledge, 2015).

3 The United States sold torpedoes and large-caliber ammunition, provided artillery firefinder radar, and upgraded the avionics of Chinese fighter aircraft. The United States also sold the civilian equivalent of the UH-60 Blackhawk helicopter to China via a direct commercial sales program. Kerry B. Dumbaugh and Richard F. Grimmett, "U.S. Arms Sales to China," Congressional Research Service, Report, no. 85–138 F, July 8, 1985, 41, www.disam.dsca.mil/pubs/Vol%208-1/Dumbaugh%20&%20Grimmett.pdf.

4 Richard C. Bush, *Untying the Knot: Making Peace in the Taiwan Strait* (Washington, DC: Brookings Institution Press, 2005), 183.

5 A PLA intelligence officer stated in 1998 that the Chinese side "was glad the United States had gotten the message." Author Interview, Boston, September 1998.

6 Roy D. Kamphausen, "Developments and Digressions in PLA Studies Since 1989" (unpublished conference paper, 2006).

7 Shirley A. Kan, "U.S.-China Military Contacts: Issues for Congress," Congressional Research Service, CRS Report for Congress, RL32496, October 27, 2014, 57–64.

8 Campbell and Weitz, "The Limits of U.S.-China Military Cooperation," 169–70.

9 Kan, "U.S.-China Military Contacts," 61.

10 Demonstrating the interconnected relationship between mil-mil ties and the overall bilateral relationship, mil-mil ties were restored once the United States and China struck their bilateral deal as part of China's accession to the World Trade Organization.

11 Kan, "U.S.-China Military Contacts," 62–64.

12 Shirley Kan et al., "China-U.S. Aircraft Collision Incident of April 2001: Assessments and Policy Implications," Congressional Research Service, CRS Report for Congress, RL30946, October 10, 2001, 14.

13 "Cao Gangchuan Meets with Rumsfeld," *China Daily*, October 29, 2003, www.china daily.com.cn/en/doc/2003-10/29/content_276702. htm; and "China's Military Diplomacy in 2003," China Internet Information Center, 2003, www.china.org.cn/english/en-shuzi 2004/dwgx/dw-js.htm. A veteran of the 1980s period of deep engagement, General Cao had been to the artillery training programs at Fort Sill, Oklahoma.

14 "U.S., China to Resume Military Contacts," Voice of America, November 2, 2009, http://m.voanews.com/a/a-13-2009-07-28-voa45-68819637/413372.html.

15 "U.S. and China Resume Military Ties," *BBC*, September 29, 2010, www.bbc.com/ news/world-us-canada-11437758.

16 Zhou Bo, "2015 Sino-U.S. Military Relationship and Beyond," *China-U.S. Focus*, January 8, 2016; and U.S. Department of Defense, *Military and Security Developments Involving the People's Republic of China 2015* (Washington, DC, 2015), 75.

17 Li Bao, "U.S., China to Establish Military Dialogue," *Voice of America*, June 13, 2015, www.voanews.com/content/united-states-china-sign-deal-on-military-dialogue/2820 468.html; and Dean Cheng, "China's Big Military Reforms," *Daily Signal*, January 11, 2016, http://dailysignal.com/2016/01/11/chinas-big-military-reforms.

18 In March 2016, Admiral (retired) Greenert assumed the position of John M. Shalikash-vili Chair in National Security Studies at NBR.

19 Jane Perlez, "U.S. Admiral, in Beijing, Defends Patrols in the South China Sea," *New York Times*, November 3, 2015.

20 "The Summit," *Economist*, June 8, 2013, www.economist.com/news/leaders/21579003-barack-obama-and-xi-jinping-have-chance-recast-centurys-most-important-bilateral; "Xi's U.S. Visit Clear Sign of China's Commitment to Cooperation—Expert," *Global Times*, September 8, 2015, www.globaltimes.cn/content/943246.shtml; and "Kirk, U.S.-China Working Group Emphasize Importance of U.S. China Bilateral Relationship," Mark Kirk, U.S. Senate website, November 20, 2014, www.kirk.senate.gov/?p=press_ release&id=1252. It is noteworthy that as a representative Kirk co-founded the House of Representatives' U.S.-China Working Group in 2005.

21 "President Obama's Visit to China," White House, Office of the Press Secretary, Fact Sheet, November 11, 2014, www.whitehouse. gov/the-press-office/2014/11/11/fact-sheet-president-obama-s-visit-china.

22 "President Xi Jinping's State Visit to the United States," White House, Office of the Press Secretary, Fact Sheet, September 25, 2015, https://www.whitehouse.gov/the-press-office/2015/09/25/fact-sheet-president-xi-jinpings-state-visit-united-states.

23 U.S. Department of Defense, *Military and Security Developments Involving the People's Republic of China 2015*, 63.

24 Yan Xuetong, "The Problem of 'Mutual Trust'," *New York Times*, November 15, 2012.

25 Nolan, "Why Can't We Be Friends?"

26 Mathieu Duchâtel, Oliver Bräuner, and Zhou Hang, "Protecting China's Overseas Interests: The Slow Shift Away from Non-interference," *SIPRI Policy Paper*, June 2014, http:// books.sipri.org/files/PP/SIPRIPP41.pdf.

27 It is notable, however, that China has registered its displeasure through alternative means—that is, by threatening sanctions on the U.S. companies that manufacture the equipment and materials being provided to Taiwan. For more on this development, see Bo, "2015 Sino-U.S. Military Relationship and Beyond."

28 The issue is no longer hypothetical.

29 The regional response to the 2004 Boxing Day tsunami is an excellent example of how U.S. alliances, and the patterns of interaction that flow from those relationships, were integral to the international community's swift and effective response to that enormous natural disaster.

30 NBR is in the process of exploring these issues from a multilateral perspective, and so a U.S.-China-specific dimension might bear useful fruit. The project seeks to develop a common lexicon of terms and concepts regarding how space and cyberspace interact

with nuclear strategic stability. The project further examines the impacts on escalation, resilience, extended deterrence, and other strategic concepts through the prisms of space and cyberspace.
31 Roy D. Kamphausen, "Non-Traditional Security Challenges in the Asia-Pacific Region and Implications for Taiwan," Ministry of Defense (Taiwan), Defense Security Brief, no. 2, April 2012.

7 Sino-U.S. military relations*

Interests, challenges, and solutions

Xu Hui with Yu Ying

EXECUTIVE SUMMARY

The Sino-U.S. relationship is regarded as one of the most significant bilateral ties in today's world, but so far no clear definition has emerged for explaining the military-to-military relations of this unique and complex bilateral relationship. What is the nature of the Sino-U.S. military relationship? What position does it occupy in overall bilateral ties? What incentives are there to advance military-to-military relations? And what are the challenges facing Sino-U.S. military-to-military relations? This chapter presents an analysis focusing on these questions, and offers suggestions on ways to improve bilateral military ties and build a stable and healthy Sino-U.S. military relationship.

Main argument

Since the end of the Cold War, Sino-U.S. military relations have passed through multiple evolutions and witnessed advancements and setbacks, as well as conflict and cooperation. The two sides should realize that the advancement of bilateral military ties is conducive to building a Sino-U.S. relationship based on coordination, cooperation, and stability, as well as establishing mutual trust for the maintenance of regional peace and stability. This is not only the motivation to develop the bilateral relationship, but is also in line with U.S. national interest. To resolve conflicts and advance relations, the two militaries should adopt effective measures to boost mutual trust, enhance crisis prevention and management mechanisms as a means to achieve the goal of developing a healthy and stable bilateral military relationship.

Policy implications

• The conflict and divergence between the two militaries mainly lies in the lack of strategic mutual trust. Therefore, the key to developing bilateral military ties is to take effective measures to build mutual trust. To this end, the United States should view the normal evolution of Chinese military power for purposes of legitimate national defense in an appropriate manner. In particular, it should not use the issue of military transparency as a tool to retain its predominant position and distort the image of China. Rather, the United States should squarely acknowledge the divergence in view between the two sides on this issue and respect the two sides' positions and concerns.

- The most effective means to promote the bilateral military relationship is to encourage and expand communication and cooperation. Extensive personnel communication can help increase the two sides' understanding of each other, improve military transparency, and establish mutual trust. Besides expanding military exchange, the two militaries should vigorously deepen military cooperation to elevate bilateral military ties to the next level.
- In light of the uniqueness of the current Sino-U.S. military relationship, strengthening crisis management mechanisms is an important measure to help achieve sound bilateral relations. The two sides should respect each other's security concerns and not damage one another's core interests. Furthermore, the two sides should improve crisis prevention mechanisms and build strategic mutual trust.

Despite a series of territorial disputes left over from history, the Asia-Pacific region has become the most peaceful, stable, and dynamic region in the world since the end of the Cold War.

However, since the United States unveiled its "Pivot to Asia" strategy in 2010, flashpoints such as the territorial disputes in the South and East China Seas have re-emerged, posing severe challenges to peace, stability, and prosperity in the Asia-Pacific region. With Sino-U.S. relations at a crossroads, many analysts believe the two countries' military forces are more likely to run into conflict.

Against such a background, Chinese and American leaders have proposed to build a Sino-U.S. relationship based on coordination, cooperation, and stability, one which renders Sino-U.S. military ties into a stabilizing force in the bilateral relationship. To obtain such a goal, the nature of Sino-U.S. military relations has to be defined in the first instance. What position does it occupy within bilateral ties? What profits are there to advance military-to-military relations? What are the challenges facing the Sino-U.S. military relationship? This chapter presents an analysis and discussion focusing on these questions and offers suggestions on the development of a stable and healthy Sino-U.S. military relationship.

The evolution of Sino-U.S. military relations

The establishment of Sino-U.S. bilateral military ties can be traced back to WWII. The arrival in July 1944 of a U.S. Army Observation Group, also known as the Dixie Mission, in Yan'an, marked the start of official contact and exchanges between the military force of the Communist Party of China (CPC) and the U.S. military. Their bilateral military ties have since then passed through several important stages including the Cold War and the period that followed, the post-9/11 era, and the return of the U.S. military to the Asia-Pacific. The path has been full of twists and turns, at times even like sailing against the current. The evolution of bilateral military ties indicates that it is susceptible to the impact of the two countries' political relations, the Taiwan issue, and other isolated incidents. In cooperation with each other, the two military forces can help provide public security goods. If, however, the two militaries are engulfed in an adversarial relationship, the interests of China, the United States, and other countries in the region will be seriously jeopardized.

Conflict and confrontation after 1949

During the Cold War, the United States adopted a policy of political and military containment against China. Consequently, the Sino-U.S. bilateral military relationship had for long remained in a state of conflict and confrontation. From the 1950s to the 1960s, to safeguard its national security, Chinese military forces fought, directly or indirectly, against U.S. forces in the battlefields of North Korea, Vietnam, and Laos. The U.S. military also interfered in Taiwan affairs by deploying the Seventh Fleet to the Taiwan Strait, setting up military bases in Taiwan, and conducting aerial reconnaissance missions on key targets of the mainland.

Establishment of military relations and the honeymoon period

In the early 1970s, China and the United States found common interests in resisting the strategic expansion of the Soviet Union. U.S. president Richard Nixon's historic visit to China in 1972 marked the resumption of normal communication between the two countries. Bilateral military ties began to improve with the start of some small-scale exchanges. Since the establishment of official diplomatic ties in 1979, the relations between the two militaries gradually entered what might be called the "honeymoon" period. The mil-mil ties in this period essentially consisted of three distinct aspects. First, high-level mutual visits: the visit of U.S. secretary of defense Harold Brown to China in January 1980 marked the start of regular high-level mutual visits and exchanges between the two military forces. Second, functional exchanges: since 1984, the two countries began exchange visits of military-technology teams. Third, export of weapons and technology to China: in this period, the United States exported to China a host of weapons and equipment including torpedoes, big-caliber ammunitions, artillery positioning radars, novel avionic equipment, UH-60 Black Hawk helicopters, etc.[1]

Stagnation and troubled development

After the June 4th Incident, the United States imposed comprehensive sanctions on China. The mil-mil cooperation suffered greatly as a consequence, to the extent that the bilateral military relationship plummeted from a honeymoon phase to a near freezing point. During the Gulf War, the bilateral military relationship witnessed mild restoration because of U.S. attempts to earn China's support.

With U.S. secretary of state William Perry's visit to China and Deputy Chief of Staff of the PLA Xu Huizi's visit to the United States in 1994, the exchange of visits by senior officers of the two military forces returned to normal. However, bilateral military ties took a plunge once again with the outbreak of the 1995–96 Taiwan Strait Crisis, triggered by the Clinton administration's approval of Taiwan leader Lee Tenghui's visit to the United States. With the exchange of visits by the Chinese minister of defense and the U.S. secretary of defense from 1996 to 1998, the bilateral military relationship achieved rapid restoration but was followed by a grave setback due to the U.S. bombing of the Chinese Embassy in Yugoslavia in May 1999. Since 2000, the U.S. Department of Defense has submitted annual reports to the U.S. Congress under the title *Military Power of the People's Republic of China*, playing up the threat posed by growing Chinese military power. The two countries' military relations suffered another devastating blow with the EP-3 incident in April 2001 when a U.S. EP-3 reconnaissance plane violated Chinese air space and crashed into a Chinese jet fighter.

9/11 and the U.S. Pivot to Asia

After the 9/11 terrorist attacks in 2001, the United States started to pursue cooperation with China because of common interests and concerns related to issues such as counter-terrorism and preventing the proliferation of weapons of mass destruction (WMD), as a result of which Sino-U.S. military relations began to improve markedly. The two countries also strengthened cooperation in counter-terrorism intelligence sharing, and a series of high-level consultations were held toward that end. The two countries normalized the exchange of visits by high-level defense officials and stepped up cooperation in exchanges between military academies, in security affairs consultations and in the administration of humanitarian aid. After years of consultation, the two sides agreed to establish a Sino-U.S. military hotline in 2007 to boost communications in the military-security field.[2] In the same year, China sent senior military leaders and scholars to attend the Shangri-La Dialogue to elucidate its defensive-oriented national defense policy. After Sichuan Province was hit by a massive earthquake in May 2008, the U.S. military dispatched two C-17 air freighters to transport relief materials. In the same year, China decided to send a navy formation to the Gulf of Aden, joining the U.N.-mandated counter-piracy escort missions, along with the U.S. Navy and the navies of other countries. Part of the PLA naval escort formation visited the U.S. Navy base on the way home. During this period, cooperation between the two military forces in counter-terrorism, humanitarian aid, and other security-related areas witnessed steady but significant improvement.

U.S. Pivot to Asia to present day

During the 2012 Shangri-La Dialogue in Singapore, U.S. secretary of state Leon Panetta declared that the United State would deploy 60% of its naval forces to the Asia-Pacific region, marking the return of the U.S. military to Asia.[3] With more expansive U.S. military presence in the Asia-Pacific region as a result of the Pivot to Asia policy, military activities in the region had become more frequent and intense, raising the possibility of confrontation between the two military forces. Apparently, there are frictions between the two militaries even when their cooperation is moving in a forward trajectory. The U.S. military has regularly dispatched warships and aircraft to conduct close-in reconnaissance missions in violation of China's sovereignty and territorial integrity. Warships of the two navies even ran into a standoff in December 2013.[4] The Chinese military set foot on U.S. territory for the first time during the joint live exercise on humanitarian aid and disaster relief (HADR) held in Hawaii in November 2013. The Chinese military also participated in traditional exercises led by the U.S. and U.S. allies, such as the Golden Cobra and RIMPAC exercises in 2014. Troops from the two countries performed mixed formations and combined operations during the Sino-U.S. joint live HADR exercise in January 2015.[5] In June 2015, Vice Chairman of the Central Military Commission General Fan Changlong paid a visit to the United States and signed the Framework Document for the Army-to-Army Dialogue Mechanism of Exchange and Cooperation with the U.S. side. The document was the first cooperation agreement signed by the militaries of the two countries in recent years. The U.S. Army chief of staff Raymond Odierno stated that the signing of the document "marked a new phase in Army-to-Army cooperation and dialogue between China and the U.S."[6] The two sides also decided to elaborate on relevant content of the Memorandum of Understanding on Rules of Behavior for the Safety of Air and Maritime Encounters signed earlier as a way to reduce the possibility of miscalculation and conflict between the two militaries. Generally speaking, despite frictions in some cases, development of Sino-U.S. military relations remained relatively stable since the advent of the U.S. Pivot to Asia. In its annual report to Congress entitled *Military and Security Developments Involving the People's Republic of China 2016*, the U.S. Department of Defense stated that "the relations between the two militaries maintained an active momentum."[7] This period was marked by the coexistence of conflict and cooperation between the two militaries.

Benefits for China to develop mil-mil relations

Fundamentally speaking, the Chinese government, the military, and the public all wish to establish a sound bilateral relationship with the United States. The advancement of bilateral military ties is conducive to building a Sino-U.S. relationship based on coordination, cooperation, and stability, and to maintaining regional peace and stability.

Important components in establishing a Sino-U.S. relationship based on coordination, cooperation, and stability

During Chinese president Xi Jinping's meeting with U.S. president Donald Trump in Buenos Aires in December 2018, the two leaders agreed to build a Sino-U.S. relationship based on coordination, cooperation, and stability.[8] Developing bilateral military relations is the key to building such a Sino-U.S. relationship. Since the establishment of official diplomatic relations between China and the United States, the two countries, despite differences and frictions, have developed broad cooperation and communication in a variety of areas including the economy, culture, science, education, and other fields, all of which have driven the overall bilateral relationship in a sound and positive direction. Owing to the unique nature of military affairs, the advancement of bilateral military relations has been relatively sluggish in comparison to other facets of the overall relationship, so unfortunately Sino-U.S. military ties have become a weak point in Sino-U.S. relations. The Pentagon divides military relations into eight levels of descending order: exchange of high-level visits; exchange of staff intelligence; symposia between two military forces; training of foreign officers in the U.S. and exchange of observers; joint exercises in engineering, medical affairs, and other areas; small-scale military drills; joint military exercises; and multinational military exercises.[9] Although exchanges between the Chinese and American militaries cover the aforementioned fields at different levels, the bilateral military relationship by and large remains at the third or fourth level. That the ties between the two militaries hover at a low level has to some extent constrained the development of the overall relationship between the two countries. Against the background of U.S. strategic adjustment and increasing U.S. military presence in Asia, the contact between the Chinese and American militaries will undoubtedly increase, and it becomes more likely for the two militaries to encounter frictions. It therefore becomes all the more necessary for the two militaries to enhance exchanges and cooperation, build a sound bilateral relationship, and lay a solid foundation for the two countries to build a Sino-U.S. relationship based on coordination, cooperation, and stability.

Maintaining regional peace and stability

China is a developing country and at the same time a regional power in the Asia-Pacific with global influence. China's greatest priority as it concerns security is to uphold peace and stability in the Asia-Pacific region in order to create a sound external environment for its peaceful development. Meanwhile, China also shoulders responsibility commensurate with its capacity. China and the United States hold differing positions regarding the latter's deploying of missile defense systems and strengthening of military alliances in the Asia-Pacific, but the greatest possible convergence of interests is that both countries prefer stability to conflict in this region.[10] The two countries have common interest in maintaining peace and stability in the Asia-Pacific region. Since the end of the Cold War, relations between the two militaries, despite multiple sharp fluctuations (the 1995–96 Taiwan Strait Crisis, the 2001 EP-3 incident, etc.), have reached a relatively stable position. It is of great importance to further promote the stable advancement of Sino-U.S. military relations for the purpose of maintaining peace and stability in the Asia-Pacific region, as the bilateral military relationship is the most sensitive one compared to other aspects of the relationship.

Establishing mutual trust and promoting cooperation

First, developing military relations is conducive to building mutual trust and promoting cooperation. The U.S. frequently accuses China of lacking military transparency and proceeds to apply various restrictions on exchanges with the PLA, in addition to conducting close-in reconnaissance on China's peripheral areas, often in violation of China's sovereignty. All these acts are signs of an absence of mutual trust. Such a situation will negatively affect the development of bilateral relations between the two countries, or even lead to crisis and conflict. Closer communication and cooperation can help improve the two sides' mutual understanding and trust and serve as an effective means to enhance military transparency and advance bilateral military relations. China is committed to deepening understanding and consensus and building mutual trust through enhanced military exchanges and cooperation, thereby creating sound conditions for the development of Sino-U.S. military relations. The development of bilateral military relations is a win-win outcome with mutual benefits. Minimizing the weakness in military ties can help contribute to the two countries' bilateral relations.

Furthermore, advancing bilateral military ties can help in providing public goods in the security domain to the region and to the world. It is manifested in the regularized and institutionalized arrangements between different governments.[11] Thanks to the significant influence of China and the United States on regional and global security, tighter Sino-U.S. military relations and improved communications can help promote tacit understanding between the two militaries, build mechanisms of trust and cooperation, and reduce the risks of crises and frictions so that the two countries can join hands in responding to various nontraditional security threats and provide the Asia-Pacific and the world with public security goods.

Major challenges to the Sino-U.S. military relationship

The reason that there have been ups and downs in Sino-U.S. military relations is that while the two militaries have common interest and thus valid grounds for cooperation, the bilateral relationship also faces a number of cross-cutting challenges.

The negative impact of political relations

First, bilateral political relations have over the years exerted a great impact on the development of Sino-U.S. military relations. And Sino-U.S. military relations have in a sense become a barometer for the overall bilateral relationship.

Containment against China

Although the United States has always publicly claimed that it welcomes China's rise, in reality it has engaged in a policy that combines engagement with containment.[12] The use of this sort of containment strategy is difficult to comprehend and does not really convince China or, for that matter, the international community that the United States truly welcomes China's rise. For instance, *Time* magazine published an article in 1995 entitled "Why We Must Contain China," which claims that one of the cornerstones of America's China policy is to build or improve security relationships with China's neighboring countries so as to contain the enlargement of China's influence.[13] Some American scholars even argue that America's China policy is indeed not really engagement combined with containment, but rather engagement is just a continuation of containment.[14] George Kennan's 1947 *Foreign Affairs* article "The Sources of Soviet Conduct"[15] signified the formation of America's containment strategy. After the end of the Cold War, the U.S. government has repeatedly stressed that China is different from the Soviet Union in that the United States does not seek a containment policy against China. But in actuality, there is still some shadow of U.S. containment strategy directed at the successor state of the Soviet Union, namely the Russian Federation. While giving a speech at the U.S. Naval Academy in May 2016, U.S. secretary of defense Ashton Carter mentioned China 22 times, accusing China of erecting "a Great Wall of self-isolation."[16] Such a statement reflects typical American hegemonic thinking. China and the United States share common interests and face common challenges in the Asia-Pacific region. The two sides have everything to gain from cooperation and everything to lose from confrontation. Clinging to the Cold War mindset will serve no one's interest.

Divergence of ideology and values

Many American analysts believe that although China is on the way to a market economy, it still has not changed its political system as a socialist country. The so-called Democratic Peace Theory holds that democracies do not tend to fight or otherwise use force to settle differences. With deep-seated liberal anti-communism ideology, the United States has been extremely reluctant to accept the rise of China as a socialist country.[17] The United States has always promoted American values such as freedom and democracy in the world and has tried to use American values to influence and mold other countries. China believes that ideology and values belong to the sphere of sovereignty, and its basic political interest revolves around maintaining China's own social system and ideology. Interference in political values and ideology is therefore viewed as intolerable and unacceptable. It is obvious that divergence in ideology and values between the two countries poses a great challenge to the development of mil-mil relations.

Anti-China forces in the United States

Anti-China forces in the U.S. Congress, the Pentagon and other circles are significant constraining factors in the development of the relations between the two militaries. Due to the political system of separation of powers, U.S. Congress has played a very important and oftentimes negative role in the Sino-U.S. relationship. Michel Oksenberg, a leading China expert, once noted that Congress could often take away policymaking powers regarding China from the president and that congressional influence on the Sino-U.S. relationship would be profound as long as Congress is determined to play such a role.[18] Using its legislative power, the U.S. Congress has passed legislation to limit Sino-U.S. military exchanges. Also, the Pentagon is known for propagating the "China threat" narrative in order to gain a bigger share of the budget and maintain its status in the bureaucratic system. Moreover, some anti-China elements in the United States are always active, and they readily oppose anything involving China, such as the ABC (Anyone but China) club when it comes to the issue of the TPP.[19] All of these have posed severe challenges to the normal development of bilateral military relations.

Absence of strategic trust

One final reason for the glacial pace of development of Sino-U.S. military relations is the lack of strategic trust or the strategic distrust between the two sides. In particular, the United States has long held suspicion when it comes to China's military buildup.[20] The annual report on China's military development, issued by the Pentagon, also helps fan the flames of the "China threat" discourse in the United States and elsewhere. It should be noted that although China's military development has made some progress, there remains a great gap between the two militaries. As China has been committed to the foreign policy of "peaceful development" as well as the policy of active defense, the development of China's military capability should be viewed as an opportunity for rather than a threat to the United States.

The abnormal relationship between the U.S. and Taiwan

According to international law, after the United States established diplomatic relations with the People's Republic of China, it should not have maintained any political or military relations with Taiwan, which is an integral part of the PRC. However, regarding Taiwan as an "unsinkable aircraft carrier" which holds important strategic value, the United States continues to maintain an abnormal relationship with Taiwan, in violation of the three China-U.S. joint communiqués. This is a serious infringement on China's sovereignty and territorial integrity and has become the most severe obstacle for the bilateral relationship. When the United States sells arms to Taiwan or interferes in Taiwan affairs, it sends the wrong signals to the Taiwan independence forces, causing serious damage to Sino-U.S. military relations.

Concerning China's sovereignty and territorial integrity, the Taiwan issue is one of China's core interests. Relations between the United States and Taiwan, especially their abnormal military relations, have become the most sensitive, destructive factor in Sino-U.S. military relations. Even so, in an attempt to pursue the strategy of "balancing the Chinese mainland with Taiwan," the United States maintains special relations with Taiwan. In 1995, by agreeing to the visit of Taiwanese leader Lee Tenghui to the United States and sending aircraft carrier fleets to Taiwan's surrounding waters, the United States seriously violated China's sovereignty, directly causing a major crisis in cross-Taiwan relations. The 1995–96 Taiwan Strait Crisis also led to an interruption of security consultations and military exchanges, serving as a serious setback in relations between the two countries and two militaries. The Foreign Relations Authorization Act, Fiscal Year 2003, passed by the U.S. Congress in September 2002, stated that Taiwan shall be designated as a "major non-NATO ally," further confirming the de facto alliance relationship between the United States and Taiwan.[21] Since then, the United States and Taiwan have cooperated on cutting-edge military technology research, intelligence sharing, and military personnel training.

Sino-U.S. relations have witnessed ups and downs, and one of the important reasons is U.S. arms sales to Taiwan. The China-U.S. Joint Communiqué of August 17, 1982, states that "arms sales to Taiwan will not exceed, either in qualitative or in quantitative terms, the level of those supplied in recent years since the establishment of diplomatic relations between the United States and China, and that [the United States] intends gradually to reduce its sale of arms to Taiwan, leading, over a period of time, to a final resolution."[22] However, after the end of the Cold War, the United States increased the level of arms sales to Taiwan, which seriously violated the aforementioned joint communiqué and became a huge obstacle to the smooth development of the mil-mil relationship. In 1993, U.S. senator Frank Murkowski proposed an amendment which declares that the provisions of the Taiwan Relations Act supersede provisions of the China-U.S. Joint Communiqué of August 17, 1982.[23] This amendment was finally approved by the U.S. Congress and became the legal basis for U.S. arms sales to Taiwan, causing the level of arms sales to increase year by year. Merely two years after President Obama took office, U.S. arms sales to Taiwan amounted to a record high of US$12.2 billion.[24] That the United States constantly increases the level of arms sales to Taiwan will surely render the already fragile mutual trust between the two countries even worse and severely damage the overall Sino-U.S. bilateral relationship. As the Trump administration implements the "Indo-Pacific strategy" and increases U.S. military presence in the Indo-Pacific region, U.S. arms sales may potentially lead to a crisis situation and pose a great threat to regional peace and stability.

The "military transparency" trap

Military transparency is like a double-edged sword. On one hand, it is conducive to demonstrating sincerity and therefore establishing mutual trust; on the other hand, it may become a tool in a great-power competition. The issue of "military transparency" has been a key problem in the development of Sino-U.S. military relations. China has always attached great importance to military transparency, and has made great efforts to improve its military transparency. Nevertheless, the United States still often criticizes the level of China's military transparency as being insufficient. One of the key reasons for such a gap is the different understanding of the term "transparency" between the two countries. Whereas the United States focuses

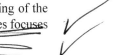

on transparency in capability, China gives priority to transparency in intention. Some American scholars acknowledge that China's lack of military transparency is increasing not only in intention but also in capability.[25] The United States generally believes that transparency is absolute, and it thus imposes its own standards to other countries.[26] The Chinese opinion, however, holds that transparency is relative and should be evaluated based on each country's own security environment, safety assessments, and requirements, as well as on international consensus.

Some Chinese analysts argue that the issue of transparency has become a policy tool of the United States to pressure China in an effort to maintain its leading position. The pursuit of military transparency presumably is to build an open information system and strengthen mutual trust in one another's militaries; however, the United States has long treated military transparency as a tool rather than a goal. For the U.S. military, the issue of military transparency has already become an effective means to obtain intelligence and put political pressure on a rival power. Arguably, the United States can create a "transparency trap": if the opponent complies with U.S. requirements for transparency, its national security might be compromised; if the opponent refuses to comply with U.S. demands, it will then be accused of lacking transparency.[27] A 1951 National Security Council document, *NSC-112*, set the tone for the U.S. policy on military transparency and treated military transparency as a tool rather than a goal per se.[28] Policy related to the U.S. military's interest in transparency derives from the Cold War, when the United States played up the Communist threat and sought to tarnish the international image of the Soviet Union by launching a "transparency offensive." In a sense, the policy centered on military transparency as an integral part of the American containment strategy and played an irreplaceable role in the winning of the Cold War.[29] Since the end of the Cold War, U.S. military policy toward China carries traces of its Soviet policy, which includes exaggerating the non-transparency of the Chinese military and promoting the "China threat" narrative so as to maintain a dominant position for the United States.

Abuses of freedom of navigation

Over time, the United States has, in the name of freedom of navigation, implemented frequent close-in reconnaissance missions by sending warships and aircraft to surrounding areas along China's coast. Every year the United States conducts about 500 air sorties of close-in reconnaissance of China, each of which can stay in the air for more than ten hours.[30] The EP-3 incident in April 2001 has weighed heavily on the Sino-U.S. military relationship. The United States has increased the intensity of close-in reconnaissance in the South China Sea in recent years, resulting in the close encounter between the USS *Cowpens* and the *Liaoning* in the South China Sea in 2013 and the U.S. B-52 bombers' provocative flight near South China Sea islands in 2015. Furthermore, the USS (DDG) *Larson*, *Wilbur*, and *Lawrence* have entered the surrounding waters of islands in the South China Sea since 2015.[31] Some analysts note that the United States' excessive freedom of navigation operations (FONOPs) in the South China Sea have humiliated

China and could force China to push back. As a result of excessive U.S. FONOPs, the situation has become more intense and the probability of a Sino-U.S. military conflict in the South China Sea has greatly increased, posing a threat to the peace, stability, and development of East Asia as a whole.[32]

It should be pointed out that the two countries have established a series of tactical and technical rules for naval and air encounters to prevent accidents from escalating into crises. However, there is no denying that the tactical rules for encounters can only solve the tactical and technical problems. Excessive naval and air close-in reconnaissance by the United States of China has sent a wrong strategic signal to the region and could lead to severe consequences such as conflict or even war. It is time for the United States to reflect on these actions.

Excessive commitment to allies

U.S. president Barack Obama has claimed that the United States "will monitor China's military modernization program and prepare accordingly to ensure that U.S. interests and allies, regionally and globally, are not negatively affected."[33] U.S. secretary of defense Leon Panetta reaffirmed the Rebalance to Asia strategy at the Shangri-La Dialogue in June 2012, emphasizing that the United States will strengthen traditional alliance relations and enhance its military presence in the Asia-Pacific region.[34] America's security commitment to its allies, however, often shows partiality to its allies and damages the legitimate rights and interests of China. For example, the United States has repeatedly claimed that it does not take any position on the Diaoyu Islands dispute between Japan and China,[35] but it nevertheless affirmed that the U.S.-Japan Mutual Defense Treaty applies to the Diaoyu Islands.[36] Just shortly after the Huangyan Island standoff occurred in April 2012, the United States declared that it would deepen its strategic and security partnership with the Philippines.[37] America's security commitment to its ally should be conducive to maintaining peace and stability in the Asia Pacific region; it should not be injurious to the interests of third parties such as China, nor should it send wrong strategic signals to encourage its allies to take provocative actions. Unfortunately, this is not the case. Emboldened by U.S. support, in January 2013 Japanese prime minister Shinzo Abe publicly called for countries in the Asia-Pacific to "counter China."[38] The United States also reinforced its partnerships with India, Vietnam, Mongolia, and other nontraditional Allies and conducted more in-depth cooperation in the field of military trade, military exercises, personnel exchanges, etc. The United States is trying to draw/co-opt China's neighbors over to the American side so as to contain China's development, which makes the "third party factors" (*disanfang yinsu*) more complicated.

Addressing challenges in bilateral military ties

In order to effectively deal with the challenges facing the development of bilateral military ties and to establish mechanisms conducive to the long-term, healthy development of such ties, the two sides must focus on the following aspects, such as enhancing mutual trust, expanding exchanges, and enhancing crisis prevention and management.

Establishing mutual trust

Establishing mutual trust is aimed at reducing the probability of conflict caused by miscalculation and misunderstanding.[39] To meet this end and to enhance mutual understanding and reduce strategic misjudgment, the priority is for the United States to develop the right strategic orientation toward China. U.S. strategic orientation toward China has been adjusting in accordance with the development of the bilateral relationship between the two countries. Immediately following the end of the Cold War, U.S. strategy toward China vacillated between engagement and containment. The China-U.S. Joint Statement of 1997 stated that both sides should build "a constructive strategic partnership" between China and the United States. In 2001 when George W. Bush took office, China was regarded as a challenger and strategic competitor; it quickly changed with the 9/11 terrorist attacks. By 2005, the Bush administration introduced the concept of the "responsible stakeholder." The 2011 China-U.S. Joint Statement stated that China and the United States should commit themselves to building a "cooperative partnership based on mutual respect and mutual benefit" in order to promote the common interests of both countries.[40] In June 2013, Chinese president Xi Jinping and U.S. president Barack Obama met in Annenberg, California, and declared that both sides should work together to build a "New Model of Major-Country Relationship."[41] In December 2018, Chinese president Xi Jinping and U.S. president Donald Trump jointly declared that the two countries should aim at building a China-U.S. relationship based on coordination, cooperation, and stability. Only with correct strategic positioning can mutual trust be effectively established and a good foundation be laid for the healthy development of bilateral military ties.

China has repeatedly stressed its policy of peaceful development and has disavowed any intention to seek hegemony. Nevertheless, many American leaders, especially military officials, still regard the normal development of China's military power as a threat to the United States. The Pentagon is required by congressional mandate to submit an *Annual Report on the Military Power of the People's Republic of China*, therefore trumpeting in a sense the military threat of China on a regular basis. The United States has the most powerful armed forces in the world, and despite progress in recent years, the Chinese military lags far behind its U.S. counterpart. Moreover, China upholds a defense policy that is defensive in nature, and it has no intention of competing with the United States for hegemony. Therefore, whether from the perspective of intention or capability, the United States should treat the development of China's military properly and should not regard its normal evolution as a threat. Dr. Henry A. Kissinger once pointed out that the "U.S.-Chinese relationship should not be considered as a zero-sum game, nor can the emergence of a prosperous and powerful China be assumed in itself to be an American strategic defeat."[42] Jeffrey Bader, former senior director for Asian affairs for the National Security Council under Obama, also noted that China "has not attacked any island in the South and East China Sea occupied by another claimant," adding that "it asserts it has no intention to challenge the United States for global supremacy and has not built an alliance system to support its goals."[43] The United States needs to put into correct perspective the development of China's military power, and China's actions to defend legitimate rights and interests should not be viewed as pushing the United States out of the Asia-Pacific region or eliminating U.S. influence there.

In addition, the two sides should have a proper understanding of their differences on the issue of military transparency and show mutual respect for each other's standpoints and concerns. In particular, the United States should not view the issue of transparency as a tool for pressuring China and safeguarding its hegemony. Instead, the United States should consider China's tremendous efforts to increase the openness of its military. In 1998, China issued its first defense white paper entitled *China's National Defense*, regarded by American analysts as "an important step toward openness of China's armed forces."[44] From then on, the defense white paper has been issued biennially, introducing such aspects as the development policy and the progress of the Chinese military. In 2008, the spokesperson system was instituted in the Ministry of National Defense, and in 2009, the official website of the Ministry of National Defense was launched. By the end of 2013, the PLA and the seven major units of the Armed Police had all set up the spokesperson system, which is primarily responsible for releasing authoritative information concerning important activities in each unit, responding to public concerns, responding to media inquiries and questions, and so on.[45] All of these developments show the increasing transparency in the Chinese military, which helps create a good environment for expanding exchanges and enhancing mutual trust.

Expanding exchanges and deepening cooperation

Expanding the scope and level of exchanges and mutual visits is an important way to enhance bilateral military ties. Through extensive mutual visits and exchanges, including visits to military units and exchange of military doctrine and defense policies, mutual understanding will naturally be deepened. Such activities are also effective ways to enhance military transparency. For a long time, bilateral military exchanges were limited to high-level visits and talks, which only cover some aspects of military ties. Since 2013, when the heads of both states agreed to establish a "New Model of Major-Country Relationship," military exchanges between the two countries have increased significantly. In 2015 alone, the two militaries carried out four high-level visits, three high-level multilateral meetings, six regular exchanges, ten academic exchanges, and numerous functional exchanges, which cover broad content and tend to be pragmatic.[46] As some military analysts note, "Military exchange will not pose a threat to national security, nor can it enhance the combat effectiveness of a country. On the contrary, it helps prevent conflict resulting from miscalculation if the two sides learn more about each other's security strategy through exchanges."[47]

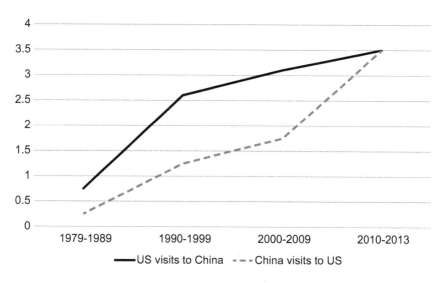

Figure 7.1 Frequency of Sino-U.S. military exchanges[48]

In addition to expanding military exchanges, the two sides should also strive to deepen military cooperation so as to elevate bilateral military ties to a higher level. Of the eight levels of U.S. military ties with foreign countries, the bilateral military ties between China and the United States have long stagnated between the third and the fourth levels. However, after 2013 when the two countries agreed to establish a "New Model of Major-Country Relationship," the two sides began to organize joint exercises, which have the effect of both intensifying and deepening the level of cooperation. From 2013 to 2015, the number of Sino-U.S. joint military exercises had increased significantly, and historic breakthroughs had been made in many areas.[49] In addition, Chinese and American militaries share a wide range of common interests in nontraditional security areas such as counter-terrorism, counter-piracy, and HADR, which provides a good opportunity and broad space for both sides to strengthen cooperation in the nontraditional security domain and is conducive to building mutual trust and deepening cooperation for both sides.

Focus on crisis prevention and management

First of all, each side must respect the security concerns of the other without prejudice to the other side's core interests. For a long time since normalization, there have been ups and downs in the development of the Sino-U.S. military relationship. Although the specific reason for each interruption of the normal development of bilateral relations varies, one common thread we discern in all cases tends to be that the United States undermines China's major security concerns and core interests. The Taiwan Straits Crises, the bombing of the Chinese embassy in

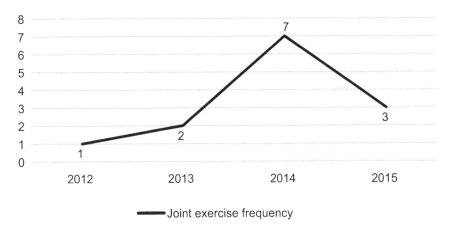

Figure 7.2 Statistics of Sino-U.S. joint exercises, 2012–15[50]

Belgrade, and the EP-3 incident were all provoked by the United States and detrimental to China's core interests. The United States tried to either harm China's core interests or force China to compromise on core interests, so as to maintain its dominant position in the region, which is in fact the root cause of problems in the Sino-U.S. relationship. To establish a mature and constructive relationship, it is necessary for the United States to make fundamental adjustments to its relevant policies and earnestly respect China's core interests, which is the key to building a China-U.S. relationship based on coordination, cooperation, and stability.

Secondly, both sides should pursue limited objectives and abjure any sort of zero-sum mentality. Although the two sides have some disagreements over their strategic objectives from the perspective of overall development of bilateral relations and of safeguarding regional peace and stability, both sides should pursue limited strategic objectives. This can be achieved by maintaining restraint and in particular by exerting control over sensitive military elements involved in crisis scenarios so as to avoid the unnecessary escalation of conflict. For example, it should be noted that in the normal construction of facilities on the islands and reefs in the South China Sea, China used civilian vessels and non-military personnel in order to avoid direct military confrontation.[51] Through mutual accommodation and mutual understanding, the two countries will be able to gradually move away from zero-sum games and create a sound, win-win bilateral relationship. In particular, the United States, as the world's sole superpower, should take full account of the Chinese stance on its core interests regarding the Taiwan issue. Doing so will not only be conducive to expanding the two countries' cooperation on regional and global security issues, but is also very much in accordance with U.S. national interests.[52]

Finally, both sides must endeavor to strengthen crisis prevention and management mechanisms to prevent the escalation of conflict. An effective crisis prevention and management mechanism will enable China and the United States to deepen strategic trust and to better understand the strategic intent of each other. In particular, it enables both sides to conduct rapid communication of information in case of emergency, accurately grasp each other's psychological expectations, and reduce the possibility of strategic misjudgments. Currently, the two militaries have established many mechanisms, such as defense consultations at the ministerial level, strategic security dialogue, bilateral military hotlines, defense working meetings, and maritime security consultations. Furthermore, the two sides should continue to improve military exchanges, bolster crisis prevention and management mechanisms, and establish an active military cooperation system to better respond to contingencies or challenges to bilateral relations resulting from strategic misjudgments.

Conclusion

On January 20, 2017, Donald Trump took the oath of office as the 45th president of the United States of America on Capitol Hill in Washington, D.C. From the very beginning of Trump's campaign, he remained a controversial figure. He has repeatedly broken protocols, made controversial remarks, and criticized American foreign policy. On the campaign trail, China was one of Trump's one favorite targets of attacks. After getting elected, Trump publicly stated on December 11, 2016, via a Fox News broadcast that "I don't know why we have to be bound by a 'One China' policy."[53] Even before that, Trump responded to a congratulatory call from Tsai Ing-wen, the pro-independence Taiwan leader, breaking with diplomatic practice since the establishment of diplomatic relations between China and the United States and seriously undermining the basis of bilateral relations. After sending shockwaves through the foreign policy community in the United States, Trump then took the step to assure Beijing that Washington would continue to honor the "One-China policy" during a phone call with Chinese president Xi Jinping on February 10, 2017.[54] From the Clinton administration to that of President Obama, every U.S. president has expressed blessings during the Spring Festival of the Chinese Lunar New Year. Donald Trump, however, broke that tradition by not expressing blessings to the Chinese community on the occasion of the first Spring Festival after he took office. Nevertheless, Trump sent his daughter Ivanka Trump to celebrate the Spring Festival at the Chinese Embassy in Washington on February 1, 2017, thereby transmitting a positive signal to Sino-U.S. relations. In terms of defense policy, in a March 2016 interview, Trump suggested that the United States had spent too much money on troop deployments in Europe, Asia, and the Middle East and that it should instead focus more on internal affairs.[55] Such a statement was inconsistent with Obama's Rebalance to Asia strategy, casting doubt on America's stance vis-à-vis Asia and indicating a strategic retreat to some extent. However, Trump proposed more military spending in a speech at the Union League on September 7, 2016, calling for an end to the mandatory cap on defense spending as a result of the 2011 Budget Control Act.[56] In November 2017, Trump proposed the concept of the "Indo-Pacific strategy" in a public speech. In

December 2017 and January 2018, two key documents—the 2018 U.S. National Security Strategy and the 2018 U.S. National Defense Strategy—were released, which further expounded the "Indo-Pacific strategy" and signified the formal unleashing of the strategy.

Over the past several decades since normalization, the Sino-U.S. bilateral military relationship has witnessed ups and downs but on the whole, it is advancing in a positive direction despite twists and turns. With the increase in military exchanges, the two sides have become increasingly mature in dealing with bilateral military ties. Forming bilateral military relations that are anchored in constructive developments is of benefit to jointly promote the China-U.S. relationship based on coordination, cooperation, and stability and is a means to safeguard regional peace and stability and enhance mutual trust and cooperation. This also conforms to the common interests of both countries. China adheres to a defensive-oriented national defense policy and will not compete with the United States for world hegemony. But China will definitely take effective measures to ensure and safeguard its core interests. China is now building a modern military force in line with its own national security requirements and commensurate with its present situation. The United States should recognize this and assume a reasonable position on the development of bilateral military ties, rather than frequently take provocative military actions in surrounding areas of China which unquestionably aggravate regional tensions. Chinese and U.S. militaries should, on the basis of mutual respect, mutual trust, and mutual benefit, deepen cooperation and exchange and take effective measures to prevent crisis and conflict, which is not only beneficial to win-win cooperation of the two sides, but also conducive to regional peace and stability.

Notes

* This chapter represents the personal views of the authors.
1 Kerry B. Dumbaugh and Richard F. Grimmett, "U.S. Arms Sales to China," Congressional Research Service Report, No. 85–138 F, July 8, 1985, 41.
2 "China, U.S. 'to Set up Military Hotline'," *The Sydney Morning Herald*, June 3, 2007, www.smh.com.au/news/World/China-US-to-set-up-military-hotline/2007/06/02/11802 05565181.html.
3 Leon Panetta, "The U.S. Rebalance Towards the Asia-Pacific," Remarks by Secretary Panetta at the Shangri La Dialogue in Singapore, June 2, 2011, www.iiss.org/en/events/ shangri%20la%20dialogue/archive/sld12-43d9/first-plenary-session-2749/leon-panetta-d67b.
4 Zhao Shengnan, "Pact to Reduce Sea Conflicts," *China Daily*, April 23, 2014, www.chinadaily.com.cn/china/2014-04/23/content_17455623.htm.
5 Zhao Xiaozhuo, "Zhongmei Xinxing Junshi Guanxi Chengwei Liangguo Guanxi Xinde Zengzhangdian" [The New Type of Military Relationship between China and the U.S. Has Become a New Growth Point in the Bilateral Relationship], in *Jiefangjun Bao* [PLA Daily], September 30, 2015, 3.
6 "China, U.S. Sign Agreement to Boost Army Cooperation," http://eng.chinamil.com.cn/special-reports/2015-06/15/content_6540579.htm.
7 Department of Defense (DoD) of the U.S., "Annual Report to Congress: Military and Security Developments Involving the People's Republic of China 2016," Office of the Secretary of Defense, April 26, 2016, III.

8 South Daily Commentator, "Zhongmei Xinxing Daguo Guanxi Juyou Qiangda Sheng-mingli" [New Type of Major-Country Relationship between China and USA Has Strong Vitality], *Nanfang ribao* [South Daily], September 26, 2015, http://news.xinhuanet.com/world/2015-09/26/c_1116686437.htm.

9 You Lin et al., "Xinxing Daguo Guanxi Kuangjia Xia Goujian Zhongmei Xinxing Jun-shi Guanxi De Biyaoxing Yu Kexingxing Fenxi" [Analysis of the Necessity of and Fea-sibility for Building a New Type of Military Relationship between China and the U.S. Under the Framework of New Type of Major-Country Relations], *Haijun Gongcheng Daxue Xuebao* [Journal of Naval University of Engineering of the PLA] 12, no. 2 (June 2015): 22.

10 John D. Negroponte, "The Future of Political, Economic and Security Relations with China," the Testimony before the House Committee on Foreign Affairs, Washington, DC, May 1, 2007.

11 Yang Luhui, "Zhongguo Jueqi Beijing Xia De Zhongmei Xinxing Daguo Guanxi" [New Type of Major-Country Relations between China and the U.S. Against the Back-ground of China's Rise], *Shandong Daxue Xuebao (Zhexue Shehui Kexue Ban)* [Jour-nal of Shandong University], no. 6 (2013): 2.

12 Aaron L. Friedberg, *A Contest for Supremacy: China, America, and the Struggle for Mastery in Asia* (New York: W. W. Norton & Company, 2011), 115–19.

13 Charles Krauthammer, "Why We Must Contain China," *Time*, July 31, 1995, 72.

14 Christopher Layne, "A House of Cards: American Strategy Toward China," *World Policy Journal* (Fall 1997): 77–95.

15 X (George Kennan), "The Sources of Soviet Conduct," *Foreign Affairs* 25 (July 1947): 575.

16 "Foreign Ministry Spokesperson Hua Chunying's Regular Press Conference on May 30, 2016," www.fmprc.gov.cn/mfa_eng/xwfw_665399/s2510_665401/2511_665403/t1367853.shtml.

17 Wang Jisi, "Ezhi Haishi Jiaowang" [Containment or Engagement], *Guoji Wenti Yanjiu* [International Studies], no. 1 (January 1996): 3.

18 Michel Oksenberg, "Congress, Executive-Legislative Relations, and American China Policy," in *The President, The Congress, and Foreign Policy*, ed. E.S. Muskie, K. Rushand, and K. W. Thompson (Lanham, MD: University Press of America, 1986), 218.

19 David Pilling, "The Anyone But China Club Needs a Gatecrasher," www.ft.com/intl/cms/s/0/62613e6a-6b5a-11e5-aca9-d87542bf8673.html#axzz48Q6mEYtQ.

20 Wang Jisi and Li Kanru [Kenneth Lieberthal], *Zhongmei Zhanlue Huyi Jiexi Yu Yingdui* [Addressing China-U.S. Strategic Distrust] (Beijing: Social Science Academic Press, 2016).

21 It is stated in the document that "Taiwan shall be treated as though it were designated a major non-NATO ally (as defined in section 644(q) of the Foreign Assistance Act of 1961(22 U.S.C. 2403(q))." See *Foreign Relations Authorization Act, Fiscal Year 2003*, www.congress.gov/107/plaws/publ228/PLAW-107publ228.pdf.

22 "Joint Communiqué of the People's Republic of China and the United States of Amer-ica," www.china-embassy.org/eng/zmgx/doc/ctc/t946664.htm.

23 JianYang, *Congress and US China Policy, 1989–1999* (Huntington, New York: Nova Science Publishers, 2000), 189–90.

24 Zhao Yingzhe,"Aobama Zhengfu Duitai Junshou Yanjiu" [Study on Arms Sales to Tai-wan by the Obama Administration], Master Dissertation of China Foreign Affairs Uni-versity, June 2015.

25 David Shambaugh, "China Engages Asia," *International Security* 29, no. 3 (Winter 2004): 64–99.

26 Brendan S. Mulvaney, "Zhongmei Junshi Guanxi Zhong De Toumingdu Wenti" [Trans-parency Issue in China-U.S. Relations], *Xiandai Guoji Guanx* [Contemporary Interna-tional Relations], no. 10 (2005): 61.

27 James J. Marquardt, *Transparency and American Primacy in World Politics* (Surrey: Ashgate Publishing Limited, 2011), 93.

28 Xu Hui and Han Xiaofeng, "Meiguo Junshi Touming Zhengce Jiqi Dui Zhongguo De Yingxiang" [U.S. Military Transparency Policy and Its Influence on China], *Waijiao Pinglun* [Foreign Affairs Review], no. 2 (2014): 80.

29 Xu Hui and Han Xiaofeng, "Meiguo Junshi Touming Zhengce Jiqi Dui Zhongguo De Yingxiang" [U.S. Military Transparency Policy and Its Influence on China], *Waijiao Pinglun* [Foreign Affairs Review], no. 2 (2014): 83.

30 "Mei Junji dui Zhongguo Zhencha Meinian yue 500 Jiaci, Meici Liukongchao 10 Xiaoshi" [U.S. Military Reconnaissance to China Has Reached 500 Sorties Each Year and Exceeded 10 Hours Each Time], *People.cn*, August 27, 2014, http://world.people. com.cn/n/2014/0827/c1002-25545168.html.

31 "U.S. Navy Destroyer 'Illegally' Sails near Disputed Chinese Island Damaging 'Regional Peace and Stability,'" www.dailymail.co.uk/news/article-3583640/US-Navy-destroyer-illegally-sails-near-disputed-Chinese-island-damaging-regional-peace-stability.html.

32 Xue Li, "Zhi Aobama De Yifeng Xin" [A Letter to Mr. Obama], www.ftchinese.com/ story/001067611?full=y.

33 The White House, "National Security Strategy," May 2010, 43.

34 Leon Panetta, "The US Rebalance Towards the Asia-Pacific," Remarks by Secretary Panetta at the Shangri La Dialogue in Singapore, June 2, 2011, www.iiss.org/en/events/ shangri%20la%20dialogue/archive/sld12-43d9/first-plenary-session-2749/leon-panetta-d67b.

35 "U.S.: We Do Not Hold Official Position on the Diaoyu Islands Disputes, Hope for a Peaceful Solution between China and Japan," http://news.163.com/12/0816/16/891SC DCF00014JB5.html.

36 "The United States Reconfirms that U.S.-Japan Mutual Security Treaty with Japan Applies to the Diaoyu Islands," *People.cn*, April 6, 2014, http://military.people.com.cn/ n/2014/0406/c1011-24837748.html.

37 U.S. Department of State, "U.S.-Philippines Partnership," April 30, 2012, www.state. gov/r/pa/prs/ps/2012/04/188978.htm.

38 "Jane's Defense Weekly: Shinzo Abe Calls for Establishing Democratic Security Diamond to Counter China," *China.com.cn*, January 12, 2013, www.china.com.cn/inter national/txt/2013-01/12/content_27666947.htm.

39 Xu Hui, "Zhongmei Junshi Huxin Weihe Nanyi Jianli?" [Why Is the China-U.S. Military Mutual Trust Difficult to Establish?], *Waijiao Pinglun* [Foreign Affairs Review], no. 2 (2010): 23.

40 Wang Honggang, "Zhongmei Hezuo Huoban Guanxi Xin Dingwei Pingxi" [Analysis on the New Positioning of the China-U.S. Cooperatve Partnership], *Xiandai Guoji Guanxi* [Contemporary International Relations], no. 2 (2011): 12–13.

41 Wang Jisi, "ZhongMei Guanxi Ru Nishui Xingzhou" [China-U.S. Relations are Like Sail against the Current], *Zhongguo Qiyejia* [China Entrepreneur], no. 15 (2013): 40.

42 Henry Kissinger, "The Future of U.S.-China relations: Conflict Is a Choice, Not a Necessity," *Foreign Affairs*, March/April 2012.

43 Jeffrey Bader, "A Framework for U.S. Policy Toward China," *Foreign Policy at Brookings*, May 2016, 3, www.brookings.edu/wp-content/uploads/2016/07/us-china-policy-framework-bader-1.pdf.

44 Kenneth W. Allen, "China's Approach to Confidence-Building Measures," *The Stimson Center*, www.stimson.org/images/uploads/research-pdfs/cbmapchina.pdf.

45 "Tell the Stories of the Chinese Army to the World," Ministry of the National Defense of the PRC, December 28, 2014, http://news.mod.gov.cn/headlines/2014-12/28/content_ 4561033.htm.

46 DoD of the U.S., "Annual Report to Congress: Military and Security Developments Involving the People's Republic of China 2016," Office of the Secretary of Defense, April 26, 2016, 103–04.

47 Brendan S. Mulvaney, "Zhongmei Junshi Guanxi Zhong De Toumingdu Wenti" [Transparency Issue in China-U.S. Relations], *Xiandai Guoji Guanx* [Contemporary International Relations], no. 10 (2005): 62.

48 Zhang Fang, "Zhongmei Xinxing Junshi Guanxi De Neihan Yu JianGou Lujing" [The Connotation and Construction Paths for the New Military Relations between China and the United States], *Fudan Meiguo Wenti Yanjiu* [Fudan American Review], no. 1 (2014): 105.

49 See Figure 2.

50 DoD of the U.S., "Annual Report to Congress: Military and Security Developments Involving the People's Republic of China 2013," May 7 2013, 69; "Annual Report to Congress: Military and Security Developments Involving the People's Republic of China 2014," April 24, 2014, 71; "Annual Report to Congress: Military and Security Developments Involving the People's Republic of China 2015," April 7 2015, 74; "Annual Report to Congress: Military and Security Developments Involving the People's Republic of China 2016," April 26, 2016, 104.

51 Wang Hanling and Peng Sixiang, "South China Sea Militarization: the Chinese Perspective," *China-U.S. Focus*, October 3, 2016, www.chinausfocus.com/peace-security/south-china-sea-militarization-the-chinese-perspective.

52 Xu Hui, "Zhongmei Junshi Huxin Weihe Nanyi Jianli?" [Why Is the China-U.S. Military Mutual Trust Difficult to Establish?], *Waijiao Pinglun* [Foreign Affairs Review], no. 2 (2010): 29.

53 Eric Bradner, "Trump: U.S. Doesn't 'Have to be Bound' by 'One China' Policy," *CNN*, December 12, 2016, http://edition.cnn.com/2016/12/11/politics/donald-trump-china-taiwan/index.html.

54 "Foreign Ministry Spokesperson's Regular Press Conference on February 10, 2017," www.gov.cn/xinwen/2017-02/10/content_5167146.htm#1.

55 "Donald Trump's Interview with the *Washington Post*," *The Washington Post*, March 22, 2016, www.washingtonpost.com/news/the-fix/wp/2016/03/22/donald-trumps-interview-with-the-washington-post-is-totally-bananas/?utm_term=.784413067b81.

56 Sopan Deb, "Donald Trump Says of Hillary Clinton 'She's Trigger-happy and Unstable,'" *CBS News*, September 7, 2016, www.cbsnews.com/news/donald-trump-calls-for-more-defense-spending-outlines-defense-policy/.

Conclusion

Dong Wang and Tiffany Ma

The rise of the People's Republic of China is one of the most consequential developments in the Asia-Pacific, and growing uncertainties about the future of U.S.-China relations make this study particularly timely. Taken together, the chapters in this volume offer a fresh approach to addressing areas in the bilateral relationship where the two sides currently do not see eye to eye—from well-established strategic domains, such as maritime and nuclear, to newer ones, such as cyber and space. Given the importance of U.S.-China relations, our study underscores the need to make progress in these domains so that future developments will not destabilize, or derail, the overall relationship.

As a baseline, a consensus exists among the authors that, despite the current challenges, there exists room for cooperation in each of the domains studied. Indeed, China's growing set of strategic interests creates new opportunities, and even incentives, for cooperation. At the same time, China's expanding international profile raises the costs of escalation, especially if divergences between the United States and China on key issues remain an obstacle to crisis management. This is especially true in the newer domains where there is a relative lack of experience and established norms. Going forward, it may be possible to apply lessons from some domains toward strengthening cooperation in other domains. In the international context, the United States and China are also not the only players in the maritime, nuclear, cyber, and space domains, which heightens the stakes for global security as the two countries blaze their paths forward in these areas.

The challenges in these domains, however, are well documented by the authors. As is evident throughout this volume, these domains are sources of friction because both sides' interests are firmly rooted in broader geopolitical, security, and economic interests. Moreover, these same factors—coupled with disparity in levels of capabilities in some cases—drive U.S. and Chinese perceptions of the other side's interests, resulting in assumptions and narratives that widen the gap in rhetoric and action. As such, this volume's inclusion of each country's perception of the other's interests in these domains makes a valuable contribution to the understanding of U.S.-China relations by shedding light on why the two sides have difficulty reaching agreement on these issues. Given that a significant change in one country's position will most certainly alter the calculus of the other, our study's recommendations underscore an urgency in managing the risks of escalation—whether this is through strengthening frameworks and norms, developing confidence-building measures, or even addressing distrust through a more nuanced understanding of each other's positions.

Various forms of bilateral engagement on strategic domains could play a role in managing risk and building cooperation. The special studies in this volume highlight the potential for exchanges at the people-to-people and military-to-military levels to push forward bilateral discussions. Beyond establishing good habits of engagement, these two modes of exchange can cut across issues in all the strategic domains and tap into the broader policy communities on both sides. More importantly, the outcomes of these discussions can add content and substance to the relationship, setting it on a more durable and constructive course. In this sense, official and nonofficial discussions complement each other in addressing critical issues in the strategic domains.

While challenges in the strategic domains will remain salient in the U.S.-China relationship, the authors identify areas of convergence for fostering cooperation and recommend steps that policymakers can take to manage tensions in areas of divergence. As is evident in this volume, the key is not to disregard the areas of disagreement—or let them diminish the possibilities for cooperation—but rather to foster an understanding of each side's approach in order to talk about these issues more constructively. The future course of the U.S.-China relationship has ramifications both for regional security, even in contingencies not directly involving the two countries, and for the international system as China carves out its global role. Looking ahead, the methodology employed in this book might be useful for understanding areas of convergence and divergence on other substantive issues, including views of global governance, the broader functions of the international system, and the importance of innovation to economic development.

While China has continued to rise against the backdrop of the Obama administration's Asian rebalance strategy, the Asia-Pacific region as a whole has become a global hotspot for both competition among rival powers as well as an arena for substantial economic cooperation. The level of uncertainty in U.S.-China relations has increased considerably since the advent of the Trump administration. Prior to and following his inauguration, Donald Trump issued confrontational remarks on trade, cyber security, the North Korea nuclear issue, and the South China Sea, causing many observers to wonder whether he would push U.S.-China relations towards greater antagonism. However, since the start of the Trump presidency, the Chinese government has actively engaged the Trump team and suggested that the leaders of both countries meet and discuss ways to constructively move forward in the new era of U.S.-China relations. Constructive steering of the U.S.-China relationship requires leaders in both countries to maintain a positive outlook toward the future. Cooperation between China and the United States should be expanded in various issue areas, despite the existing structural contradictions that remain.

Whether or not China and the United States can avoid the 'Thucydides Trap' and chart a new course for the relationship between a rising power and an established power will have tremendous consequences to the peace and stability of the 21st century. We are of the view that there are reasons to believe that China and the United States do not necessarily have to fall into a "new Cold War" and that Beijing and Washington can successfully avoid the 'Thucydides Trap' and together forge a relationship based on coordination, cooperation, and stability. In order to do so, a rational and pragmatic attitude must be adopted by way of which we may examine and discuss U.S.-China relations from a positive-sum rather than from a zero-sum perspective. In this sense, the studies compiled in this book represent a small step in that direction.

Index

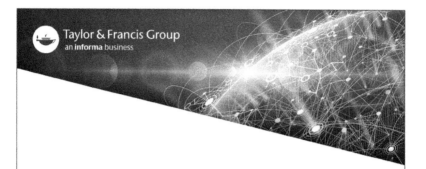

CPSIA information can be obtained
at www.ICGtesting.com
Printed in the USA
LVHW081839291122
734259LV00005B/344